Laura
Bush

ALSO BY RONALD KESSLER

A MATTER OF CHARACTER: Inside the White House of George W. Bush

THE CIA AT WAR: Inside the Secret Campaign Against Terror

THE BUREAU: The Secret History of the FBI

THE SEASON: Inside Palm Beach and America's Richest Society

INSIDE CONGRESS: The Shocking Scandals, Corruption, and Abuse of Power
Behind the Scenes on Capitol Hill

THE SINS OF THE FATHER: Joseph P. Kennedy and the Dynasty He Founded

INSIDE THE WHITE HOUSE: The Hidden Lives of the Modern Presidents and
the Secrets of the World's Most Powerful Institution

THE FBI: Inside the World's Most Powerful Law Enforcement Agency

INSIDE THE CIA: Revealing the Secrets of the World's Most Powerful Spy Agency

ESCAPE FROM THE CIA: How the CIA Won and Lost the Most Important KGB
Spy Ever to Defect to the U.S.

THE SPY IN THE RUSSIAN CLUB: How Glenn Souther Stole America's Nuclear
War Plans and Escaped to Moscow

MOSCOW STATION: How the KGB Penetrated the American Embassy

SPY VS. SPY: Stalking Soviet Spies in America

THE RICHEST MAN IN THE WORLD: The Story of Adnan Khashoggi

THE LIFE INSURANCE GAME

Laura Bush

An Intimate Portrait of the First Lady

RONALD KESSLER

Doubleday
New York London Toronto Sydney Auckland

PUBLISHED BY DOUBLEDAY
a division of Random House, Inc.
1745 Broadway, New York, New York 10019

DOUBLEDAY and the portrayal of an anchor with a dolphin are
trademarks of Doubleday, a division of Random House, Inc.

Book design Michael Collica

Library of Congress Cataloging-in-Publication Data

Kessler, Ronald, 1943–
Laura Bush : an intimate portrait of the first lady / by Ronald
Kessler.—1st ed.
p.   cm.
Includes bibliographical references and index.
1. Bush, Laura Welch, 1946– 2. Presidents' spouses—United States—
Biography. I. Title.
E904.B87K47 2005
973.931092—dc22
2005051983

ISBN 0-385-51621-5

PRINTED IN THE UNITED STATES OF AMERICA

1   3   5   7   9   10   8   6   4   2

First Edition

For Pam, Greg, and Rachel Kessler

CONTENTS

Contents

Laura
Bush

PROLOGUE

When the call came in just after 6 P.M. on October 20, 2004, Laura Bush had just finished an hour-long yoga session with Pamela Hudson Nelson, her high school friend from Midland, Texas. The day before, *USA Today* had run an interview with Teresa Heinz Kerry. When asked how she would be different from Laura Bush as first lady, the wife of the Democratic presidential candidate sniffed: "I don't know that she's ever had a real job. . . ."

Within hours, Heinz—who would drop "Kerry" from her name after the election—issued an apology. Now she was calling the first lady. Having finished their yoga in the exercise room on the third floor of the White House, Laura and Nelson were on the second floor of the residence in Laura's dressing room. Off the first couple's bedroom, the dressing room had a chaise longue, a fireplace, a small desk, drawers for jewelry, and racks of clothes in cleaner's bags. Pinned to the bags were lists of when and where each item had been worn.

With a touch of drama, Daniel Shanks, an usher, came in and announced Heinz's call. Also present were Lindsey M. Lineweaver, Laura's assistant and personal aide, and Maria Galvan, the Bushes' personal housekeeper from Austin. In photos, Lineweaver could be seen with Laura carrying a huge bag that held the first lady's extra contact lenses and Cover Girl makeup.

It was twelve days before the election, and Laura had been out campaigning in New York, New Hampshire, and Pennsylvania. Today was her only break from the campaign, and she and her husband were planning to enjoy a rare dinner together with their daughters and Pamela Nelson. The next day, Laura was set to leave again for New Hampshire. The president was heading for Pennsylvania.

Earlier that afternoon, after Heinz's public apology, Laura had told reporters that there had been no need for her to do so.

"I know how tough it is, and actually I know those trick questions," she said.

Laura did not take Teresa's call. Instead, she turned to Andrea G. "Andi" Ball, her chief of staff in the White House and during the years Laura had been first lady of Texas. "Let's not make this into anything," she said. "Call her back and tell her that Mrs. Bush understands that when you talk to the media, things get quoted that you didn't quite say or mean to say."

Ball went back to her office in the East Wing and called Heinz's assistant. Unlike Hillary Clinton, who moved the first lady's office to the West Wing, Laura has her office in the East Wing. However, she operates most of the time out of a small office in the residence portion of the White House. That office is also where she has her hair done. Ball told the assistant that if Teresa was calling about her comment, there was "no need for either of them to take time out of their day to talk about it. Mrs. Bush thinks nothing of it. I don't think Mrs. Kerry meant that she never worked."[1]

Pamela Nelson had been staying overnight at the White House for several days each month for meetings of the Commission on Fine Arts, which reviews and approves architectural plans submitted by the federal and District of Columbia governments. As Laura continued selecting clothes to pack, she explained to Nelson, "If I took the call from Mrs. Kerry, it would escalate. The next story will be: 'Mrs. Kerry Talked to Mrs. Bush.' I don't want this to be news. I don't want reporters to grab this and start beating up on Teresa Kerry. She doesn't know how to talk to the media. She blurts things out. You can't blurt."[2]

Despite Laura's excuses for Teresa Heinz, her comments in the *USA Today* interview were not off-the-cuff responses during a high-pressure press conference. They were part of a recorded Q&A. Heinz had apparently forgotten that, for ten years, Laura had been an elementary school teacher and librarian at inner-city schools. Heinz also appeared to be implying that women who don't have jobs and devote themselves to raising a family are unworthy of respect.

Soon after this, press secretary Gordon Johndroe called Laura at the residence to say that a new Gallup Poll for *USA Today* and CNN showed that 74 percent of Americans had a favorable opinion of her.[3] Only 16 percent had an unfavorable opinion. "We're going to get those sixteen percent," Johndroe told Laura jokingly. "We're going to wring their necks and get them over to us." The following year, Laura's approval rating would soar to 85 percent, according to a Gallup Poll. Since opinion polls first began asking about them in 1939, no first lady had received a higher rating. After Hillary Clinton and Oprah Winfrey, Laura Bush was the most admired woman in America.

At the table that night in the pale green family dining room, Laura took the same positive approach to Teresa Heinz's remark as she had in public. Bush had been campaigning that day in Iowa, Minnesota, and Wisconsin. His arrival for dinner at 8 P.M. did not have to be announced. Laura and Pamela Nelson could hear the helicopter—*Marine One*—landing on the South Lawn.

After Bush took his place at the dinner table, he said grace.

"Sometimes, I've been asked to say grace, which is a little nerve-racking because of where you are and maybe who is sitting around the table," Nelson observed. "You never know who is going to be asked, so you have a little prayer just in case he goes, 'Pam, go pray.' One time I kind of waited too long; I was taking deep yoga breaths."

"Are you going to come out with it?" Bush asked.

"Wait, it's coming out," Nelson responded.

That October 20, 2004, evening, as a butler passed cheese and chicken enchiladas, daughters Jenna and Barbara Bush expressed outrage at Teresa's comment. Typically, Jenna was the more vocal.

"You know, Mom, she put down every woman who raised their children," Jenna said. "She was saying that's not a real job. That was what was so bad about it. Not that she forgot you had a teaching job, but that she was putting down raising children."

Meanwhile, Nelson, a vegetarian, selected a chicken enchilada by mistake. Laura plucked it from her friend's plate and put it on her own. She then talked about how easy it was for words to be twisted and taken out of context.

"You know that comment, 'Bring them on,' " Laura said, referring to Bush's July 2003 statement challenging those who would attack American forces in Iraq. "It had so many political repercussions. Everything can be used a million times against you."

"This has to be the meanest campaign ever," Nelson said.

"No, the leaflets they dropped when Lincoln was running that disparaged him and his family were horrible," Laura said. "People blame everything that happens on this office."

Bush was tired from his trip and expressed no opinion about Heinz's comment. Instead, Nelson recalled, "Every time the butler came in, the president asked who was ahead in the St. Louis Cardinals versus Houston Astros National League Championship." After dinner, Bush went into his office in the residence and worked a hand-cut mahogany jigsaw puzzle lent to the White House by Elms Puzzles of Maine. Another Elms puzzle was a present from the White House staff. Imprinted on it was the face of Barney, the Bushes' omnipresent Scottish terrier.

Among themselves, members of the Bush campaign staff were expressing joy over Heinz's comment. On behalf of the campaign, Karen Hughes took the offensive, saying on television that Heinz's remarks were "indicative of an unfortunate mind-set that seeks to divide women based on who works at home and who works outside the home."

Donald L. Evans, Bush's close friend who had attended Bible study with him and had been present at the dinner that precipitated Bush's decision to give up drinking, was in Florida when he heard about Heinz's comment.

"I couldn't believe it," Evans, Bush's commerce secretary, said. "When I first heard it, I thought it had been misreported."[4]

In fact, the comment reflected a prevalent view among the 16 percent of Americans who said they did not have a favorable opinion of Laura. While that view rarely appeared in print, in certain liberal circles it was fashionable to express disdain at the mention of Laura Bush. In those circles, she was thought to be a Stepford wife, someone with no life of her own, subservient to her husband. If she looked glowing, it was attributed to plastic surgery or Botox. If she smiled a lot, she must have been on tranquilizers.

"The chattering classes in New York City, the Hamptons, and Hollywood have a view of Laura Bush which they express to each other with giggles of contempt over cocktail party canapés and at dinner parties," said Ed Klein, a contributing editor of *Vanity Fair* and a noted author of books about the Kennedys. "They claim that Laura Bush is a prefeminist figure who has accomplished nothing while she has been the first lady, has no influence on her husband or in the White House, and is basically a neuter within the Bush administration."[5]

The truth, carefully concealed because the Bushes prefer to keep their private lives private, is quite the opposite. When Laura entered the White House on January 20, 2001, everyone wanted to know what kind of first lady she would be. Would she be like Mamie Eisenhower? Would she follow in Barbara Bush's footsteps? Would she be another Hillary Clinton?

"I think I'll just be Laura Bush," she would say.

On Saturday, April 30, 2005, the world got a glimpse of what she meant by these words when Laura pushed aside the leader of the free world and stole the show at the White House Correspondents Association dinner. Wearing a shimmering lime-green Oscar de la Renta gown, Laura wisecracked that she was a "desperate housewife" married to a president who was always asleep at nine. She said she had to find ways to amuse herself, like going to Chippendale's, where partying bachelorettes shower male strippers with greenbacks.

Replayed constantly on the air, Laura's stand-up routine with its impeccable comedic timing turned the first lady into a glittering star. But while the routine catapulted her to a new status, it did not answer the question of who she really was or just what role she plays in influencing her husband and shaping his administration. The Bushes are better than the FBI or the CIA at keeping secret what goes on behind the scenes.

Unknown to the public, the Bush administration asks for Laura Bush's opinion and for any suggestions she might have on possible appointments and on issues affecting a range of agencies dealing with subjects that she has committed herself to promoting or in which she has a strong interest. They include such areas as education, the arts, women's rights, juveniles with social problems, AIDS, libraries, and the humanities. Because of her, budgets for some agencies have been increased or not cut. In one case, a well-connected top political appointee who had engaged in deceit never took his post because of her take on the issue.

Craig Stapleton, who is married to Bush's cousin Debbie, was a partner with Bush in the Texas Rangers baseball team and is one of the Bushes' close friends. Since the 1980s, the Stapletons have vacationed each year with George and Laura, have spent every election night with them, and are frequent visitors at the White House, Camp David, and the Crawford ranch.

"Laura has tremendous influence," Stapleton said. "She doesn't say, 'I think you ought to put private accounts in Social Security.' But she has a tremendous sense of what the right thing to do is at the right time. He listens to her more attentively than to anyone else. Sometimes when you talk to him, he's a busy guy, and he's thinking of other things. When Laura is talking to him, he is all ears. She is invariably right even in situations where he misses. She doesn't miss."

Stapleton, who was named by Bush to be ambassador to the Czech Republic and later to France, said Laura "shapes his view of the world in a broad sense, which influences his policy. All the volunteerism, the church groups, the arts and cultural affairs. People who are in poverty in the U.S. AIDS sufferers in Africa. She influences what the president thinks about the world."

When it comes to administration appointments, "She gives her view on people she knows who might be cabinet selections," Stapleton said. "He asks her. She is not trying to be the chief of staff. Her job is not to be the guardian of the gate. But if she sees some issue with somebody, she says, 'You're making a mistake. This person isn't the right person.' Or 'This person is fabulous.' She has great instincts about people."[6]

Andrew H. "Andy" Card, Bush's chief of staff, often has dinner with the Bushes in the residence with his wife, Kathleene, a United Methodist minister. "I think the great influence Laura has had on his life is one of discipline," he observed. "She has a great sense of what is right, and she is also not a preacher. She is more like a conscience to the president. But she never wraps his conscience with her conscience. She kind of exposes his conscience to himself."

Laura is "a quiet listener, [while] he will interrupt your sentence and finish it for you," Card said. "He does that much less now. She has shown him how to be a good listener, how to absorb, and how to be patient. But she's done it in such a way that it truly is quiet counsel."[7]

If Laura feels that the staff is offering counsel that is "inconsistent with what she sees in the president's heart, she is not bashful about telling us," Card said. Laura knows, he said, that she was not elected president. But when important appointments or appointments to agencies in which she has an interest are under consideration, Bush will ask her opinion. "He will say, 'Why don't you check with Laura and see if she has any ideas?' Or he'll say, 'Did you run that by Laura? What's Laura's reaction?' "

According to Secretary of State Condoleezza Rice, it was Laura's "initiative and her idea to really fully and completely expose what the Taliban regime was doing to women, emphasizing violations of women's rights prior to the U.S. invasion of Afghanistan."[8]

Beyond such examples of direct influence, "Laura reads almost everything," Card said. "She reads the newspapers, the magazines, and the books. She reads things that would not be of interest to the president. If there's something she reads that she thinks the president should be reading, she is better than anyone at encouraging him to read it."

Besides being an unofficial adviser, Laura is an aggressively supportive wife. Only those who have a strong marriage know how important this is, how their success or failure can ride on the reactions—however subtle—of their partner.

As he talked about Laura, Card was sitting on a couch in his West Wing office, where Laura had selected the sandstone paint for the walls.

"Just today," Card said, "there was a very touching moment. The president was getting ready to go off in the helicopter to Kentucky to talk about Social Security reform. He had had a meeting with members of the House on Social Security reform measures. He came out of the cabinet room. The helicopter had landed. People were getting on their coats to run off to the helicopter."

Karen Keller, Bush's personal secretary, ran outside.

"The first lady is calling for you," she said.

"Is it an emergency?" Bush asked.

"I don't think it's an emergency, but she'd like to talk with you before you leave," Keller said.

"He goes back into the Oval Office and calls her on the phone," Card said. After a minute he opened the door to the Oval Office and looked out with a smile on his face.

"That was great," Bush said to his chief of staff. "She was just calling to tell me she loves me."

Hostile Terrain

From the air, Midland looks as if a hurricane had just hit. The few trees are short, like Christmas trees. The grass is yellow, the land flat. Dust coats the paved roads. There are no lakes or rivers. Visitors could be forgiven for thinking they were stepping off onto the moon.

With annual rainfall of only thirteen and a half inches, Midland is so arid that, to keep their lawns green in summer, residents must water them every day. To create flower beds, they often have to use jackhammers to cut through the brittle crust formed from caliche, a weathered soil rich in calcium. Until the city started mixing more surface water from the Colorado River Municipal Water District with its own well water, tap water would cause brown stains on teeth because it had excess levels of fluoride.

Two or three times a year, usually in the spring, a bad sandstorm hits, obscuring the sun as in a total eclipse. The sand stings and enters the nostrils. Drivers peering through their windshield cannot see the front of their car. The sand seeps through the frames of windows and doors and piles up on floors and windowsills. Sand frosts the panes as well.

The wind uproots the tumbleweeds—tangled balls of light, stiff branches that can balloon to the size of a Volkswagen. The tumble-weeds roll before the wind and clump together in masses of five or ten along the cinderblock walls residents build around their back-yards to try to keep out the sand. Into this inhospitable environment, on November 4, 1946, Laura Lane Welch was born.

Located 335 miles west of Dallas in what is known as West Texas, Midland was named for Midway Station, a section house where railroad employees could stay overnight. The Texas and Pacific Railway built the station in June 1881 halfway between Dallas and El Paso, an area crisscrossed by a Comanche trail and wagon roads. The name was changed from Midway Station to Midland on January 4, 1884, when a post office was established. Until Herman N. Garrett moved his herd of sheep there in 1882, the area had no permanent residents. In 1885, Midland County was established with Midland as the county seat.

Soon, Nelson Morris, a Chicago meatpacker, bought 200,000 acres from the state for his Black Angus ranch and introduced cattle to the area. Farmers began moving in, and by 1920 over 4,600 acres in Midland County were devoted to cotton. In 1923, oil was discovered seventy miles southeast of Midland, touching off a boom that has continued, off and on, to this day. Located at the center of the Permian Basin, which has 22 percent of the nation's oil reserves, Midland would become one of the greatest petroleum-producing areas in the country.

Laura's ancestors on her father's side can be traced back to England and to Christopher DeGraffenried, a Swiss nobleman born in 1691. DeGraffenried moved to Philadelphia and eventually to Charleston, South Carolina. Laura's paternal grandfather, Mark Anthony Welch, was born in Texas in 1873. He began as a carpenter and became a homebuilder. According to family legend, he became a friend of Samuel Langhorne Clemens, better known as Mark Twain, and sometimes traveled with him. His wife, Marie Lula Lane, was born in Arkansas in 1873. They moved to Lubbock, Texas, 120 miles north of Midland, in 1918.

As with her father's ancestors, Laura's mother's side goes back mainly to England, except that she is "one-eighth French," according to genealogist Robert Battle, who, along with William Addams Reitwiesner, has traced Laura's origins. In doing so, they discovered that Laura, on her father's side, is a very distant cousin of Senator John McCain. Both are descendants of Allen Valentine, who lived in Virginia in the 1700s and served as a lieutenant colonel with the North Carolina Troops during the American Revolution.

On her mother's side, Laura also has an ancestor who fought in the Revolution: John Wiseman, a private in the Pennsylvania militia and a descendant of one Abraham Wiseman, who lived in Philadelphia in the early 1700s. While his name sounds Jewish, he was probably a Mennonite, according to the two genealogists.

Laura's maternal grandfather, Halsey Sinclair Hawkins, was born in 1894 in Little Rock, Arkansas. While delivering mail for the U.S. Post Office, he met his future wife, Jessie Laura Sherrard. Laura's mother, Jenna Louise Hawkins, was born in Little Rock in 1919. But having been gassed in combat during World War I, Hawkins sought out a dry climate, and they settled first in Tyler, Texas, then in the tiny village of Canutillo about twelve miles northwest of El Paso, where they opened what was known as a tourist court on Nuway Road. A precursor of a motel, it had guest cottages, a restaurant, and a small grocery store.

Laura's father, Harold Bruce Welch, was born in Oklahoma in 1912 and moved with his parents to Lubbock when he was six. In 1944, he married Jenna Hawkins in the military chapel at Fort Bliss. Jenna had attended Texas Western College—now the University of Texas at El Paso—and had been working as a bookkeeper at an El Paso department store when a mutual friend introduced them.

Harold served during World War II with the Army's 555th Anti-

Aircraft Artillery Battalion as a master gunner. On April 11, 1945, he was among the soldiers who liberated Mittelbau-Dora concentration camp in Nordhausen in central Germany, 150 miles southeast of Hamburg. An estimated 20,000 prisoners were killed at the top secret camp, where prisoners made V2 rockets in underground tunnels as long as two miles. As the Allies advanced, Hitler began sending prisoners to the Bergen-Belsen camp. In what became known as death marches, tens of thousands of prisoners died of starvation or cold in the winter or were shot by SS guards when they could no longer walk.

"It was said we discovered six thousand political prisoners, but alas, five thousand were corpses," said Father Edward P. Doyle, a Catholic chaplain in the 104th Infantry Division, who participated in the liberation with the 555th. "A sight beyond description, mutilated, beaten, starved skeletons. A thousand were 'living' in various stages of decay, merely breathing among the already dead."

"I can still remember the smell of burning bodies as we entered the camp," said Marvin S. Brettingen, who served with Welch and played cards with him while on maneuvers in Louisiana.

A month after the liberation, on May 14, 1945, Major General Terry Allen commended Harold's battalion and its efforts against a "fanatic enemy."

"Frequently in forward positions, under hostile observation, and suffering casualties from deadly direct enemy fire, all members of the 555th AAA Battalion have proved their courage and skill," Allen wrote. Besides destroying eleven Nazi planes and "probably" destroying another eleven planes, the battalion rendered close ground support to the infantry on thirty-four occasions.[1]

After the war, Harold took a job as a district manager with Universal CIT Credit Corporation in El Paso. When an oil boom created a need for homes for workers, Harold and Jenna moved to Midland, where he became a homebuilder. For some ventures, he joined forces with Lloyd E. Waynick, another builder, and together they formed Waynick and Welch Company. Eventually, Harold would build 200 homes.

Harold maintained his office in a tiny room off the kitchen of his home at 2500 Humble Avenue. On Sundays, the Welches attended the First United Methodist Church, where Laura was baptized and would later marry. Harold and Jenna were a team. He built the houses, drawing up a rough floor plan and then taking it to a drafts-man to finish. Jenna kept the books.

Jenna was a traditional stay-at-home mother, which was the norm in those days. As in the television show *Father Knows Best*, Jenna knew all Laura's friends and spent most of her time in the kitchen. She often made chili with red beans, rice, and guacamole.

"Laura's mom always fixed three meals a day," remembered Jan Donnelly O'Neill, who became friends with Laura in the ninth grade. "Her dad would often be home for lunch. So she was always in the kitchen."[2]

After living at two other homes in Midland, in 1961, Harold built the three-bedroom ranch house on Humble Avenue that would be Laura's home until she went to college. It was a typical fifties-era sub-urban neighborhood—kids biking, playing baseball. Laura's friends and neighbors from those days would be her friends for life.

Harold was a warm man with a slight paunch and a ruddy face. Outside the house, he always wore a fedora, which covered a large bald spot. He was a cutup, full of energy and always cracking jokes. "Harold was really funny, had a great sense of humor," recalled Laura's cousin Mary Mark Welch, whose father was Harold's only sibling. "He was boisterous, happy-go-lucky, and had a very positive attitude." In this respect, friends observe, he was very much like the man she later married.

"I remember the first time I met her father in Midland," said Janet Kinard Heyne. A Kappa Alpha Theta sorority sister of Laura's, she roomed with her when Laura was working in Dallas and Houston. "Harold was the kind who had so much nervous energy and paced around all the time," she said. "When I first met George, I thought he was like her father. Super-energetic and couldn't sit still."[3]

Also like her future husband, Harold was intensely sociable. Almost every morning, he would smoke and drink coffee at Johnny's Barbecue with the owners, his friends John and Betty Hackney. Harold called the small restaurant the "Sick Pig" because he thought the pig on a spit painted on the sign outside the place looked like it had been stricken with a grave illness. Occasionally, Harold ate at the restaurant, where customers savored succulent barbecue beef brisket, pork ribs, turkey breast, ham, or German sausage with barbecue sauce lovingly ladled over them. When asked for the secret to his barbecue, Johnny would say, "You want to know how the hell we make barbecue? Barbecue is the simplest thing in the world. We don't do a damn thing! Just put it in a big ol' pit and cook it slow with oak all night long."

Also like George, Harold was an ardent sports fan. He was a bit of a gambler, too. Either with friends or through a broker, he would place bets on college and professional football games.

"They had football parties at their house," Mary Mark Welch remembered. "They watched the games and bet on different teams. Harold would do research. He would call around and find out which player on which team had an ingrown toenail."[4]

Because of the possibility that it might become a politically embarrassing issue, "Harold quit betting completely when George Senior became vice president," Johnny Hackney said.

He also quit smoking after his brother, Dr. Mark Lane Welch, a general surgeon, reviewed Harold's chest X-ray and found a suspicious spot on his lung. It turned out to be lung cancer, and Harold had successful surgery to remove part of his lung.[5]

Like her mother, Laura was an only child—unusual for a family in those days. From an early age, she was a self-sufficient child, immersing herself in books. She also always had a dog as a companion, the last one being Marty, short for Martini. When Laura was an infant, the Welches had a dog named Bully. Laura could say "Bully" before she could say "mom" or "dad," according to what Jenna Welch told Mary Mark Welch.

"Bully was a mutt who would just run away," Mary Mark Welch said. "He was always being picked up by the dogcatcher. He would go to a department store. They had a pneumatic-tube system for getting change. The central office sent back the change. The dog would go and watch it. The dog thought it was really neat. Aunt Jenna was in there one time. A salesperson said, 'Do you know who that dog belongs to? He is in here all the time.' She told me she said, 'I don't know.'"

When Bully ran away, Harold would have to go to the pound and pay a dollar to get him back. "The next day, Bully got out again and was picked up again. Harold went down to pick him up a few days later," Mary Mark Welch explained. "The dogcatcher said, 'That will be a dollar.' Harold said, 'I don't know if he's worth a dollar.' The dogcatcher said, 'Well, just take him.'"

Laura's parents had not intended to have so small a family. At a young age, Laura was aware of her mother's difficulties bearing children. Both before and after Laura was born, her mother had several stillborns. One child, born before Laura, died when it was a few days old. Once, Laura's parents took her on a visit to the Gladney Center for Adoption in Fort Worth. In the end, however, they decided against adopting. Later in life, Laura and George would consider adoption when she, too, was having trouble conceiving a child.

Being conceived after such trauma affected Laura's personality. As she herself once explained, "I felt very obligated to my parents. I didn't want to upset them in any way."

Perhaps in response to the hardships they had faced, both Laura's parents adopted an irreverent, lighthearted approach to life. Laura and her father were constantly poking fun at each other, and Laura's mother never took herself seriously. Laura was so close to her father that after her twins were born in Midland, Harold would drop in almost every day to see her and the girls. But Laura's mother was the stronger influence on her. Her calm competence and quiet virtues, though of a kind that may be easily overlooked, were an enduring legacy to her daughter.

For twenty years, until Jenna moved to a retirement home in June 2004, Kathy Robbins lived across the street from her on Humble Avenue. The woman she describes is, like her daughter, first and foremost a loyal and constant friend.

Jenna "always had all the time in the world for conversation," said Robbins, who continues to be her friend. "She was the best neighbor in the world. We would call each other whenever for sugar, coffee, whatever we were out of. If her dishwasher was broken, she was at my house and vice versa. I watched the way she is with other people. It's all about them, not her. She always sees the best in people, and she always gets that in return."[6]

The only time Robbins heard Jenna say anything negative was when the press was beating up on the twins. "She thought you can say whatever you want about the grown-ups, but leave the kids alone," Robbins said.

Jenna had a range of interests, from astronomy to bird-watching. But most of all, she loved to read. "Jenna wore heavy glasses, so she didn't get involved in sports," her childhood friend Jackie Stubblefield Ball recalled. "Her family attributed it to reading too much."[7]

Jenna is "very educated about astronomy," Kathy Robbins said. "She would say, 'Did you know there is going to be an eclipse? Let's take your kids. Let's get our flashlights and meet in the front yard. Let's spread our blankets out and look at the stars.' She would show the children all of these things. Or she would call in the fall and say, 'Butterflies are migrating.' We would meet in the front yard, and she would show me all these different birds. She would do a bird count twice a year with her birding group."

Laura adopted most of her mother's interests, especially reading.

Later in life, she kept a birding journal and went on bird-watching trips with her mother to places like Belize.

"Oh!" Jenna would say when she learned a new fact. Some might think that Jenna's enthusiasm for the wonders of nature was born of naïveté. But—very much like her daughter in this respect—it reflects a conscious choice to go through life with a positive attitude. "It's how she chooses to view the world and the people around her," Robbins said.

That attitude, in turn, reflects the culture of West Texas, and of Midland in particular. Laura is much like the strong pioneer women who were her forebears. They came on creaky wagons and stagecoaches and endured blizzards, prairie fires, malaria, wolves, horse kicks, and Indian raids. In winter, the wind whistled through the walls of their log cabins. In summer, dust blew through. If a horse or farm animal was gored, the pioneer women cleansed the wound and stitched it. The women preserved and dried fruit and butchered and cured meat. They cooked in kettles suspended from a wire over a fireplace. They washed clothes in iron kettles filled with water hauled from a well. The women administered herbal brews to reduce fevers and used a strong dose of whiskey as an antiseptic. The pioneer women were practical women who had no time for theorizing, ruminating, or complaining. They developed the virtues of fortitude and resilience to overcome the deprivations, the loneliness, and the hardship. And they kept their eyes on the horizon.

"Can you imagine coming here in the late 1880s, trying to find water?" asked Martha Holton, who lives on Humble Avenue three blocks to the east of Laura's childhood home. "Ranchers and farmers had to be made of pretty good stock to survive that." Holton's late husband, Walter, helped George Bush get started in the oil business, teaching him how to be a land man, someone who searches courthouse records to determine who owns property and whether they own the mineral rights. "These women had to be really optimistic, independent people to raise a family while the husband is trying to plow, and the wind and sand are blowing," Holton said. "It took strong people to survive out here in the beginning, and a lot of that carried over."[8]

If the terrain was hostile, it also fostered a sense that men and women could achieve anything if they were determined enough. The flatness and the open, clear skies made it seem as if there were no limits—no impediments to success and realizing one's dreams.

"The sky's the limit" became Midland's motto.

Laura would tell the *Midland Reporter-Telegram* that she thought this spirit of freedom had "something to do with the landscape because the sky is so huge . . . There is a real feeling of unlimited possibilities here. Also, I think the people that the oil business attracts to living here are risk-takers and optimists, or they would not be in that business."[9]

At the same time, as fortunes were made and lost in oil and gas, Midland residents were quick to see that anyone could become a millionaire or a pauper overnight. This kind of economic uncertainty engendered a spirit of humility, directness, and friendliness, one that encouraged helping others and focusing on what's important in life.

Despite extreme disparities of wealth, the spirit of Midland has always been egalitarian and "small *d*" democratic. "You can see somebody in a grocery store who looks like he just came off a ranch, and he could be a multimillionaire and you'd never know it, and he wouldn't want you to know it," Holton said.

"You're not going to get very far here if you think you are better than anybody else," said Tammy Smith, Holton's daughter, who is a land "man" herself. "We are brought up to think that everybody is the same, everybody is equal. If you walk downtown and you see people you don't know, they speak to you and say hello."[10]

"People in Midland are very generous as far as helping other people," Holton said. "If there's a tragedy and they need money, it's usually taken care of, and you never know who contributed to get them over the hump. Those things are just done. Neighbors help neighbors."

Above all, Midlanders keep their word. "If I tell you I'm going to do something, it's what I'm going to do," Holton said. "We don't have to get a notary. You can set your sights on a goal, and if you have integrity and want to, you can accomplish a lot."

The Midland of Laura's youth was a place frozen in time—a throwback to a lost era of American innocence. It was here that Laura and George Bush both absorbed the bedrock values that would guide them through the tumultuous times ahead.

2

A CRUSH ON GEORGE

A November baby, Laura was too young to enter first grade in the Midland schools. So her mother sent her to Alyne Gray's Jack and Jill for first grade, according to her friend Susie Marinis Evans, who attended school with her and later walked to school with George. In the second and third grade, Laura attended North Elementary, a public school. When North closed and Bowie Elementary opened at 805 Elk Avenue, she went there until the sixth grade.[1]

Coincidentally, Bowie was just fourteen blocks to the northeast of Sam Houston Elementary, where Laura's future husband was enrolled. It was one of several near misses that occurred before they met and married.

While Bush's grandparents came from wealth—Barbara's father was president of McCall Publishing Company and a descendant of Franklin Pierce, fourteenth president of the U.S., while George H. W. Bush's father was an investment banker and a U.S. senator—Bush's parents themselves had little money when he was growing up in Midland. When George Walker Bush was born on July 6, 1946, his father was finishing Yale. In 1948, after a distinguished tour of duty as a naval pilot in the Pacific, Bush Senior moved his family to

Odessa, Texas, where he hoped to make it in the oil business. There they moved into a tiny one-bedroom duplex apartment on East Seventh Street. They owned the only refrigerator on the block and shared a bathroom with a mother and daughter who moved in later. The women turned out to be prostitutes.

At first, the senior Bush worked as a $375-a-month oil-drilling-equipment clerk. Then he became an independent oilman, scouting out land that had petroleum-producing potential. He also negotiated with owners for mineral rights. He worked from morning until night and traveled the oil patch extensively. By then, George W. Bush, their first child, was two.

By 1950, they had moved to Midland. Their first home, at 405 East Maple, was so small it looked like a shack.

Little George played Little League baseball and climbed over fences to get to his friends' houses. In Midland in those days, no one locked their doors. Car keys were left under the seat, in an ashtray, even in the ignition. At night, the scream of freight-train whistles filled the air.

On almost every other block, there was a church. On the radio, preaching, punctuated by cries of "hallelujah."

"When you see the bad things and you start sinking, get your eyes back on Jesus," a preacher would exclaim.

Midlanders picked up only two television stations with a rooftop antenna or the rabbit ears on top of their black-and-white sets. At 11 P.M., the stations played "The Star-Spangled Banner" and went off the air. *Hopalong Cassidy* and *The Lone Ranger* dominated the airwaves. Cowboys were the good guys who saved the day and won the pretty girls.

These shows promulgated the American creed in its simplest form. "I believe that to have a friend, a man must be one," the Lone Ranger declared. "That all men are created equal, and that everyone has within himself the power to make this a better world. That God put the firewood there, but that every man must gather and light it himself. In being prepared physically, mentally, and morally to fight when necessary for that which is right."

In these respects and others as well, George's childhood, like Laura's, was typical of its time and place—part of an almost forgotten world of childhood innocence. George brought baseball cards to school for show-and-tell. He was "the class clown and flirt," Linda Mills Wofford, a classmate, recalled. "He would sit behind me and pull on my ponytail. He would chase me around on the playground and tease me."[2]

Sometimes a teacher might say, "Someone in our class could be president of the United States someday!" recalled Christine Mast Gilbert. "You might have looked around and wondered which boy it would have been. No one would have thought it could be a girl. We probably would have picked Lyle Burkhead," Gilbert said. "I don't think we'd have picked George. He was too normal, average in school, kind of a prankster, and not what you thought of as presidential material."

In the first grade, Gilbert recalled, "our classroom had long, low tables that sat four children, with two boys on one side and two girls on the other side. George sat across the table from me. He was cute and freckled, and I had a crush on him all through grade school, but I was shy and not one of the 'popular' girls.

"Girls always wore dresses to school back then," Gilbert added. "George and the other boys often peeked under the table trying to see up our skirts, and the other girls and I would sometimes let them! We got a lot of giggles out of that."[3]

In the third and fourth grades, Gilbert still had a crush on George. By then, the children had individual desks with tops that lifted up, under which they kept their school supplies.

"One of the most embarrassing moments of my childhood happened one day when a note fell out of my crayon box and the boy sitting in front of George picked it up and read it, then showed it to George. They tapped me on the shoulder and handed it to me and asked if I wrote it. It said, 'I love George Bush.' I probably blushed a dozen shades of red, but I adamantly denied that I wrote it."

On Fridays, "our big event was trying to see who could blow the biggest bubble," Linda Wofford said. "I remember competing with George and sitting there blowing these huge Bazookas. We put like twenty pieces in our mouths and tried to blow these huge bubbles. Mine were so big it would get in my hair."

"We were on the safety patrol at Sam Houston," said Susie Marinis Evans, whose husband, Don Evans, would later become Bush's commerce secretary. "We thought we were really big on the safety patrol, directing kids crossing the street, and we were only sixth graders. George won the safety-patrol award."[4]

"We played spin the bottle in my garage for my sixth-grade birthday," Wofford said. "My parents said you can play music, but you have to be in the garage. I'm sure George was there. When my parents came to the door and asked what we were doing, we would put the lights on and act like we were dancing."

Wofford was in George's second-grade class when his mother and father came to pick him up and tell him that his little sister Robin, who was three, had died of leukemia.

"My mom and dad and sister are home!" George shouted to a teacher. "Can I go see them?"

He raced to the car and thought he saw Robin.

"I got to the car still certain Robin was there," Bush said later, "but of course, she was not."

"We felt devastated by what we had to tell him," Barbara Bush wrote in her memoirs. "As I recall, he asked a lot of questions and couldn't understand why we hadn't told him when we had known for a long time."

"In those days, you didn't talk about cancer or dying much," said Bush's sister Dorothy "Doro" Bush Koch. "He kind of wished my parents had told him she was dying. But they wanted to protect him."[5]

At night, Bush had nightmares about Robin. He asked his father if "my sister was buried standing up or in a prone position . . . because the earth rotates, they said so at school, and . . . does that mean Robin is standing on her head?"[6]

George felt an obligation to comfort his mother, who leaned on her son for support while her husband traveled. When he came home from school, he was her constant companion. He would joke and laugh to make her feel better. But the loss also gave him a sense of how fleeting and arbitrary life can be.

"I believe the death of his sister was a major event in his life," said Elsie Walker, a cousin of George's whose sister also died early. "Robin was a beautiful child. I think her death broke his heart. But, on the other side, I think it deepened him and made him more compassionate. It also might have helped to turn him into a clown because he tried to make things better around the house and tried to keep things light. My guess is that he repressed a lot of his grief. Incidentally, I think the fact that he was close to Robin and close to his mother after her death is one reason he gets along so well with women."[7]

In contrast to George, Laura was perceived as shy or, as she later liked to say, "reserved." She was not unsociable by any means, however. Like other girls her age, she joined the Brownies and the Girl Scouts, attended Girl Scout camp, sang in the church choir, and took ballet and swimming lessons. But most of all, she liked to read.

In those days of no Internet, no e-mail, and no instant messaging, each house had one telephone line and usually one telephone. There were no answering machines and no area codes. Operators placed long-distance calls. If a line was busy, that was tough: there was no such thing as call waiting. The television set was in the living room, so watching TV was a family activity, and often involved friends and neighbors as well.

Laura had a vivid memory of her trips to the public library with her mother. By then, Midland's population had grown from 20,000 when Laura was born to 62,000, but the library was still housed in the Midland County Courthouse, then a white Art Deco structure.

These trips to the library were a defining part of her childhood. As Laura later said, "Even at three and four years of age, I remember thinking how special the library must be. Here were so many books with people of all ages enjoying them, located in the most important building in our town."

Laura's favorite books were from the *Little House on the Prairie* series by Laura Ingalls Wilder. "I loved the main character, Laura, because we shared the same name," she said. "But what I loved even more was sitting with my mother, listening to her read." Laura's mother read *Little Women* to her. "I remember both of us crying when Beth died," she said.

Laura's friend Pamela Nelson, who first got to know her in junior high when she borrowed her lipstick in the girls' room, recalled that their favorite entertainment was reading, usually in Laura's bedroom at the back of her house.

"We would lie there and tell each other what the other one was reading," Nelson said in her soft, crooning drawl. "It was so comforting to be around her and sit on her bed and read. She didn't have sisters or brothers, but she collected friends. People liked to be around her because of how solid she was. It was a peaceful place around her."

Much later, Laura told her close friend Anne Sewell Johnson, "Introverts are very happy people. We don't need all the feedback that other people need."

Girls in those days were not expected to have a profession. In a section about the school's homemaking department, Laura's high school annual or yearbook would say, "To help each girl reach her ultimate goal of becoming a successful wife and mother, Lee's Homemaking Department offers a variety of courses in domestic skills." Beneath a photo of students looking warily at the food they had prepared is the caption: "Home Ec girls, realizing their way to their future husbands' hearts, try out their cooking skills with teacher, Marlene Wesselman."

Despite these expectations, back as far as age two, Laura wanted to be a teacher. "That's what girls did a lot in those days," said her cousin Mary Mark Welch. "You became a teacher, a dental hygienist, or a flight attendant if you wanted to have a job."

Laura would practice teaching on her dolls. Looking back, she joked that she had "the best educated dolls in America." Her mother remembered that when Laura had a friend over, they set up a classroom in Laura's bedroom but then struck up a conversation in the hallway. When her mother asked why she was talking in the hall, Laura said, "This is what our teachers do!"[8]

Like her future husband, Laura also had a remarkable capacity to remember names, and she liked to give nicknames to people.

"Laura would sometimes call her father Harold Bruce," said Mary Mark Welch. "They are a very relaxed family. And she called her mother and father MoBini and PoBini, terms of endearment. Or just Mo and Po."

When Laura and George entered seventh grade, they were, for the first time, in the same school, San Jacinto Junior High, a beige brick building just nine blocks southeast of Laura's house. While they later said they "sort of" remembered each other, they were never in the same classroom.

"For art class," recalled Marge McColl Petty, who became a friend of Laura's, "George and I spent a good deal of time one year creating a mosaic on the wall of the San Jacinto cafeteria of Santa Anna surrendering to Houston, sitting with his broken leg under a sycamore cottonwood."[9]

George was elected class president, but while Laura was popular and one of the prettiest girls in school, she liked to remain in the background.

"Laura was always one of the nicest girls in our class," said Christine Gilbert. "Girls can be so snotty and stuck-up, and in Midland there was a social strata [sic] with the working-class kids, the smart kids, the popular kids. I was in the smart-kids group, accepted by others but not popular. Laura was very shy but was also very well liked, an egalitarian, nice to everyone."

"Our parents would say, 'We want you to be like Laura Welch,'" said Pamela Nelson. "They would say, 'We want you to be friends with Laura Welch. We want you to run around with Laura Welch.' It was because she was like a perfect girl to her mother and dad. She just had this manner, and everyone thought she was perfect."[10]

Normally, a girl who was held up as a model in this way would be resented by other girls. But because she was nice to everyone, the remarkable thing about Laura was that she wasn't disliked.

In 1959, at the end of the seventh grade, George and his family moved to Houston. Their last home in Midland was half a mile from Laura's house.

3

ROCK 'N' ROLL

When Laura started at Robert E. Lee High School in the fall of 1961, the rock-'n'-roll craze was in full effect, challenging established balladeers like Perry Como, Frankie Laine, and Bing Crosby. Laura relished the tunes and had a collection of well-worn 45s.

Regan Kimberlin Gammon first knew Laura when they were in Brownies together, and they became best friends in seventh grade. Music "was a huge part of our lives," Regan said. "We danced around to music all the time. Friday night was about dancing. Saturday night was all about dancing. Laura and I loved to listen to the radio and dance around and sing along. Music was the background of our lives."[1]

Laura's tastes ranged from Elvis and the Beatles to the Neville Brothers, Ray Charles, Joan Baez, the Crickets, Little Richard, Muddy Waters, Bo Diddley, the Big Bopper, Lenny Welch, and Little Willie John. She especially liked Buddy Holly, who was from Lubbock, and Roy Orbison, who was from Odessa.

Robert E. Lee High School had just opened that year on Neely Avenue. A handsome building made of beige brick, it was fifteen blocks from Laura's home. Everyone west of Garfield Street went to

31

Lee. The school flew a Confederate flag, and its football team was called the Lee Rebels.

Midland had two other high schools, Midland High and George Washington Carver High. Having gone to the same elementary and junior high schools, the students at Midland and Lee were used to mixing socially with one another. However, Midland was segregated, and Carver was an entirely black school in a black section of town called the Flats. It was literally on the other side of the railroad tracks. Most of the streets there were unpaved. Even though Carver was a mile from Midland High and four miles from Lee, no one at Carver—now closed—mixed with students from the other schools except when the boys played in summer baseball leagues.

Ann Gerhart, a *Washington Post* reporter, wrote in her book *The Perfect Wife: The Life and Choices of Laura Bush*, "What Laura Bush never mentions in her accounts of growing up in Midland—not in interviews nor in all the speeches she has given as first lady of Texas and the United States to commemorate Martin Luther King Day— is that she grew up in a time and place where segregation ruled completely." Gerhart went on to scold both Laura and George for remembering Midland as a place where "people only had good values." It was, she wrote, "an odd view of America, to look back on this town and see it as a paradise without mentioning this shame." Indeed, Gerhart wrote, the history of bias in Midland is "uglier and more persistent" than "elsewhere."[2]

The truth was that Midland's racial bias was no worse than it was in other places. As anyone who lived in the 1960s knows, not only was the entire South segregated; the North imposed a more subtle prejudice that was just as devastating.[3] It would take years of civil-rights marches, sit-ins, and deployment of federal troops before federal legislation was passed that finally began to make an impact on discrimination in America. Growing up when and where they did, Laura and her friends simply accepted that this was the way things were.

"We just didn't realize that segregation was terribly wrong," Regan Gammon said. "That's the age we lived in."

Like teenagers everywhere in America at the time, Laura and her friends were largely unaware of world events, poverty, or social issues. To be gay meant you were in a laughing mood; a "queer" person was an unusual one. Drugs were unheard of. A Coke party meant that Coca-Cola was served. No one knew about the Beat generation. Few had heard of the Bay of Pigs. What teenagers in Midland did know was how to drive around aimlessly in cars that sprouted tail fins modeled after jet planes.

"In Midland, there wasn't much to do," said Don Aiken, a classmate of Laura's who dated some of her friends. "There was no lake, no pond, no parks to speak of. We had a ten-mile loop. We cruised. We went to Agnes' Drive-in and had a Coke or we had a fifteen-cent hamburger and french fries. It was the place to see and be seen. We would see someone and say, 'Did you see him? Where was he before?' We'd cruise for another hour or so and maybe go back there and have another Coke. Then we'd loop around again. We'd wave at our friends as they were going east. Then we'd wave and they're going west. It was like *American Graffiti*."[4]

Dating meant going to a dance or a movie, usually at a drive-in. Midland had three: the Fiesta, the Texan, and the Chief. Sometimes the theaters showed 3-D movies, requiring patrons to wear Polaroid glasses. To avoid the one-dollar admission charge, kids would hide in the trunks of cars.

Girls wore sweaters or white blouses and skirts made of felt with a patch in the shape of a poodle glued on. Under their dresses they wore petticoats. Skirts came to just below the knee. Girls wore penny loafers and bobby socks and would slip a penny into the notch of their penny loafers.

"Besides driving around, we would do our hair," said Peggy Porter Weiss, who was in Brownies with Laura and became friends with her in high school. "We had big old hair dryers and big rollers. It was a big challenge to straighten out hair and then get it high. But it was kind of a social thing. I would say to Laura, 'Why don't you come over and let's do our hair?' "

The bubble hairdo was especially popular. "We all rolled it, ratted, and sprayed it," Christine Gilbert said. "Some girls sported pony-tails."

Boys wore tan chino pants with pink shirts. They had crew cuts or ducktails (known as DAs) and put Brylcreem, Wildroot, or Vitalis in their hair. They might buy condoms and put them in their wallets, but that was mainly for show. Over time, the unused packet would leave a round impression on their wallets.

"See you later, alligator" and "In a while, crocodile" were favorite expressions.

Boys would proudly place "Caution" signs on the front lawns of girls' houses, either because they liked them or because they didn't. In the summer, for entertainment, boys might shoot rattlesnakes or rabbits on the outskirts of town. Even though they drove their families' cars, what car they drove was important. Cars had names like Thunderbird, Spitfire, and Wildcat. New models with entirely different bodies came out each year. Car designers were like rock stars. No one worried about fuel economy, and General Motors was the largest corporation in the world.

The first issue of *Playboy* came out in December 1953 with Marilyn Monroe on the cover, but few of the boys in Laura's circle ever saw a copy.

"Getting a copy of *Playboy* was wishful thinking," Don Aiken said.

Nor did most of them see, much less read, Grace Metalious's steamy 1956 novel, *Peyton Place*, which lifted the lid off a small New Hampshire town.

With few exceptions, dating followed certain rules, laid down by the girls. No kissing on the first date. On the second date, a girl might allow a kiss at the front door as her father anxiously peered out the window. On subsequent dates, the girl might make out in a car, meaning she would engage in prolonged kissing, not petting. Otherwise, the boy would not "respect" her.

"No kissing on a first date was the rule," Regan Gammon said. "It was like *Leave It to Beaver*," she said. "You don't call boys. You wouldn't make out with somebody unless they were really, really your best boyfriend and then you might kiss him for a while. Petting would not be allowed. There would be a few girls with bad reputations, but that was because I think they would openly smoke cigarettes."

"I read *Peyton Place* in my sister's room," said Linda Mills Wofford, who became a cheerleader at Lee High. "But Laura was squeaky-clean. She might have kissed someone. She had an impeccable reputation. No one was talking behind her back."[5]

"Having a drink of whiskey on a ski trip with our church was what we might do," Pamela Nelson said. "But Laura would never be accused of doing anything."

"Laura was never party to a rumor that I knew of," her high school classmate Don Aiken said. "If you kissed her good-bye at the front door, wow!"

Laura had several overlapping circles of friends. They were neither overly intellectual nor necessarily athletes.

"Everyone was mixed in together," Gammon said. "It was a free-for-all. There were circles of friends, but you didn't have to be with certain people all the time. As wealthy as some of the people were, nobody cared."

"Midland didn't have a lot of places to go," Nelson said. "We just went to each other's houses. It made for strong friendships."

Laura earned respect because she did not gossip. Instead, she had a ready laugh and was a good listener.

"In high school, I was always having boy problems," said Candy Poague Reed. "I would go over to Laura's, and she would try to help me out. We would sit in her bathroom on the side of the tub, and she would tell me to be patient or offer other advice. She was a good listener and would say, 'He's not worth it,' or 'Be patient.' "[6]

"Laura was the way she is now," said Peggy Porter Weiss. "She was fun and funny, interested and interesting, and always calm. You just wanted to be around her. She doesn't take up all the oxygen in the room. She is more likely to ask you questions than to tell you what she thinks."[7]

At the beginning of her sophomore year, Laura began dating Harvey Kennedy, a gangly six-footer who was a year ahead of her at Midland. They met because a friend of his was dating Regan Gammon. While each of them occasionally dated others, Laura and Kennedy essentially went steady for two years.

"What we did was just a lot of hanging out," Kennedy said. "We drove around in a circle, as goofy as that sounds."

With the money he made working summers and a gift from his father, Kennedy was able to scrape together enough to buy a used 1957 Chevrolet with big fins.

"It was powder blue with a white top," Kennedy said. "It had an AM radio that picked up two stations, one country and one popular. We would go to Agnes' Drive-in, where we got a Coke (Laura preferred Dr Pepper) and hung out and saw other people. We hung out at Laura's house a lot. My best friend Todd Southern was dating Regan Kimberlin Gammon. A lot of times it was a foursome. We listened to music like her Joan Baez album and hung out until it was time to go home."[8]

Laura and Harvey went to dances at their respective schools or at the Midland Youth Center next to Midland High. Laura was a good dancer, and Harvey would try to master the Stroll, the Mashed Potato, or the Twist.

Laura was "a good student," Kennedy said. "Her parents would never have let her have any social life if she didn't have good grades. She was very smart. If she wasn't straight A, she was close to it."

Kennedy had never taken a date to a sit-down restaurant, but Laura introduced him to Luigi's, an Italian place with red-checked tablecloths. It was the first time he had had pizza. She also introduced him to music recitals and musicals like *The Music Man*.

"The restaurants and movies had separate sections for blacks," Kennedy recalled. "In movies, we would sit down below. Blacks sat in the balconies. No one asked why blacks didn't go to school with us. It was the culture. My kids ask why people would think like that. I don't have a good answer because I don't know why we thought like that, either. My kids ask where the laws were. I explain there weren't laws against that.

"In the summer, I saw her almost every day," he said. "We'd go swimming a lot and go to pool parties. We didn't do anything on school nights. On a Friday night or Saturday night, maybe we went to a movie. Sometimes we saw each other after school."

For someplace different to go, Harvey and Laura would drive to Odessa, down a twenty-two-mile stretch of road to the southwest that was dotted with oil wells.

The two would park in the mesquite on the outskirts of town.

"Things were pretty straitlaced," Kennedy said. "Preserving your reputation was important. We would go parking in the woods to make out. That was that. A few girls in high school got pregnant. They would drop out of school. A lot of guys talked about sex, and a lot of guys lied. They would say they went all the way on the first date."

While Harvey and Laura were necking in front of her house, Laura's father would often blink the porch lights.

"When the lights started blinking, it was time to come in," Kennedy said. "Harold was gruff, so you didn't want to cross him. That was the way you were supposed to be when you had a daughter."

Kennedy took Laura to his senior prom, and Laura took him to her junior prom. Because they were supposed to bring dates only from their own schools, they registered other classmates as their dates.

But if Laura almost never broke the rules, she was still no Stepford girlfriend.

"I can still remember being told regularly not to contradict her," Kennedy recalled. "She did not like to be contradicted. I was probably the biggest jerk in the world," he said.

When Harvey went off to college in El Paso, the two stopped seeing each other. "I don't think there was a specific breakup," Kennedy said. "There was an understanding that I was leaving and she was staying and that this was a high school romance."

Kennedy would reappear twice in Laura's life, both times under surprising circumstances.

4

THE END OF THE WORLD

Just before Laura entered ninth grade, her father introduced her to Judy Dykes Hester, who would wind up being tied to Laura through tragedy. Judy was also about to enter ninth grade. Her father sold used oil-drilling equipment and knew Laura's father from when they both lived in Lubbock. Harold had built Hester's parents' house on Neely Avenue in Midland. The two men liked to watch football games on TV together and drink a beer or two. One weekend, Harold brought Laura over to meet Judy. They wound up in honors English together and became fast friends.

"She had her own room to herself and her own bathroom," Hester said. "I was impressed by that. I would spend the night with her. I liked her as a friend because she was someone I could talk to. I was a little shy. She was a little shy. I could be open with her. We were not very wild. We shared some life values. You didn't want to disappoint your parents. You were respectful of them. You were a good friend. You kept your promises. Her parents would encourage her to be friends with me. She said, 'My parents really like you.' They thought I was fairly reserved, too."[1]

Judy and Laura often went to slumber parties at friends' homes.

Once, for a special occasion, they got their hair done at a beauty shop. They heard their first Beatles song together on a car radio.

"We thought that's kind of cool—a different sound," Judy said.

Laura introduced Judy to Lenny Welch. The fact that Laura liked a black musician's work was a little on the edge. Many disc jockeys refused to play records by black musicians or even Elvis Presley records because, they said, he sang like one.

Laura especially liked Welch's "Since I Fell for You," which ended, "I can't get you out of my heart."

Every school day, Judy and Pamela Nelson, Laura's close friend, carpooled to Lee High, alternately driving one of their parents' cars.

As they entered their junior year in high school, Laura and Judy Hester often double-dated. Laura was going with Harvey Kennedy, and Judy was going with Dewey "Bud" Corley. Kennedy remembered that one afternoon when Judy's father and Laura's father were watching a football game, Harold offered him a beer. Since Kennedy's father was a teetotaler, he never told his parents.[2]

"We went to Agnes' Drive-in for hamburgers and milk shakes," Corley remembered. "Because their parking lot was small, everyone was parked bumper to bumper. There would be three or four cars parked back-to-back up to the awning. They would bring hamburgers and french fries out to your car. If someone wanted to leave, everyone else would have to back out. It was a rotating circus of people. Everyone knew each other."[3]

In their senior year, Laura and Judy occasionally smoked in each other's car. But when it came to dating, Judy was even more conservative than Laura. Both Judy and Corley described their relationship with the same word: *wholesome*. Don Aiken remembered taking Judy out five times and never getting a kiss good night.

"I don't recall any discussion with Laura about sex," Judy Hester said. "Occasionally, we would say, 'Did you kiss him?' "

Then an event occurred that shattered this idyllic teenage world and left its mark on young Laura forever.

On the evening of Wednesday, November 6, 1963, Judy and Laura went to Luigi's on Wall Street for a pizza. The next day was a teachers' meeting, so they had the day off from school. Otherwise, they would not have been out. Two days earlier, Laura had turned seventeen.

Laura was driving her parents' brand-new Chevrolet Impala. After dinner, as was the ritual, the girls went for a drive. They drove north toward the outskirts of town, then looped east on Farm Road 868 in the country. Originally called a farm-to-market road, a farm road is a secondary two-lane road without a shoulder. The roads were designed to carry produce from a rural area to town. Teenagers used this particular road, now a highway called the Loop, as a drag strip.

At 8:28 P.M., according to the Midland police accident report, Laura ran a stop sign at the intersection of State Highway 349 and slammed into a 1962 Corvair sedan driven by Michael D. Douglas. Douglas, who had olive skin, perfect teeth, and big ears, was a close friend of Laura's and one of the most popular boys in her class. Douglas lived a mile away from the scene of the accident on Solomon Lane. That night, he had a date with Peggy Weiss, who had just been practicing for a dance recital with Regan Gammon. Before his date with Weiss, Douglas was driving south toward the city. His father was following him.

"He was going to see his sister, whose child needed some physical therapy," said Regan, who had previously dated Douglas. "Mike and some other friends would go and help with that baby. So he was on his way into town."[4]

"I remember seeing the stop sign all of a sudden," said Judy Dykes Hester, who was in the passenger seat.* "The intersection had no lighting. I remember it was extremely dark. There was nothing to let us know that it was coming. All of a sudden, it was upon us. I said,

---

*Prior to this book, Judy Dykes Hester received only one other request from the media to tell her story. She declined.

'Laura, there's a stop sign!' By then, it was too late. I don't remember seeing the other car. I remember ducking. I bent my knees. If I hadn't, I could have gone through the windshield. There were no seat belts. Then I was on the floorboards."[5]

In those days, safety was the last thing on car designers' minds. The auto industry had the attitude that it was up to drivers not to get into accidents. They maintained that safety features would add to the cost of cars and make people less willing to buy them. Cars had no seat belts or air bags. Dashboards were made of steel with no padding, and they had sharp edges that were supposed to be stylish. In an accident, the protrusions slashed open the heads of occupants hurled against them. Steering wheels were rigid and would not collapse in an accident. Because their centers did not have padded panels as they do now, steering-wheel columns would impale drivers unfortunate enough to have accidents. Upon impact, car doors flipped open easily, so passengers were thrown to the street.

Neither Laura nor Judy drank, and Judy said Laura always drove cautiously.

"We weren't doing anything bizarre or going excessively fast," Judy said. "We were probably listening to the radio.

"I remember getting up and getting out," Judy said. "Laura had been thrown from the car. I heard her calling my name. It was dark. I remember people running to us. I saw a body on the ground. It was a form. I was somewhat in shock. In the background, a woman was saying, 'Oh my gosh, oh my gosh.' Then there were police. The ambulance was there. They put us in the ambulance, and it took us to the hospital."

Douglas died of a broken neck at the scene. Both cars were totaled.

The police report said Laura had been going fifty miles per hour, just under the speed limit of fifty-five. She was not cited for any infractions.

"Vehicle Number 2 [Laura's car] did not see stop sign or Vehicle Number One," the report said.

As with car designers, highway engineers in those days had the attitude that if drivers had accidents, it was their fault. They gave little thought to warning drivers to slow in advance of a stop sign, even on a road with a speed limit of fifty-five miles per hour. Today a stop sign planted in the middle of a high-speed road without any warning signs or lighting would be considered an invitation to disaster.

A photo taken the day after the accident and attached to the police report shows that the stop sign was located in a field at least twenty feet to the right of the road, so headlights were unlikely to pick it up until a car was almost on top of it. In fact, of Midland's nine traffic fatalities up to that point that year, two were at that intersection, the *Midland Reporter-Telegram* said in reporting the accident two days later.[6] A few years after the accident, Judy returned to the scene and found that traffic lights had been installed at the intersection. The intersection had been widened and was now lighted.

At Midland Memorial Hospital, the same hospital where Laura was born, a doctor stitched up a cut on her right knee. Judy, whose back hurt, stayed in the waiting room.

"First I called my home," said Judy. "The line was busy. I called her home. There was no answer. She had already told me that her parents were out visiting friends. I called my line again. I told my mother we had been in an accident. My parents somehow got in touch with her parents."

Judy noticed a distraught family in the waiting room.

"A member of that family came over to ask me if I was all right," Judy said. "I asked who they were, and that's when I realized the driver of the other car was Mike. The man told me that yes, he had died. So that's when I knew."

Both Judy and Laura were released to go home. Regan Gammon learned about the accident from her father, who had heard about it on the radio. She drove to the hospital. Told that Laura had left, she drove to Laura's house. When she arrived, Laura's mother told Regan, "She doesn't know who was in the other car. She doesn't know it was Mike. She doesn't know that the person died."

"I just hope the person in the other car is okay," Laura said to her friend as she lay in bed.

"Laura had been in Mike's car so many times," Regan said. "It was a yellow Corvair. But she didn't know it was Mike."[7]

Regan left, but then she returned to ask Jenna if she should spend the night. By then, Laura's parents had given her the awful news. Laura was sleeping, and Jenna said there was no need for Regan to stay over.

"There was numbness, everyone feeling so sad," Gammon said. "It was all too bizarre. Mike and Laura were best friends. They did projects together in school. They talked on the phone all the time. They didn't date because he had been my boyfriend."

Indeed, according to Jan Donnelly O'Neill, Douglas had nominated Laura for Rebelee Court, similar to homecoming queen.[8]

The day after the accident, Harold Welch visited Judy, who was resting in bed. Then Laura called her.

"We were both just very shocked," Judy said. "We were still in disbelief that something like this had occurred."

Laura went back to school on Friday, but Judy was out for several days because of her back. She had to walk slowly. Neither girl went to Mike's funeral at St. Mark's Methodist Church that Saturday. The other students sympathized with Laura and tried not to make her feel bad by bringing up the accident.

"Everyone supported Laura so much," Gammon recalled. "It might have broken friendships apart or been weird or tense. But everyone had this innate sense to try to mend and carry on."

"Nothing much had happened in our lives that was tragic," Pamela Nelson said. "This was unreal. It was like the end of the world. I had never known anyone who had died. It was hard on her parents. Laura was their only daughter, and it was such a tragedy."

Laura never discussed the details of the accident. But Judy was sure it had a lasting impact.[9]

"It was frightening at such a young age to have to take it all in," Judy said. "For a couple of years, I would shake when I talked about it. I couldn't control the feeling in my stomach and the trembling voice." Even though Hester wasn't the driver, "It's like a nightmare," she said. "I wonder if it really happened. It changed the way I felt about life and the way people felt about me. All of a sudden I had to accept and deal with death."

Judy never thought of Laura as being frivolous. "But I think it made her more serious, more introspective," Judy said. "She was quieter than a lot of her friends. It probably made her more quiet, maybe more reflective. She had to have inner strength not to go off the deep end. As teenagers, we did not look at our own mortality."

Laura never talked about the accident or mentioned to friends that a tiny scar on her right knee was a reminder of it. It was just too painful. Nor was she the type to seek solace by discussing her problems and heartaches with others. She would go on with her life, accepting whatever it brought her. But the loss of her close friend, like her future husband's loss of his sister, deepened her understanding of how precious life was and made her grateful for what she had.

THE GO-TO GIRL

Just two weeks after Mike Douglas's death, another tragedy struck: the assassination of John F. Kennedy. It was the first time that world events made an impact on many of Laura's friends. "It was such an emotional time because of the JFK assassination," Regan Gammon said. "We cried all the time it seemed for a month."

Because Kennedy had been visiting Dallas, televisions were set up in homerooms so students could watch the procession. Sandra Moore-Dyrenforth was watching in her eighth-grade homeroom at Stephen F. Austin Junior High. The previous year, she had attended the all-black Carver High, which was a combined junior high and high school. Because hers was one of a handful of black families who lived in the white section of Midland across the tracks from the Flats, Sandra was allowed to go to Austin Junior High, which, with the exception of a few Hispanics, was almost all white.

"When JFK was shot, the room went silent," Moore-Dyrenforth recalled. "Everyone was speechless until a student by the name of Arnold spoke. He had flaming red hair and freckles. Arnold said, 'I bet a nigger shot him!' "[1]

"Who else would do such a thing?" the teacher responded.

"My heart dropped because now I was the focus of every student in the class," Moore-Dyrenforth said. "I stood up and said a colored—as we were called then—person wouldn't have done this."

The teacher told Sandra to sit down and shut up.

"The rest of the class started to talk about what should be done to the nigger who just shot Kennedy," Moore-Dyrenforth continued. "Only one person in the class came to my defense. He told Arnold to be quiet and said the rest of the class should 'leave her alone.' He was Mexican, Epifonio Ramiez. But in saying what he did, he angered the teacher. She then told both me and Epifonio to get out of the class and go to the principal's office and wait for her. We went to the office and waited for about thirty minutes. The teacher told the principal that we had been unruly and were 'sassing' her. I tried to tell my side of the story. I was told to 'shut up.' I was also told that I should 'get on my hands and knees' and be 'thankful you are able to attend such a wonderful school.' "

The principal suspended both students for three days.

Sandra Moore-Dyrenforth became friends with Epifonio. He dropped out of high school and served in Vietnam, where, in 1967, he was killed.

"I attended his funeral," Moore-Dyrenforth said. "I have told my children this story just to let them know how much things have changed since that day in Midland, Texas."

For all the pain in her life, when the *Rebelee*, Robert E. Lee's annual or yearbook, came out in the spring of 1964, it listed Laura as the girl with the best smile. Then, as now, she had a mischievous look. The yearbook ran a head shot of Mike Douglas, a photo of him in his track uniform, and a poem dedicated to his memory.

Under Laura's photo, the *Rebelee* listed "Junior Council, '63, '64; *Rebelee* staff, '63; advisory officer, '64; homecoming queen nominee, '64; Rebelee Court nominee, '64; 100 Club, '62; Student Council alternate, '64; Physiology Club, '64." This last club was for students interested in the life sciences, including medicine.

Laura was not a member of the Future Teachers or Future Homemakers. While she played tennis and swam with friends, she did not play any organized sports. Even if she had been interested, the only sports open to girls at school were tennis and powder-puff football, a game played with flags.

At the end of the summer, Judy Hester's parents were moving from Midland, and Laura gave her a going-away party. Everyone brought their yearbooks. In Judy's copy of *Rebelee*, Laura wrote:

Judy, gosh, I just don't know what to say. You know what a dear friend of mine you are. We've been through some good times and some bad times, too, sweetie. I hope you have the very best in life, for it is exactly what you deserve. Remember the two Jan. Firsts we were all together. Perhaps we can all be together again sometime. Who knows? I'm going to miss you this year, so write to me lots and lots. Look out for those college boys. Remember they are all on the make. Please come visit me every summer. I love you, Laura. P.S. Excuse the grammar and spelling.

Laura's warning about college boys apparently did not make an impression. Just before she was to go to college in Lubbock, Hester double-dated with Laura and Robert McCleskey, who had been George Bush's friend in grade school and would become his accountant. McCleskey dated Laura briefly. At the time, Judy was staying at Laura's house because her parents had already moved. Judy was with a blind date who was already in college.

"We pulled into the driveway of Laura's house," Judy said. "We were getting ready to go inside. I think I was tired, and he was older and already in college. When he bent over to kiss me, I kissed him back. It wasn't just one kiss, either. I finally said, 'Time for us to go in.' I'm not sure if Laura and Robert kissed. How embarrassing for them because we were kissing in the front seat."

"I can't believe you did that!" Laura said when they went in her house.

"I don't know what was wrong with me," Judy replied. "I guess I was tired."

In junior high, Laura decided she wanted to go to Southern Methodist University, a Dallas school known for its conservatism. When she was accepted as a member of the class of 1968, she jumped at the chance to live on the bucolic, tree-lined campus. Dallas was a 335-mile drive from Midland, but it was not the proximity of the university that drew her to SMU. Indeed, Laura was already somewhat of a world traveler, having taken Spanish and cultural-studies courses at a summer school in Monterrey, Mexico, after her sophomore year in high school. What gave her the idea of attending SMU was a book.

"When I was in the seventh grade, I read a biography of Doak Walker," she once said, referring to the SMU football legend. "From that point forward, I wanted to attend SMU."

Kappa Alpha Theta had a stately brick sorority house at University Boulevard and Airline Road. Theta wanted Laura to join, but there was a slight problem.

"Our freshman year, when we all went through rush, the Theta sorority that we all ended up pledging was cited for rush infractions," said Janet Kinard Heyne, who lived with Laura in the sorority house and became her friend. "I think the infraction was hot boxing. You're not supposed to have a rushee with more than one sorority member alone in the room. There were several of them with one rushee. The idea was they would pressure a rushee into doing something she didn't want to do. So they cut the pledge class the last night after everyone had put in their preferences. What happened was a fair number of girls got cut out completely, and that's what happened to Laura."[2]

"Two other sororities accused the Thetas of dirty rushing," said Anne Lund Stewart, who was the sorority's head of standards and who became a suite mate and friend of Laura's. "There was a quota of thirty-eight new members. The National Pan-Hellenic Executive Board, which rules on such things, decided the Thetas had to be slapped on the hand, so they cut the pledges to nineteen. They said we had kept people over and hot-boxed them. Laura was in the bottom nineteen nominees. So she and the others got cut because of this charge. So the next year, we picked everyone who lost out the first year."

Laura lived in Peyton Hall, a standard dorm, during her first year at SMU. She pledged in November of her sophomore year and moved into the sorority house at midterm.

"Everyone was upset," Heyne said. "It was a poor way to handle it because people got cut out, and it wasn't their fault. Laura handled it pretty well. She always was pretty levelheaded."

SMU, like most colleges, had curfews for girls but not for boys.

"We had to sign in at night when we came in from dates," said Laura's friend Marie Dodson Maxwell. "The house mother would flick the lights on the front porch if you were out there with your boyfriend at the curfew. We had to be in at ten and at midnight on Saturday."

"We were not allowed to wear slacks or pants on campus unless it was snowing," Stewart said. "It was the Dark Ages compared to now."

As in high school, Laura had a wide circle of friends.

"I just remember every morning she would brush her wonderful hair and being so envious that she had such great hair," said Stewart. "She was very soft-spoken. Not to say that she didn't have fun. She did have some fun. You just knew from the beginning she was your friend. She was very nonjudgmental, a great listener. Not to say she didn't tell somebody, 'Hey, you're way off base.' "

Laura could have been elected an officer in the sorority, but she preferred, as always, to remain in the background.

"You don't think of her as being a leader, but quietly she was the one everyone counted on and trusted," Janet Heyne said. "She is a no-nonsense person. One good pair of gold earrings and one pair of pearl earrings. That was not like SMU, which is very fashion-conscious. She had fewer clothes than the average coed and could have cared less about them."

Like everyone else, Laura often went to fraternity parties and drank beer and a drink called Purple Passion.

"We played music in our pajamas and danced and drank Cokes with each other," said Susan Byerly Nowlin, who was Laura's big sister at Theta. "That's where we learned our great moves. There were always fraternity parties with kegs."

During this time, President Lyndon Johnson was escalating the Vietnam war, and protests were erupting at campuses on the East and West Coast, but not at more conservative colleges like SMU.

"The boys we were going to school with worried about the draft," said Pamela Nelson, who followed Laura to SMU and joined Theta. "We would discuss who was going and whether it was right to go. But there weren't many protesters. In college, we were probably self-centered. But the bigger world was knocking on our doors, taking away people to go to Vietnam. It was grim."[3]

While Laura took part in these discussions, she displayed no interest in politics or the civil-rights issues of the day. Having already decided she wanted to become a teacher, she majored in education. Her favorite course was a one-semester survey of children's literature taught by Dr. Harryette Ehrhardt.

"I remember Laura because she was one of the few students who made an A in my class in the many years I taught at SMU," Ehrhardt said.[4]

While it may not sound challenging, some fundamental works of Western civilization fall under the heading of children's literature—books by Lewis Carroll, Rudyard Kipling, C. S. Lewis, Jonathan Swift, and Mark Twain, to say nothing of the Brothers Grimm.

Years after Laura took the class, when George Bush was governor of Texas, Ehrhardt was a Democratic state representative. "The governor would remind me that Laura was in my class and that she made an A," Ehrhardt said.

When they were juniors, Laura and Pamela Nelson were debutantes at the Midland Country Club. Like everything else in Midland, it was a low-key affair.

"Your daddy brings you down on his arm," Nelson said. "You bow and have a dance with your father."

In their senior year, Laura and Janet Heyne, who also planned on being a teacher, began teaching second graders at the Highland Park United Methodist Church's Sunday school, a half mile south of SMU. They thought it would help prepare them for teaching careers.

"We just laughed," Anne Stewart, Laura's friend and suite mate, said. "We would be up smoking cigarettes into Sunday morning and they would roll out of bed and go teach Sunday school."

In her 2004 book, *The Family: The Real Story of the Bush Dynasty*, Kitty Kelley claimed that Laura was "known in her college days [at SMU] as a go-to girl for dime bags of marijuana."[5] The charge provoked uproarious laughter among Laura's friends from SMU.

"If she was the go-to, I missed that," said Pamela Nelson, her Theta sister at SMU. "I was there. She was the go-to for a lot of things that were uplifting."

"In the South, there was virtually no marijuana. It was so new," said Laura's big sister Susan Byerly Nowlin. "It leaves you in awe that someone would say that."[6]

Kelley attributed the claim to Robert Nash, identified as an Austin public-relations executive who was a friend of "many" in Laura's SMU class. Tracked down by Alan Murray of the *Wall Street*

Journal, Nash said that he did not know any of Laura's SMU class-mates. He said he merely told Kelley he had heard a rumor about Laura selling dope.

"She is taking a kernel of cocktail chatter that was ill-advised and stupid on my part, and she has blown it up," Nash said.[7]

Laura knew so little about drugs that when she was discussing Kelley's charge with Gordon Johndroe, her press secretary in the White House, she mistakenly said Kelley had accused her of selling "dime boxes" of marijuana.

Kitty Kelley also claimed that after Laura and George married, they would visit Jane Purucker Clarke, one of Laura's sorority sisters, and her boyfriend Sanford "Sandy" Koufax, the former baseball star, on the island of Tortola in the British Virgin Islands and attend "heavy pot-smoking parties."* But when the Bushes visited Jane Clarke on Tortola, "Jane had not met Koufax and was married to her husband, John Clem Clarke, the artist," said Nelson.

"The Kitty Kelley story is a lie," Jane Clarke said.[8]

During spring break in their senior year, Laura and her sorority sisters Janet Heyne, Susan Ritchey, and Bobby Jo Ferguson, who has since died, drove to Florida to take a three-day cruise to the Bahamas. They were passing through Selma, Alabama—then a hotbed of racial confrontation and violence—when their car broke down.

"It was six-thirty A.M.," Heyne recalled, "and we were looking for a place to have breakfast while our car was in the shop. The chief of police and the sheriff drove up and said we were walking around in a bad neighborhood. They said to get in the squad car, and they would take us to a good place for breakfast. The sheriff radioed ahead to the jail."

"We're bringing four prisoners in," the sheriff said. "Have breakfast ready for them when we arrive."

---

*Kelley incorrectly spelled Jane Clarke's name "Clark."

"So the four of us had breakfast in jail," Heyne said.[9]

Laura graduated in the spring of 1968 with a bachelor's degree in education. That summer, Laura and her cousin Mary Mark Welch traveled to ten European countries as part of a two-week trip arranged by Mary Mark's father. Dr. Welch was attending a medical meeting in Munich and had invited Laura's parents to accompany them, but Harold said, "I walked my way through Europe, and I don't want to go back again."[10]

"Jenna would not leave him," Mary Mark Welch said. "They had a wonderful marriage, and she didn't want to be without him."

Traveling mainly by bus, the two girls visited Monte Carlo, Brussels, Paris, London, Nice, Rome, Florence, and Venice. From a gondola on the Grand Canal, Laura pointed to a palace and joked, "I used to be a princess up there."

She had no idea how close to the truth she was.

6

CHATEAUX DIJON

Laura began teaching at Longfellow Elementary School in the Dallas Independent School District in the fall of 1969. After a year, she moved to Houston, where she briefly held a clerical job in the bond-trading department of a brokerage firm. She then taught fourth grade and later second grade at the inner-city John F. Kennedy School.

In Dallas, Laura lived with Janet Heyne and three other roommates. Heyne moved to Houston and convinced Laura to move there, so they wound up living together again for a total of four years.

Like Laura, Heyne taught school but soon decided teaching was not for her.

"Laura always wanted to be a teacher," Heyne said. "I, however, was not really motivated. I just was miserable and hated it and quit."

Heyne remembered the racial turmoil in the school district.

"A lot of black parents didn't want a white teacher," she said. "With any new teacher, they test them. Being a brand-new teacher in a racially diverse school was hard for me. I wasn't cut out to be a teacher. Laura had to prove herself to the kids."

When the kids acted up, Laura projected a calm confidence and demonstrated her genuine interest in them.

"She finally won them over and had a real good class," Heyne said.[1]

Laura and Janet Heyne lived successively in three different apartments at the Chateaux Dijon. Located on Beverly Hill Drive on the southwestern edge of town, the complex attracted singles and billed itself as "the place to live." It included three hundred tree-shaded garden apartments overlooking a courtyard and pool. Unknown to Laura, in yet another eerie coincidence, George Bush was living in a different section of the same apartment complex in what was known as the wild side because of its reputation as a pickup place with loud parties.

"Laura said we were on the staid side," said sorority sister Anne Stewart, who lived four doors down from her at the Chateaux Dijon. "I think it was true. I was always afraid to go to the other side."

Laura turned out to be a neatness freak who enjoyed cleaning with Clorox and Windex. "Laura is the Clorox queen," said her close friend Nancy Weiss. "When she dusts her bookshelves, she takes the books out and sprays Formula 409 on the shelves. Clorox, Formula 409, and Windex are her three favorite substances." During the uncertainty over the results of Bush's first presidential election, Janet Heyne called Andrea G. "Andi" Ball, Laura's chief of staff in the governor's office and later in the White House, and asked her how Laura was doing. Ball told her Laura was at the ranch in Crawford.

"She is just cleaning that kitchen," Ball said.

"That tickled me so much because Laura used to always get these little sponges at the grocery store when we lived together in Houston and almost polish the kitchen sink whenever she was sort of nervous or had extra energy," said Heyne, who shared a bedroom with Laura. "That was so Laura. It gives her a sense of control."

Even before she became a librarian, Laura insisted on arranging her books according to the Dewey decimal system. She named her cat Dewey.

During college, Laura dated a number of boys but never went steady with any of them. However, in Houston, she became involved in two serious relationships. The first was with Jimmy McCarroll, a stockbroker at Eastman Dillon. Having quit teaching, Janet Heyne was working there, and she fixed Laura up with Jimmy, who also happened to live at the Chateaux Dijon. McCarroll knew George Bush because they were both members of the same bachelors' club.

McCarroll remembered how, on her own time, Laura often went in to school on Saturdays to do remedial work with kids who were having trouble reading. "She would help them on her own time," McCarroll recalled. "She met them at their school. Everyone else on Saturday mornings was trying to get over their hangovers."[2]

"During the campaigns, they stereotyped her as a librarian," Janet Heyne said. "I lived with Laura during her misspent youth. She was teaching inner-city kids to read."

After slightly less than two years, Laura and Jimmy McCarroll drifted apart, and she began dating Ralph W. Ellis, who was a friend of her sorority sister Mary Shultz Brice. Ellis also lived at the Chateaux Dijon. The relationship lasted slightly more than two years.

"When we dated, we saw each other practically daily," said Ellis, who was then a purchasing agent for an engineering construction firm.* "We did not live together."[3]

Like Jimmy McCarroll, Ralph Ellis knew George Bush. They played basketball together at the YMCA.

Ellis remembered going to movies and Willie Nelson concerts with Laura. On Sundays, they would drive around looking at houses. She introduced him to the novels of Texas writers like Larry McMurtry.

---

*Like former boyfriends Harvey Kennedy and Jimmy McCarroll, Ralph Ellis never spoke to the media about Laura Bush before doing so for this book.

"She liked margaritas and wine. She loved Mexican food," Ellis said.

Often, the two drove to Midland to see Laura's parents.

"Her father was a frugal person. So was she," Ellis said. "She would spend an hour in the grocery store picking out the right tomatoes. Her cars were plain-Jane Chevrolet models."

Laura smoked occasionally, a habit she had difficulty breaking in later years.

After more than two years of teaching at the Kennedy school, Laura decided she wanted to become a librarian.

"Laura read all the children's books," Janet Heyne said. "I think that was her favorite part of teaching. So it was a natural progression to being a librarian."

Laura moved to Austin to attend the University of Texas, where she obtained an MA in library science in 1973. Ellis, along with Regan and her husband, William Gammon III, helped her move. Asked if they discussed marriage, Ellis said, "I guess you always think about marriage, but we never talked about it."

As with Jimmy McCarroll, Laura and Ellis drifted apart. Eventually, he moved to Colorado. However, they remained friends. Laura invited Ellis and his wife to the White House a few times for Christmas parties, and they attended the inaugurations of George as governor and as president.

"With Laura, there was never a huge dramatic breakup," Regan Gammon said. "Laura is not a drama queen."

7

"I Kinda Like Him"

After obtaining her advanced degree in Austin, Laura wanted to return to Houston. In 1973, Laura began working at the Kashmere Gardens branch of the Houston Public Library. But she missed Austin, and the following year, she moved back there and became a librarian at Dawson Elementary School.

"She lived in the university area," said William Gammon. "She was a beautiful young woman, and guys were courting her all the time. I never understood why Laura had any free time. If she had any eccentricities, it was that she was so clean. She would move into a little dump, and in a matter of weeks, everything would be washed and scrubbed and freshly painted, and she would have planted flowers."

Dawson was an inner-city school with black and Hispanic children, including many who were handicapped or had Down syndrome.

"We did a lot of extra stuff for the kids because they had parents who did not have the time or the finances to do it," said Judy Harbour, a Dawson teacher who became a friend of Laura's. "So the teachers were terribly dedicated, and Laura jumped right in. She adored the children. She had a very open library. She wasn't worried about losing books. She wanted kids to come in and check out books."[1]

To expand the children's horizons, the school staged special events, called Armadillo Days.

"Laura fixed up the library as if it were a restaurant, with table-cloths on the tables," Harbour said. "She served cookies and punch and taught the children manners—how to place your napkin in your lap and which utensil to use."

In 1975, Laura's high school friend Jan Donnelly O'Neill wanted her to meet George Bush in Midland. Bush was about to help his father on his Senate campaign. Laura later said she understood that George was "real political." She was on the liberal side and considered herself a Democrat, as were her parents. She was not a fan of the Vietnam War but was not passionately against it. Laura was "so uninterested in politics," as she later put it, that she declined to meet Bush, who had helped in his father's race for Congress.

Bush had been dating a succession of girls, none of them seriously. Back in college, he became engaged to Cathryn Wolfman, a blond former high school cheerleader who was an economics major at Rice University in her hometown of Houston. They began going out together during Christmas break of his sophomore year. By Bush's senior year, they had broken up.

"I know his brothers tease him about Cathy," Anne Stewart said. "One time, I was in Dallas at their house and his brother Marvin was there. Marvin was kidding George unmercifully.

" 'George, I rented a tuxedo! I paid for it, and it was called off!' Marvin complained."

In fact, Marvin was twelve years old when George became engaged.

Having graduated from Yale, George had applied to the University of Texas Law School but was rejected. So was Donald B. Ensenat, a fraternity brother from Yale who roomed with Bush in Houston. According to Ensenat, a friend of George's father's who was on the board at the University of Texas later asked him, "Why didn't you tell us you were applying?"

"We were a little naive," Ensenat said. "We just took a shot. We were told they gave the same weight to grades from Yale as grades from an easier school. So our grade averages didn't stack up. Our LSAT scores did."[2]

Bush enrolled at Harvard Business School, where he obtained an MBA in 1975. Thrilled by the entrepreneurial spirit in Midland, he settled there and entered the oil and gas business.

Midland attracted risk takers. Anyone could buy a stake, drill for oil, and become a millionaire. Just as quickly, they could hit a dry well and lose everything. What people don't understand about the oil business, observed Robert McCleskey, the Midland accountant and Bush's friend from childhood, is that you can do everything right and still wind up broke. "The great thing about this place is that you get a chance to get up to the plate," he said.

Bush's father had lived in both the East and the West and felt comfortable in both. Having grown up in Midland, George embraced Texas and its values. When asked to define the differences between himself and his father, Bush would say that his father "went to Greenwich Country Day School in Connecticut, and I went to San Jacinto Junior High" in Midland. Or he would say, "He grew up in Greenwich. I grew up in West Texas."

"I think George wanted to differentiate himself from his father, as most men do, consciously or unconsciously," his cousin Elsie Walker said. "His father is more polished, and George is more rough-hewn. For years George was a tobacco chewer and spitter. I can't really picture his father with a wad in his mouth. George always felt more comfortable in the wide-open, nonjudgmental country of Texas than on the East Coast, which he considered more formal and uptight. With George, there isn't much artifice, and he doesn't like it in others. He likes the simple life."[3]

After Bush graduated from college, his father gave him $15,000 left over from a trust fund he had set up for his education. Bush invested modestly in oil leases and exploration across West Texas and eastern New Mexico. He didn't borrow, and he didn't take big risks. Like his parents when they started out, he had few resources.

Clay Johnson III, his friend from Phillips Academy at Andover and roommate from Yale, called him one day and asked how his oil hustling was going. "Well," Bush said, "I won a hundred dollars in a poker game last night, and that's my income for the week."

In Midland, Bush lived in a guesthouse at 2006 Harvard above a cinderblock garage. The apartment, which had a tiny window overlooking an alley, was crammed with shucked-off clothing, discarded newspapers, and a bed literally lashed together with neckties. Bush wore jeans and T-shirts. He often wore slippers outside, ones his parents had brought him from China.

That same year, Donald L. Evans, who had married Laura's friend Susie, moved from Houston to Midland and became a "roughneck" working on oil rigs for Tom Brown, Inc., a large independent energy company. Ten years later, he rose to CEO.

"George would bring his dirty clothes over to our house, and my wife would wash them," Evans recalled. "We were painting a couple of rooms in the house, so he paid us back a little there by helping us paint," he said half-jokingly. "Material things have never been important to him. If you give him a couple of good books and a pair of running shoes, he's happy."

When friends were about to throw their clothes away, Bush would say, "You gonna throw that out?"

"He's not frugal, he's cheap," said Bush's friend Bob McCleskey.

In August 1977, two years after Jan Donnelly O'Neill's abortive attempt to play matchmaker, Laura was visiting her parents in Midland. Jan again tried to introduce her to George. Jan and her husband, Joe O'Neill III, an independent oilman, invited Laura to meet George at a barbecue in their backyard. This time, Laura accepted.

Laura always had plenty of dates and was satisfied with her life. In that sense, she was ahead of her time, feeling no urgency about getting married, despite being over thirty. "I would guess she was pretty rational about the fact her friends were all getting married and she was not," Janet Heyne said. "She always had a boyfriend, so I don't think she was real frantic about it."

If her parents were worried, they never expressed it. "Their approach was always to be positive and encouraging," Pamela Nelson said.

"Certainly during those years I wondered if I would ever find anyone to marry," Laura told A&E's Biography Channel in 2004. "Which made me really happy when I found George."

"I thought they would be good together because they were both really intelligent, savvy people," Jan O'Neill said. "They both read a lot. They both had a great sense of humor. They both loved to laugh and tell jokes."[4]

O'Neill could tell something was brewing when Bush stayed beyond 9:30 P.M. Normally, he would leave by then to go to bed.

"I knew the next night when she agreed to go out to play miniature golf with him that it was mutual," O'Neill said. "Then six weeks later, she called me and said they were getting married. She was excited. They were making plans. They weren't going to let any grass grow under their feet."

"Laura was never one to say, 'Oh my God, who am I going to find?'" Regan Gammon said. "She came back from that weekend in Midland and said, 'I had dinner with this guy George Bush. I kinda like him. He kinda likes me.' Then he started coming to Austin. A lot."

"One Monday, Laura said she met this really cute guy; his name is George," Judy Harbour, her friend at Dawson Elementary, said. "We said, 'We have to check him out.' She brought him around, and he seemed quite taken with her, so we agreed she could go out with him."

At the time, George's father was director of Central Intelligence.

"His last name meant nothing to us," Harbour said.

"Don said, 'Guess who George is taking out?' He said, 'Laura Welch.' I said, 'Perfect,' " said Susie Evans, Laura and George's friend.

Bush's parents knew something was going on when George cut short a visit to their home at Walker's Point in Kennebunkport and flew back to see Laura.

"He left Maine in the middle of vacation," Barbara Bush said. "Laura wasn't answering the phone, or she'd answer and say, 'Sorry, I'm busy. Can I call you back?' We sort of got the word when he left early that summer."

"I was enthralled," Bush said later. "I found her to be a very thoughtful, smart, interested person—one of the great listeners. And since I'm one of the big talkers, it was a perfect fit."

"I knew when he asked me to marry him that he would make me laugh for the rest of my life. And that's important to me," Laura said.

Laura quit Dawson, saying she hoped to return to teaching someday.

"I think teaching in minority schools opened my eyes," Laura said later. "It made me realize how unfair in a lot of ways life is."

Before the wedding, Bush brought her to Kennebunkport to meet his parents. When Barbara Bush asked her what she did, Laura said, "I read."

The Bush family wasn't quite sure what to make of her. At one point, George's father asked Donald B. Ensenat, who had been his personal aide, "What do you think?"[5]

"A ten," said Enzo, as the younger Bush called him. The elder Bush looked slightly surprised.

"Laura was different from the people who had married into the family before," Craig Stapleton, husband of George's cousin Debbie, said. "She's very self-confident, very independent."

"She was an only child and married into our family, which I'm sure at first she thought was total chaos," said Doro Bush Koch,

Bush's sister. "We come out of the woodwork at every event like an army. But she is the most inclusive, warm person who loves to have people around her constantly."[6]

"We were always so grateful that my brother found her," Doro added. "We were so impressed with her. We thought, 'Wow, how did he find her?' I think she taught him patience, just by example. She was very calm. That rubbed off on him. She doesn't say, 'You need to be calm.' She demonstrates it with her own demeanor."[7]

"Laura entered the picture when George had a lot of restless energy and was probably drinking too much," his cousin Elsie Walker said. "Everyone was relieved because he fell in love with this angel who was also very witty."

"She wasn't competitive, which was just refreshing in our family," said Debbie Stapleton. "She didn't have this need to have to succeed and be the best at this and the best at that. She was very centered and secure within who she is. She doesn't have to best somebody else to feel good about herself."[8]

"I think Laura was born a couch potato, and her boyfriends were like that," Janet Heyne said. "George, on the other hand, is very active like her father was. We always kidded Laura about being tight, but then when she married George, he was so tight with money that she looked normal."[9]

"Jenna Welch called Janet Heyne and me and said, 'I can't get Laura down to earth,' " Anne Stewart said. "It was just a small wedding, but they had all these announcements to send out. Jenna asked if we would go over to help address them. So we did. We sat at a card table in the living room and addressed them. I remember Harold Bruce stood over me and said, 'You just be real careful with the ones addressed to Averell Harriman and those people. You don't have to worry about my friends."[10]

At the wedding rehearsal, "Harold made mention of the fact that Laura was such a blessing, that they had buried at least one child, and they never thought that they would ever, ever have a child," said Stewart, who was one of the seventy-five guests.

On November 5, 1977, a day after Laura's thirty-first birthday, she and George were married at First United Methodist Church in Midland. They had met just three months earlier.

8

MIRACLE GIRLS

Having quit her job in Austin, Laura moved to Midland, where the newlyweds lived at 1405 West Golf Course Road and later at 910 Harvard Avenue. Before the wedding, Laura had made Bush promise she would never have to give a speech. The thought made her stomach churn. But after a brief honeymoon in Mexico, they spent the next year campaigning for Congress.

On July 6, 1977, Democratic representative George Mahon announced he was retiring after forty-four years. Ten days before Bush accepted the O'Neills' invitation to attend the barbecue with Laura, he had declared his candidacy for the seat. By then, George had worked in three of his father's campaigns and had been on the campaign staffs of two Republican Senate candidates, Edward J. Gurney in Florida and Winton Blount in Alabama.

Going back to George's grandfather, Senator Prescott S. Bush, the family had always had a sense of noblesse oblige. Prescott declared that a man's first duty was to secure a fortune and provide for his family. Then he might turn to public service.

"The seed began with his grandfather Prescott Bush and his father's service, going to Washington in 1989," Bush's cousin Debbie

Stapleton said. "The American people who haven't supported him don't get it. It's not about a desire for power or prestige. He genuinely cares about service to his country. It is in the fabric of his being."

Bush staked out moderate positions, but his opponent in the primary election, Odessa mayor Jim Reese, attacked him as a liberal East Coast Republican aligned with the Rockefeller wing of the party. While Bush said he was personally opposed to abortion, he was against a "pro-life" amendment to the Constitution.

Reese called Bush "junior" and tried to tie him to the Trilateral Commission, of which his father was a member. The Trilateral Commission was a group of international political and corporate leaders viewed by many conservatives as sinister elitists plotting to establish a world government. Referring to the wild charges and conspiracy theories, Clay Johnson asked his friend, "How can you stand it?"

When he thanked his cheering supporters after beating Reese in the Republican primary, Bush said to Johnson, "That's how I stand it." Bush explained that there were benefits to having people "excited about what you're trying to do."

In the general election against Kent Hance in 1978, the Democrat accused Bush of being a "dilettante" who was "riding on his daddy's coattails." He said, "George Bush hasn't earned the living he enjoys. I'm on my own two feet, and I make my own living."

Full of frustration, Bush responded at one point, "Would you like me to run as Sam Smith? The problem is, I can't abandon my background."

Farmers would ask the candidates about the Trilateral Commission, and Hance would reply, "I don't know anything about it. But in 1973, when the Trilateral Commission was formed, what were you getting for corn and wheat? And what are you getting now?"

While Laura was not thrilled about being a politician's wife, she dutifully campaigned with George. Like a swimmer tiptoeing into cold water, she slowly became acclimated to being in the spotlight.

Bush lost to Hance, 53 percent to 47 percent.

"I got out-country'd, and it's not gonna happen again," Bush said.

Barbara Bush gave Laura one piece of advice on being the wife of a candidate: "Don't ever criticize his speeches." But one night late in the campaign, when they were driving home from Lubbock, Bush pestered Laura for her reaction to the speech he had just given. He knew he had not done well.

"I guess I was expecting her to cheer me up, to tell me I had done better than I thought I had," Bush said in *A Charge to Keep*, his campaign autobiography written with communications director Karen P. Hughes. "As we drove into the garage, I gave it one last try."

Bush said, "I didn't do very well, did I?"

"No, it wasn't very good," Laura replied.

Bush was so shocked, he drove the car into the wall of their house.

Almost every day, Bush jogged with his friend Don Evans and with Dr. Charles M. Younger, who had been a childhood friend of his and of Evans's wife, Susie. Before jogging, they would change clothes at the orthopedic surgeon's house or at his office four blocks north of Midland Memorial Hospital.

After George and Laura married, they socialized with Don and Susie Evans and Dr. Younger and his then wife every weekend. Often, the evenings included Jan and Joe O'Neill and L. E. Sawyer Jr., one of Bush's friends from Phillips Academy, and his wife, Penny. They went to Doña Anita's, a Mexican restaurant, or played Scrabble at one of their homes. The men met at Midland Country Club and played golf or tennis.

Soon, Bush's friends noticed Laura's influence. Not only did George stop bringing over his dirty laundry, he gained confidence and became more mature.

"You could see the effect of Laura's calming presence and grace," Don Evans said. "She is always in the background but always there. Close by so you can touch her or feel her. George began to draw great comfort and strength from that."

"I think one of the best things that ever happened to him is meeting and marrying her because she is a ballast and very strong," Dr. Younger said. "She's not a shrinking violet. She's not afraid to state her feelings in a very nice and polite but a very firm way. She is an anchor and a sounding board that he can bounce things off of."[1]

A few months before he met Laura, Bush had started Arbusto Energy, and he began looking for other investors. *Arbusto* is Spanish for "bush" or "shrub." Family friends invested several hundred thousand dollars, some persuaded by Jonathan Bush, Bush's money-manager uncle in New York. By then, Bush had a net worth of $500,000 from five gas wells and three oil wells.

"I can't tell you that his name and the fact that his father was respected and known didn't maybe get him in some doors that you and I might not get into easily," Charlie Younger said. "But George really struck out on his own."

In 1981, Bush renamed his company Bush Exploration Company, and he took it public. It was bad timing. The Texas oil industry was collapsing as prices fell. He raised only $1.3 million, a quarter of his goal. His partners lost 75 percent of their money as a result of dry holes.

"I made a bad mistake," Bush said. He joked that he was "all name and no money."

In late 1984, Bush merged his company into Spectrum 7, an oil-drilling firm, and became its chairman. As prices continued to fall, Bush hastily arranged to have Harken Oil and Gas buy Spectrum 7. In the previous six-month period, Spectrum had lost $402,000. It was $3 million in debt. Harken had a strategy of buying distressed oil companies. It assumed the company's crushing debts, made Bush a consultant at $80,000 a year, and gave him $530,380 in stock.

Harken hired some of his employees, and Bush made sure the rest were hired by friends.

"It was an industry that was going through a period of financial distress, and George was a part of that," Don Evans said. "He never had any problems taking care of his financial obligations business-wise or family-wise. Which was not true for many people who went through that period in the industry."

Laura and George wanted to have a large family, but in the early 1980s, Laura confided to Nancy Weiss and a few other close friends that she was having difficulty conceiving. When her mother, Jenna Welch, had become pregnant with Laura, "She had to stay in bed almost all the time to make sure the baby would not be born prematurely," according to her childhood friend Mary Bowhay.[2] It looked like Laura might have similar difficulties.

After trying for more than three years, George and Laura signed up to adopt. Meanwhile, Laura took clomiphene citrate, which induces ovulation and helps increase egg production and often leads to multiple births. When that didn't work after a few months, Laura was given a shot of gonadotropin to adjust her hormones in the hope of helping her conceive.

"Her temperature went up on a Saturday, indicating she was ovulating," said Nancy Weiss. "On Monday, she had the shot. Within a few days, they believed she was pregnant. When Laura took the second medication, it worked immediately. So the twins were miracle girls. She obviously was not able to carry children without the hormone adjustment."[3]

Anne Lund Stewart recalled the August 1981 day when George and Laura found out they were having twins. They were staying at the Stewarts' house in Houston, where Laura had been seeing a fertility expert recommended by her mother-in-law.

"George burst into my front door," Stewart said.

"Where's Bill?" Bush asked, referring to Stewart's husband. "I'm taking you all out to dinner."

"What is going on?" Stewart said.

He said the results of an ultrasound examination had just come back.

"We're having twins," he said, and began crying.

When Laura was pregnant, the Bushes vacationed with Mike and Nancy Weiss (pronounced Weese) in New Mexico. Their friendship went back to October 1977, when "George was stumping up and down," Nancy recalled. "He went into this men's store in Lubbock. He asked the guy if he could talk to him about his candidacy. The man said he couldn't talk, but his accountant was in a back room, and he might talk with George. Within about thirty minutes, Mike, the accountant, was George's Lubbock County campaign chairman. Then George and Laura married and had a short honeymoon and came back to Midland. They were quickly out campaigning. I went to meet them in Lubbock at a coffee for George. Laura opened the door and stuck her hand out and said, 'I'm Laura Bush.' She was very different from what I had expected. We started laughing."

Laura and Nancy became close friends as quickly as George and Mike had. Nancy saw the Bushes as having the same values that are prized in Lubbock. "When you have a person who brags or exaggerates, that person sticks out like a sore thumb," Nancy said. "We are common. We just be."

The campaign lasted more than a year. George and Laura were in Lubbock about half the time, often staying overnight with Mike and Nancy. "During the campaign, we were always with them," Nancy Weiss said. "We never lived in the same town, and I think you develop a different relationship when you stay with people for a weekend and have coffee with them in your pajamas. One of our friends said, 'You know, they will drop you like a hot potato as soon as this race is over.' Mike and I discussed it that night. Mike said, 'You know, we might not see them after this, but this has been one of the most fun, rewarding years we've had, so it's worth it.'"

After the campaign, the two couples continued to spend lots of time together. "We began a tradition of celebrating New Year's Eve with them," Nancy said. "Then his dad became vice president, and we thought, 'Now they'll really develop so many friends that they won't have time for us.' But they stayed the same way. Then when his dad became president and George became managing general partner of the Rangers, we thought, 'Just think of all the interesting people they know now.' But we went to many dozens of games, and even today, they have stayed the same. Mike and I are real flattered by that, because they chose to be with us. But I think it's more of a compliment to them, that they still want to be with those plain old people, not kings and queens or movie stars."

Later, when George became governor, he appointed Mike his budget director. When the Bushes had a place at Rainbo Lake near Athens, Texas, George and Mike often fished together for six to eight hours, "having very little conversation," Nancy said. "Of course, we talk and laugh a lot, but the four of us can be totally quiet. At the ranch, she has sofas facing each other, and after lunch, Laura and I each read a book or a magazine and doze off, talk a little, and doze off again. George and I can be in the same room together and go for maybe an hour without having an exchange of words."

Nancy introduced Bush at the August 2000 Republican Convention in Philadelphia. During 2004, Mike and Nancy Weiss were with the Bushes at the White House, Camp David, or the ranch at Crawford a total of forty-one days, or more than 10 percent of the year. In the past twenty-eight years, they have been with them on New Year's Eve every year but one. Other Bush friends began calling them "the Comforts."

Recalling Laura's pregnancy, Nancy said, "Laura had a fear of losing the girls. She was very careful during that time. She later developed toxemia," a condition dangerous to the mother and the fetus. "She stayed at Baylor in Dallas for seven weeks before she delivered by cesarean section five weeks before the due date."

"I knew that it was a high-risk pregnancy," Laura said. "You know

I was worried. I wanted to be sure I had those two babies. I didn't even have the courage to walk down the baby aisles at grocery stores. I was worried that I would lose one of them or maybe both of them."

The twins were born on November 25, 1981. When Regan Gammon and her husband, Billy, had their daughter on November 1, 1976, they told Laura they were naming her after Laura, spelling her name Lara but pronouncing it "Laura." When the twins were born, Laura told Regan that she had thought about naming one of them Regan. At the time, Ronald Reagan was president.

"No one thought Regan Bush was a good idea under the circumstances," Regan said.[4]

Instead, Laura told Regan that she and George had decided to name Barbara for George's mother and Jenna for Laura's mother. Barbara was just over five pounds; Jenna was just under five pounds.

"It was not easy after they were born," Nancy Weiss said. "George was precious with them, but it was a huge job, taking care of two fussy infants. They were up a lot. Laura did not get around to returning calls. It took her three or four months before she really had her feet back on the ground. She never gave them commercial baby food. She always steamed fresh vegetables and mashed them. So they didn't have salt or preservatives. She was the best mother I've ever seen."

Laura especially enjoyed reading the papers with George in the morning and feeding the twins. From the beginning of their marriage, George had made coffee for her. Back then, she called him "Georgie" or simply "GEE-o." Later they took to calling each other "Bushie," symbolizing the equality of their relationship.

"It was the sweetest time in my life," Laura said. "I was so happy and so thrilled with the way my life had turned out."

Don Evans noticed how proud George was of the girls.

"You could see it all over this guy," Evans said. "We would play golf at Midland Country Club, but we would get there at seven-thirty and get back by nine. We wanted to be back before the kids were up and moving around."

Bush had been worshiping at Presbyterian and Episcopalian churches, but after he married Laura, he switched to the First United Methodist Church, where she attended services. Having grown up in a family of strong faith, George believed in God. George's grandmother Dorothy Walker Bush had been especially interested in religion, reading the works of evangelical writers like John Stott and Francis Shaffer.

In the fall of 1985, Bush began Bible study with Don Evans through Community Bible Study, or CBS, meeting every Monday evening with a group of men in a Presbyterian-church classroom. In part, said Evans, it was a reaction to seeing what was happening to friends in the oil and gas business.

"In the early eighties, the industry was collapsing," Evans said. "We had friends who were going through bankruptcies and were moving. We saw all that pain. So that created an opportunity to strengthen our faith. You learn more from adversity than from success."[5]

Religious reawakening or not, George was his usual irreverent self. The teacher would ask, "What is a prophet?"

"That is when revenues exceed expenditures," George cracked. "No one's seen that out here for years."

The media portrayed Evans as the instigator of Bush's recommitment to his faith, but Evans said that during the two and a half years they took the course, Bush was even more disciplined than he was.

"We had these one-year Bibles we were reading," Evans said. "We were competitive and would check on each other's progress. I would have to admit that if anyone was behind a day or two or three in his readings, it was me, not him." Evans also said, "I guarantee you, he has read the Bible a lot more times than I have, from start to finish. In my view, his faith is clearly one of the places where he gets his strength and comfort and peace. He has an optimistic view of the world. He believes there's hope for everybody and that the glass is half-full—maybe more than half-full."

Billy Graham had long been a Bush family friend, and on August 24, 1986, George's parents invited Graham to their summer home at Walker's Point in Kennebunkport to speak to the Bush family and their friends. Graham talked about accepting Christ as one's personal savior. Bush called it "one of the most exciting nights I have ever spent in my life." It was, he said, "The beginning of a new walk where I would commit my heart to Jesus Christ."

"We were with Billy Graham at Walker's Point the night he spoke," Bush's cousin Debbie Stapleton said. "This was hugely important for more than just George. Hearing what Billy Graham said, many of us wanted to incorporate more of that in our lives."

Having started a family and embraced Christ, Bush was stabilizing his life. But there was still one problem that he would have to overcome if he was to achieve everything he wanted to achieve.

9

DINNER AT THE BROADMOOR

For George's fortieth birthday, on July 6, 1986, he and Laura went to a backyard party at the Weisses' home in Lubbock. With the grilled steaks, George had his usual bourbon on the rocks.

"I knew he was drinking too much, but so were most of those guys in those days," Nancy said. "But he also was very disciplined, he ran every day, and he was in bed by ten or so. He would just get louder, more feisty, and more boisterous when he drank, and also quite funny."[1]

George and Laura drove back to Midland with the twins and then went to Colorado Springs. They were to have dinner at the Broadmoor Hotel and Resort to celebrate George's and Don Evans's birthdays and spend a few days playing golf. Along with George and Laura, and Susie and Don Evans, there were Joe O'Neill and his wife, Jan; the now-divorced Penny Royall; and Bush's brother Neil.

Despite his heavy drinking, Bush ran three or four days a week, usually for three or four miles, averaging seven-minute miles. But at the Broadmoor, Bush awoke with a hangover after a dinner served with sixty-dollar bottles of Silver Oak Cabernet. He felt befuddled and had trouble running. The fact that Colorado Springs was 6,035 feet above sea level undoubtedly contributed to his malaise. Since the lungs have to work harder to get oxygen into the blood in high altitudes, alcohol is absorbed into the blood system more quickly, speeding up the effect that a couple of drinks would normally have.

Laura had been urging her husband to quit drinking for months, saying it was "necessary" and reminding him that having four bourbons at a party wasn't very smart.

"He'd say things over and over again," Laura said of his drinking. "He wasn't an alcoholic in the sense of he had to get up in the morning and have a drink to get things going. But he . . . couldn't hold his liquor, as they say."

Bush had been trying to cut down or stop for a year. At the Broadmoor, he decided to quit entirely. His religious awakening played a role, as did his near disaster in the oil business. He was also aware that he had new responsibilities. He had agreed to serve as a "loyalty enforcer and listening ear" for his father's 1988 presidential race. His role would be to come down hard on leakers and loose cannons, mediate staff disputes, and pass along to his father what he considered useful advice from others.

"He would not get drunk and pass out," Dr. Younger said. "He would get a little boisterous, a little loud, a little happy. He would get off-color. No more than the rest of us, I might add. I never considered him an alcoholic. He was more of a binge drinker. He was not someone who had to have a drink every night. He would go to a party and have a good time. He would tease Laura. He knew how to get under her skin, and he would do it. She would get a little upset with him. The next day I imagine she would speak with him. She would reprimand him a bit, and he would respond."[2]

"A couple of times I saw her rein him in when he was drinking," Anne Stewart said. "His mouth would get the better of him."

When they returned home from the Broadmoor, Bush told Laura of his decision to quit.

"He just said, 'I'm going to quit,' and he did," Laura said. "That was it. We joked about it later, saying he got the bar bill, and that's why he quit." Except for his drinking, Bush was always disciplined, she said. "And when he was able to stop, that gave him a lot of confidence and made him feel better about himself."

With Laura present, Bush jokingly said on A&E's Biography Channel, "She suggested it was either me or Jim Beam."

"Her," Laura corrected him, laughing.

"Yeah, her or Jim Beam," George said.

But giving ultimatums was not Laura's style.

"People say Laura told him to stop drinking," Nancy Weiss said. "Maybe she did, but not directly. She has a way about her of making you stop and think. At that time the girls were nearly five years old. Knowing her, I'm sure she pointed out that they need a daddy who is always the same."

"The fact that he loves her so much and loves his girls had an effect on him, making him straighten up," said Bush's sister Doro.

"She keeps me focused on what's important," Bush later said. Alcohol, he said, was "beginning to crowd out my energy level and crowd out my affections." Laura "reminded me that at some point in time I had to make a decision—whether I wanted to drink or be a productive citizen. She's helped me make many choices in my life."

"I think we all get to a certain point in our lives when you look at it and say, 'Hmm, it may not be going as well as it should be,'" Jan O'Neill said. "You reevaluate and make some decisions. We weren't aware of the fact that this was part of a big decision for him. Six months later, we were aware of it. It was a private thing. But we realized that he wasn't drinking anymore. He didn't stand up and make an announcement that he wasn't drinking anymore."[3]

"It set a very good example for lots of people, including me," Don Evans said. "I gave it up after he did. I went back to it and then I quit seven years ago. I haven't had a drink since."

George later attributed his decision in part to his religious reawakening.

"To put it in spiritual terms, I accepted Christ," Bush said. "What influenced me [to stop drinking] was the spirituality, sure, which led me to believe that if you change your heart, you can change your behavior."[4]

Laura was much quieter about her faith than her husband. Growing up in Midland, she had attended church with her parents. Although she taught Sunday school while in college, she did not attend church regularly when she was a teacher. When she married, she began going to church again.

"Laura's faith is very strong and very private," said Nancy Weiss, who has sometimes discussed it with her. "Mike pointed out that unless [George] is asked about it in a press conference or other public forum, he has never heard George bring up his faith publicly, as many politicians do. The Bushes are very private in their faith. They do always pray at the table, and you are aware that they are reading the Bible and devotional materials with inspirational affirmations." Nancy had seen such material on their nightstands at the White House, Camp David, and Crawford.

"I think George and Laura trust that there is a divine order," Nancy said. "They know that everything is going to be okay. One very pleasant night, when we were sitting on the porch at the ranch and looking out over this beautiful lake, Laura said, 'I think this is what heaven is. To be with people you love in such tranquillity.'"

For just over two years, as Bush worked on his father's campaign, George and Laura lived in Washington with the twins—who were almost five when they moved—in a classy but small town house on Westover Place. Laura's cat, Dewey, moved with them.

Laura took to Washington the way she took to everything else—with enthusiasm. With George's parents living just down Massachusetts Avenue at the vice president's residence in the U.S. Naval Observatory, Laura could stop in frequently with the twins, who loved to play on the swings and see "Gampy." Laura also liked being close to George's brother Marvin and his wife, Margaret. She em-

braced them as the brother and sister she never had. During this period, Laura and her mother-in-law often had lunch together and
bonded.

"Laura respects Barbara, and Barbara respects her because Laura
does not try to please her," Anne Stewart said. "Laura's not going to
be athletic. That's a big deal with Barbara. Laura just wasn't going
to get into a mold as such. Barbara can be pretty tough. Laura has so
much reserve and self-confidence. With everything she has been
through, she has a real sense of her own self and she is not going to
compromise it for anything. She is not going to play tennis if somebody else wants her to play tennis. She is going to play golf if she
wants to play golf. She has been exercising for the past few years, but
she did it for herself, not because George told her to or anybody told
her to."

The relationships played out at Kennebunkport, which is like "going to camp," Laura's friend Anne Johnson said. The elder Bush will
say, "Okay, Anne, you go and play tennis. Clay go to the horseshoe
game. Somebody else go to the boat." Anne said, "Laura is nowhere
to be seen. It turns out she is in the house, reading. She doesn't feel
the need to compete with anybody."

In Washington, Laura became friends with Winton Holladay,
who lived nearby, and her best friend, Sandy Langdon, the wife of
James C. Langdon Jr., Bush's lawyer friend from West Texas. Holladay remembered Laura telling her that she and George had taken
the twins to the Washington Monument three times, but because of
the long lines, they had never gone to the top.

"This was the family of the vice president of the U.S.," Holladay
said. "They are so unpretentious. They could have made arrangements to get up to the top of the Washington Monument, but they
didn't."[5]

In December 1988, after Bush Senior had been elected president,
George and Laura returned to Texas. This time, instead of returning
to Midland, they moved to Dallas. George was thinking of pursuing

business and political opportunities, and Dallas was a better base for both.

During the campaign, William DeWitt Jr., a friend who was an owner of the oil exploration company Spectrum 7, called Bush. De-Witt's father had owned Major League Baseball teams. DeWitt told Bush that Eddie Chiles, owner of the Texas Rangers, who was another friend of the Bushes', wanted to sell out. DeWitt asked if Bush would be interested in forming a group to buy the team. Bush jumped at the chance.

As a kid, Bush had dreamed of being Willie Mays, not president. If he bought this team, he could meld his business experience with his love of baseball. Now, besides his Midland upbringing, he could point to another difference between himself and his father.

Bush put the Rangers deal together in April 1989. For $75 million, he and other investors bought 86 percent of the Rangers. For his stake, Bush put up $606,302, with $500,000 of it borrowed from a bank. He became the managing general partner along with Edward W. "Rusty" Rose III. To pay off the loan, Bush sold two-thirds of his interest in Harken Oil.

As a son of the president, Bush was a brand name, and he turned it to the team's advantage. He had baseball cards printed up with his picture. Instead of sitting in one of the owners' air-conditioned sky boxes, he sat in the front row behind the dugout. Bush wore the same ratty suits over and over and eelskin boots emblazoned with the flag of Texas. He appeared almost nightly on TV sports news. Like a star player, he signed autographs and greeted fans.

"One day, we were in the owners' box watching a game," said Deedie Rose, the wife of Rusty Rose, who became a friend of Laura's. "Jenna was there. She was fourteen or fifteen. She had gotten a spider bite. George was saying, 'Jenna, you've got to get someone to look at that spider bite on your hand.'

" 'No, I'm not going to,' Jenna said.

" 'Yes, I want you to go see the team doctor,' George said.

B orn on November 4, 1946, Laura Lane Welch was an only child. Because she knew of her mother's difficulties having children, "I felt very obligated to my parents," Laura said. "I didn't want to upset them in any way." (*Laura Bush Personal Photo*)

G rowing up in Midland, Texas, Laura could say the name of her dog, Bully, before she could say "Mom" or "Dad." (*Laura Bush Personal Photo*)

L aura's mother, Jenna Welch, shown in this photo in 1955, loves astronomy and bird-watching. "She always sees the best in people, and she always gets that in return," her friend and neighbor Kathy Robbins said. (*Laura Bush Personal Photo*)

LEFT: The 1968 Robert E. Lee High School yearbook listed Laura as having the best smile. (*Laura Bush Personal Photo*)

RIGHT: Laura's high school friend Judy Dykes Hester was the only passenger in the car when Laura, at the age of seventeen, ran a stop sign and killed one of her best friends. Judy thought the tragedy made Laura "more serious, more introspective." (*Robert E. Lee High School Yearbook*)

Laura pledged Kappa Alpha Theta sorority at Southern Methodist University. Laura and Pamela Nelson, her friend from Midland, are at the right in the second row from the front. (*Courtesy of Pamela Nelson*)

TOP LEFT: Laura inherited her sense of humor from her father, Harold Welch, and her love of reading from her mother, Jenna Welch. (*Courtesy of Janet K. Heyne*)

TOP RIGHT: During a road trip to Florida that Laura and sorority sister Janet Heyne took in their senior year of college, the police chief and sheriff in Selma, Alabama, stopped them to say they were in a bad neighborhood. The officers drove them in a police car to the jail to have breakfast. (*Courtesy of Janet K. Heyne*)

LEFT: When Theta sister Janet Heyne got married in 1972, Laura was her maid of honor. Laura had a steady boyfriend in high school and two steady boyfriends in succession as a young adult, but never seemed worried about getting married. (*Courtesy of Janet K. Heyne*)

After many near misses, Laura and George Bush finally met each other at a barbecue in Midland. "I kinda like him," Laura told her friend Regan Gammon. Three months later, on November 5, 1977, they married. (*Laura Bush Personal Photo*)

BELOW: George and Laura immediately began trying to have a family. More than three years later, Laura became pregnant after taking medication. (*Laura Bush Personal Photo*)

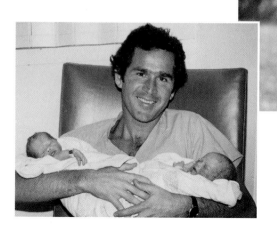

LEFT: When George Bush told Laura's Theta sorority sister Anne Stewart in August 1981 that Laura's ultrasound examination revealed twins, the future president broke down in tears. (*Laura Bush Personal Photo*)

RIGHT: Jenna, at right in 1982, was named for Laura's mother, and Barbara was named for George's mother. (*Laura Bush Personal Photo*)

Despite being beleaguered by two "fussy infants," Laura always "steamed fresh vegetables and mashed them," according to her friend Nancy Weiss, to avoid the salt and preservatives in commercial baby food. *(Laura Bush Personal Photo)*

The Bushes used this photo taken by Laura's Theta sorority sister Janet Heyne on their 1986 Christmas card. Jenna is on the left in her mother's arms, and Barbara is in front. *(Janet K. Heyne)*

Here, your highness. Sit on this," George Bush said to his mother, Barbara Bush, then first lady, after Laura purchased a thousand-dollar antique pillow when they lived in Dallas. Looking on were Clay Johnson III, George's friend from Andover and Yale, and his wife, Anne. *(White House Photo)*

L aura and her mother-in-law, Barbara Bush, bonded when George's father was vice president and George and Laura lived in Washington. This photo was taken on the South Lawn of the White House in 1989. (*Laura Bush Personal Photo*)

W hen George Bush sold his interest in the Texas Rangers in 1998, he made $12 million after taxes, according to his accountant, Robert McCleskey. He set up trust funds of $750,000 for each of the two girls and donated $250,000 to create the Laura Bush Promenade at her alma mater, Southern Methodist University. (*Laura Bush Personal Photo*)

George Bush was inaugurated as governor for the second time on January 19, 1999. As first lady of Texas, Laura started the Texas Book Festival. Later, in the White House, she started the National Book Festival. (*Laura Bush Personal Photo*)

Laura remained close to her friends from Midland, who attended the first inauguration of Bush as president in January 2001. From left are Regan Gammon, Peggy Weiss, Laura, Jan O'Neill, and Pamela Nelson. (*Laura Bush Personal Photo*)

Laura introduced her mother, Jenna Welch, who had a successful breast cancer operation, at the Susan G. Komen Foundation's Race for the Cure survivors event at the White House on June 1, 2001. Laura's friend Nancy Brinker started the foundation. (*White House Photo*)

After 9/11, Laura became the "comforter-in-chief," reassuring a nation on edge. She and the president participated in a wreath-laying ceremony near the site of the crash in Somerset County, Pennsylvania, where the passengers of United Flight 93 fought back against four hijackers. (*White House Photo*)

" 'No,' she said.

"It was clear she was going to have to go," Deedie Rose said. "Jenna turned to Laura and said, 'Mom, he's just so embarrassing!' "[6]

To attract more fans to the Rangers' games, Bush pushed for a temporary half-cent increase in the local sales tax to pay part of the $135 million cost of a new stadium. The team kicked in the rest. The new ballpark opened in Arlington, Texas, in 1994. Attendance soared from an average of 18,000 a game to 31,000. The value of the team zoomed as well.

"I like selling tickets," Bush would say. "There are a lot of parallels between baseball and politics." The success "solved my biggest political problem in Texas," he continued. "My problem was, 'What's the boy ever done?' "[7]

"He knows more about baseball and baseball history," said Craig Stapleton, a partner in the Rangers. "He would tell me exactly what happened after a game: the pitch count, who was on base, where the fielders were playing, what kind of pitch was being thrown. He could have been a sports announcer."

By the time the ballpark opened, Bush had plunged into running for governor of Texas against incumbent Ann Richards. Bush was aware of kids' declining reading scores, and a major impetus for his decision to throw in his hat was his desire to improve education in the state.

"In the late 1980s, it was clear to me that he had this strong drive to become involved in public life and the political area," Don Evans said. "He said to me, 'Education in Texas is broken. We have to fix it. It's our turn.' "

When George was thinking of running for governor in 1990, the two friends discussed the issues again. It was already apparent to Evans how much George depended on Laura for support and advice. "He was even more focused on improving education," Evans said. "He talked to Laura about it a lot, I know. Laura had the good ear and was always there providing good, sound wisdom. She would make sure that everything was well thought out."[8] But Evans warned that his friend would have to have more than one suit to wear.

Even after Bush became governor, he continued to wear old clothes. Laura told a friend, "I better find a tailor for George."

Bush ran a disciplined campaign against Ann Richards on four issues: school accountability, limiting civil lawsuits, tightening juvenile justice laws, and welfare reform. He visited one small town after another. When the press grew tired of hearing him talk about the four issues, he announced he had just added a fifth: to concentrate even harder on the other four.

"When I used to introduce him, my line was 'Anybody who is good enough to be the husband of Laura Welch is good enough to be anything they want to be," Don Evans said. "My sense was that she was his secret weapon. It was my way of saying, 'This is a very decent man who is a friend of mine, and this lady is someone very special.' "

Laura and George lived near Preston Hollow Park at 6029 Northwood Road, a ranch-style home with a limestone facade. Before they moved in, Anne Johnson, one of Laura's close friends who lived in Dallas, planted flowers at the house. In doing so, Anne remembered that the day after the twins were born, George had come to a brunch at the Johnsons' house and, at Laura's request, brought a beautiful orchid from Laura's hospital room.

Anne first met Laura at the Bushes' wedding. Her husband, Clay Johnson III, had been Bush's friend from Andover and roommate at Yale and later became his chief of staff when Bush was governor. Later, he became chief of presidential personnel in the White House. Anne is an attractive blonde with a razor-sharp wit. In 1965, along with Farrah Fawcett, she was voted one of the ten most beautiful girls at the University of Texas. Anne met Clay on a blind date when they were both in college. After the date, she sent him a letter, enticing the six-foot-four-inch-tall Johnson to ask her out again. They would often double date and attend football games with Clay's friend George. George called her "Annie"; she called him "Georgie."

Anne remembered that at Yale, George didn't have sheets on his bed.

"I'm not sure Laura would have gone out with him then," Anne Johnson said. "They were complete opposites. He was very messy. She is a perfectionist. Everything has to be organized."

"George would later say he was 'wild and irresponsible,'" Anne said. "We all drank too much on occasion, as young people do. But wild was putting twelve people in a Volkswagen. We never did drugs at all."[9]

A year after they graduated, Anne and Clay married. She was a junior executive at Neiman Marcus. Having obtained an MS from the Massachusetts Institute of Technology's Sloan School of Management, Clay became an executive at PepsiCo's Frito Lay division, Wilson Sporting Goods, and Citicorp. "When we met at their wedding, I immediately liked Laura," Anne said. "Then it turned out we both loved gardening, antiques, and books. She knows the Latin names of all the perennials. We dated some of the same boys when we were going to college. And we both have twins."

Through her sister Betty Sewell, Anne met Kenneth Blasingame, an interior designer, and she introduced him to Laura. Laura would later use Blasingame at the Crawford ranch, Camp David, and the White House. When Laura admired a large antique pillow of Anne's, Blasingame offered to bring her a similar one, and Laura bought it for a thousand dollars.

"I thought George Bush was going to go nuts," Clay Johnson said. "He's pretty tight."

When George's parents paid a surprise visit to Dallas, a White House photographer took a photo of George Junior holding the pillow and proffering it to his mother. Looking on were Clay, Anne, and Laura, who was laughing uproariously.

"Here, your highness. Sit on this," George said to his mother.

When the prints came back, George sent one to Anne.

"To Anne," George inscribed the photo. "Thanks for all your advice and help in decorating our house. Yours in poverty, George W. Bush."

One day, as George was starting his run for governor, Laura called Anne.

"I have to give a speech before the Republican Women in Dallas," Laura said. "Would you go with me?"

"George had promised her she would not have to give speeches," Anne said. "She hated the thought. She did fine. But she looked at me afterward and said, 'I was terrible.'"

Laura, the former Democrat, now described herself as a "Republican by marriage." It was not that she had given up any strong political beliefs: She had never had any. Nor had she given up her liberal views on some social issues like abortion, views that many of her friends held. Bush, on the other hand, is antiabortion except when rape, incest, or a possible threat to the mother's health is involved. No two people think exactly alike, and it was natural for Laura to hold some views different from her husband's.

"I believe Laura is pro-choice, as I am," said Regan Kimberlin Gammon. "She doesn't voice that a lot, but she has voiced it. That subject has lots of ins and outs. I don't want the government to be involved in making medical decisions about my body. The president doesn't ask me what my opinion is on that. He knows what it is, I'm sure. He either takes it into account or he doesn't. We are friends, and we choose not to discuss things we disagree on."

To support her husband, Laura did not have to adopt every one of his policies and beliefs. What she supported was Bush the man she believed in—his character, his drive, and his desire to improve the state.

First Lady of Texas

eorge Bush was elected governor of Texas on November 8, 1994, and sworn in the following January. The next month, he was in his office on the second floor of the state capitol in Austin when officials from the Texas Education Agency gave him the third-grade reading-test results from Texas schools. Some 43,000 third graders could not read. By the spring, the results had gotten worse: Some 52,000 of the state's 230,000 third graders could not read. When asked what happened to the kids who couldn't read, Bush was told that nearly all were promoted to the next grade. According to Karl Rove, then one of his aides, he had never seen Bush so angry as he was after that meeting.

Back in 1992, Bush had asked Alexander "Sandy" Kress, a lawyer and former Democratic member of the Dallas School Board, why so many kids couldn't read and what could be done about it. Bush asked him dozens of questions: What are the best ways to teach reading? What are other states doing? Taking notes on a legal pad, Bush wanted to know who had studied the issue. Kress mentioned six experts in the field.

"He was an incredible student of these issues," Kress said. "He had a voracious appetite for information. He looked into the problem and researched it. . . . I gave him six names. He called them all. They were as stunned as I was."

If Kress was amazed, Dr. G. Reid Lyon, a reading expert at the National Institutes of Health, was even more so when he answered his phone in Rockville, Maryland, and was told the governor of Texas was calling. Bush had heard that Lyon, a research psychologist and former teacher, had studied the reading problem and found that a faddish approach to teaching kids to read was behind the poor test scores. Introduced in the 1970s, the "whole language method" held that the traditional, phonics-based method of teaching kids to sound out letters was boring. Instead, under the whole language approach, kids were taught to read by simply giving them books and expecting that they would become so enthralled that they would figure out the words themselves. Essentially, that meant kids were not being taught to read at all.

Based on Lyon's advice, Bush developed a way to restore phonics to reading instruction in Texas. The results were dramatic. In 1995, 23 percent of third graders could not read. By 2003, that figure had dropped to 10 percent, according to state testing figures compiled by Kress, who became Bush's unpaid education adviser. After additional help for kids who failed, only 2 percent could not read. The greatest beneficiaries of restoring phonics to reading instruction—which includes work on comprehension, spelling, and actual reading—were minorities.

As first lady of Texas, Laura took a complementary approach, focusing on programs that would help children get ready to read that flowed from her own experience as a teacher. As she did later as first lady in the White House, Laura not only supported existing causes but conceived of new approaches.

"It was totally her idea to convene a summit of researchers on how to improve reading instruction," said Margaret Spellings, Bush's education aide who would become secretary of education in Washington. "They were dazzled that she was so well informed and so interested and that they were coming to Texas, of all places, to talk about cutting-edge research."[1]

"I became her policy adviser when she decided to take on early-childhood development," said Anne Heiligenstein. "Her concern was, how do you get good information that bolsters the health and safety of children and cognitive development into the hands of mothers?"[2]

Laura started a magazine that targeted Medicaid families with newborns. It's a monthly booklet called *Take Time for Kids* that is essentially an instructional manual on bringing up young children. Laura also conceived of Ready to Read, Ready to Learn, a program to help Head Start teachers teach kids to read.

"It was unusual for Texas to invest in a federal program," Heiligenstein said. "To push it, she hosted a forum on early cognitive learning with the legislature. She brought in top researchers and invited key lawmakers. She then hosted a lunch at the mansion. This was her idea. The Texas legislature is fairly conservative. They could have said, 'This is a federal program. We're not going to contribute to it.' The House and Senate were led by Democrats. Bob Bullock, the lieutenant governor, was a powerful Democrat. But the governor could cross party lines very easily. He would say, 'Here's my goal. How are we going to get there?' "

Bullock wound up endorsing Bush for reelection as governor and for president. Jan, his wife, became a friend of Laura's. Thanks to their efforts, the Texas legislature appropriated $17 million over two years for preschool reading programs.

In 1996, Laura started the Texas Book Festival, a three-day event promoting reading and authors. The idea arose when Bob Skimin, an author from El Paso who writes westerns, came to see her, recalled Andi Ball, her chief of staff. "He wanted to start a Texas book festival. She was intrigued and talked to the governor," Ball said. "We included any Texas author who wrote a book that year, regardless of their politics."[3]

After she met Laura at one of the festivals, Texas novelist Laura Furman sent her a list of the four other novels and short-story collections she had written. She thought that Laura would never look at them. But Laura wrote back and commented on each one.

"She'd read all of them," Furman said. "The habit of reading as a comfort and as a nurturing activity seems completely natural to her, completely one with her. But it's more than that. When you're young, you read to find yourself. When you're older, you read to find out about the rest of the world. And I think that's what she does."

"Sometimes politicians and their spouses will support causes because . . . well, they're supposed to," said Sandy Kress. "With Laura Bush, it was very different. She seemed to want to have an enduring effect, as opposed to simply being involved in something good."[4]

By the time Bush left office, the festival had raised $1.5 million for Texas libraries.

Laura's early days in the governor's mansion were tinged with sadness after her father died in April 1995. Harold Welch had suffered from Alzheimer's and, toward the end of his life, barely knew who Laura was. He would refer to George but in the wrong context. Harold lived in his own home, cared for by Jenna and a health aide who gave him showers. A week before he died, Harold was taken to Midland Memorial Hospital. He was unconscious, but Laura was with him until he took his last breath.

As she would later do in the White House, Laura redecorated the living quarters in the governor's mansion. In the meantime, she continued her lifetime habit of reading voraciously.

"She reads several books at once," Andi Ball said. "Their bedside tables in the White House are covered with books, stacks of books. Lots of times she has given me a book and said, 'This is really good.

You ought to read it.' The president likes biographies. She does, too, but she also likes mysteries and Texas authors."

After books, art was Laura's greatest passion. To promote Texas artists, she hung their works in the capitol. She loved colorful Mexican pottery, which topped her bookcases. One of her first trips as first lady of Texas was to El Paso to meet the painter Tom Lea. Adair Margo, the owner of an art gallery in El Paso and the wife of Bush supporter Donald "Dee" Margo, had gathered an oral history of Lea, who was a World War Two correspondent, novelist, and historian as well as being a painter. Lea's painting *Ranger Escort West of the Pecos* hung in Bush's office in Austin. When he became president, Bush hung Lea's painting *Rio Grande* in the Oval Office.

"Laura had read Lea's books, and because her dad was a veteran, she knew his famous war paintings that were reproduced in *Life* magazine and now hang at the Pentagon," said Margo, who became a good friend of Laura's.[5]

Within a few months, Laura had arranged for Lea and his wife, Sarah, to travel to Austin, where they met Bush and were feted at a dinner at the governor's mansion with old friends including Lady Bird Johnson. Later, Laura found a quote of Tom Lea's that she loved and shared with her husband. He used it often as governor and continues to use it as president. The quote summed up Bush's outlook on life: "Sarah and I live on the east side of our mountain. It is the sunrise side, not the sunset side. It is the side to see the day that is coming, not the side to see the day that is gone. The best day is the day coming, with the work to do, with the eyes wide open, with the heart grateful."

Nine days after Bush was inaugurated president, Tom Lea died. He was ninety-three. Laura flew to El Paso for the funeral.

As first lady of Texas, Laura remained the unpretentious person she had always been. Her office was in the basement of the capitol across from the cafeteria.

"One day she went to get a cup of coffee," Andi Ball said. "The Governor's Protective Detail was with her. They have Secret Service earpieces. She was in line. Someone said to the officer, 'Are you Secret Service?' 'No, we're on the Governor's Protective Detail.' So the person said to Laura Bush, 'Someone important is here because the Governor's Protective Detail is here. I wonder who it is?'

" 'I don't know,' Laura said."

On another occasion, Laura was in line with her daughters at a Wal-Mart in Athens, Texas, where they were vacationing at their lake house.

"A woman in line said to her, 'You look so familiar.' I'm sure the girls were rolling their eyes," Andi Ball said.

"I'm Laura Bush," Laura told the woman.

"No, I don't know you," the woman said.

Nor did Laura's new status lead her to neglect her old friends. When they turned forty, Laura and her friends from high school—Regan Gammon, Peggy Weiss, Marge Petty, who became a Democratic state senator in Kansas, and JaneAnn Fontenot, a nurse midwife in Berkeley—rafted down the Colorado River and hiked out of the Grand Canyon. For their fiftieth, they rafted the Yampa River in Utah.

"One time I overheard Laura talking on the telephone at the governor's mansion about an upcoming trip she and her friends were planning," Margo said. "Because of limited space, they had to enter a lottery with the National Park Service to camp at Yosemite National Park." Adair said to her, "Laura, you're the daughter-in-law of a president of the United States and the wife of the Texas governor and you're on a waiting list?"

"It's a very popular place," Laura said.

Busy as she was, whenever a friend asked a special favor, Laura would always try to oblige. When Pamela Nelson won the Dallas Center for Contemporary Art's Legend Award, Laura introduced her at the awards ceremonies. Pamela's work is informed by the decorative arts, such as Early American quilting and New World textiles.

The patterns, colorful and even kaleidoscopic, are hand-drawn, organic, and flowing. Because she considers Laura a gifted listener, Nelson did a painting of her emphasizing Laura's trademark earrings. The painting, called *Listening,* is displayed in the sitting room on the second floor of the White House.[6]

"Laura and I would go for walks when George was governor," Laura's close friend Penny Royall said. "We walked through the neighborhoods in Austin. During one of those walks, Laura said to me, 'At one point in my life, I thought I would marry a professor and lead a quiet life in academia and dig in my flower garden.' I looked at her and said, 'And look what you got!' We both burst into laughter."[7]

On November 3, 1998, Bush was reelected governor by 68 percent to 31 percent.

"The next morning after the inauguration, they had a breakfast for friends and family," said Anne Stewart. "George was sitting on a chair at a podium. He looked like he was about to fall off of it. I mean his eyes kept closing."

George gave a short speech.

"Thank God for the person who invented caffeine, because I really needed the coffee this morning," he said. "I also have something to say about the person who coined the word *curfew.* Unfortunately, my girls do not know the meaning of the word *curfew.*"[8]

Later, Anne Stewart asked Laura what he meant.

"The girls did not show up after the inauguration party," Laura said. "At two-thirty in the morning, I heard him frantically punching in buttons calling all of their friends, finding out where they were. Finally, he got ahold of one of the girls. He said, 'I don't care if it's my inauguration, get your booties home.'"

"They were partying and having a great time," Stewart said. "They thought, 'Dad won't mind. It's his inauguration as governor.'"

"The governor and Laura had trouble enforcing the curfews," Craig Stapleton said. "Typically, they were supposed to be in at eleven-thirty and showed up at twelve-thirty. They were not wild girls getting into trouble. They were fun-loving girls just having a good time."

"I remember when Jenna was dating Blake Gottesman, who became the president's personal aide," Anne Johnson said. "Jenna came into the governor's bedroom about one-thirty in the morning and woke him up. She said Blake had been mean to her and would the governor please speak with him. I'm sure Blake was stunned when the governor got on the phone. The boyfriend said that with all due respect, Jenna was the problem. Then George said, 'Blake, could the two of you please just work this out in the morning?' Jenna is very theatrical and had a fit. She asked her father why he didn't defend her. He told her to go to bed."[9]

"When Laura expresses irritation, it's usually involving the girls," Adair Margo said. "They were teenagers, and I think one had gotten in trouble or had boyfriend problems. There was some kind of tension. George was taking antibiotics, and he had two bottles of the pills. He started shaking them like maracas, to kind of make light of a tense moment."

In 1998, the Rangers investors had sold the team for roughly $250 million. Bush's share was $18 million. After taxes, according to his accountant Robert McCleskey, he was left with $12 million from his $606,000 investment. Bush used some of the money to set up a $750,000 trust for each of the twins.[10]

As a Christmas present to Laura, Bush donated $250,000 to create the Laura Bush Promenade at her alma mater, Southern Methodist University. The promenade consists of a tree-lined brick walkway, sitting area, gardens, and a plaque outside the entrance to SMU's Fondren Library Center. The benches are etched with quotes about friendship, including one penned by Abraham Lincoln: "The better part of one's life consists of his friendships."

At the SMU dedication on April 27, 1999, the governor of Texas literally wept as he talked about how important Laura was to him.

"This gift reflects its namesake," Bush said. "This is a serene and peaceful place—just like Laura."

"The joke in our family is that when you give a toast, the person will end up in tears along with everyone in the room," Bush's cousin Debbie Stapleton said.

George's father did not make a toast at his wedding because he knew he would wind up crying. George himself would tear up hearing Christmas carols, patriotic country songs, or tales of heroism or service to the country. Videos of his girls or notes from them set him off as well.

Laura's emotions are "very much the same as his," said Nancy Weiss, "but she is in more control of hers, more even. After he became governor, she came into Lubbock and gave a talk. Afterward, I drove her to Midland. She doesn't tear up very often, but as we were driving, she did as she talked about the free feeling she gets when the sky reaches forever.

" 'Oh, our big, beautiful sky,' she said."

With the money from the Rangers deal, Bush could fulfill his political ambitions without worrying about providing for the future of his family, following through on his grandfather Prescott Bush's dictum.

11

INTO THE WHITE HOUSE

During the summer of 1997, Karen Hughes, Bush's communications director, walked into his office in Austin and said, "You're leading in the poll."

"What poll?" Bush asked.

"The poll that shows you are a front-runner for the Republican nomination," she said.

Bush had begun thinking about running for president, but the notion finally crystallized when he attended a service at First United Methodist Church in Austin two hours before being sworn in as governor for the second time on January 19, 1999. In his sermon, the Reverend W. Mark Craig said that America was starved for honest leaders with "ethical and moral courage." At the time, Bill Clinton had been impeached for allegedly committing perjury and obstructing justice in connection with investigations of his relationship with Monica Lewinsky. The minister called for everyone to make the most of every moment and rise to the challenge.

After the service, Barbara Bush turned to her son.

"He was talking to you," she said.

Recognizing how a presidential race would impinge on their family life, Laura later said she was "somewhat reluctant initially" about a presidential campaign. "I knew it would be hard to see someone I loved criticized," she said. Laura knew that a run for the presidency and a possible win would mean giving up even more of their family's privacy. Simply taking a walk or dropping into a drugstore would require heavy security precautions.

The twins, especially Jenna, were opposed. They wanted to be normal teenagers. The thought of being different, singled out because they were in the White House, made them cringe.

Bush formally announced his candidacy on June 12, 1999. Most politicians run for the presidency to achieve glory and power. Bush's motive was a lot simpler. He told a friend he was running "to give back."

Robert McCleskey remembered being at the governor's mansion during the campaign.

"George, Laura, and the girls were there," McCleskey said. "He was kind of on his high horse, telling them to do this and do that. Laura looked over and said, 'Bushie, you ain't president yet!' "

Running for election, like drilling an oil well, entails tremendous risk. To have a partner who is hesitant, discouraging, or critical can sabotage the entire effort. When Bush lost the 2000 New Hampshire primary to John McCain, Don Evans saw how important Laura was in giving him confidence and strength.

"We expected the New Hampshire primary to be close," Evans said. "It turned out not to be close. McCain got forty-nine percent, and we got thirty-one percent of the vote. It was a moment when the world would find out how [George Bush] handles adversity. I can remember being in the room with him and Laura when that news came in. She didn't have the attitude of 'Oh, my gosh. What has happened?' Her attitude was much more 'We're going to win this. You're going to be strong in the upcoming South Carolina primary, in the upcoming debates.'

"When you're in that position, that's what you need to hear from somebody close to you," Evans observed. "Some people could go the other way and say, 'Let's fire everybody.' She wasn't for that. Instead, she said, 'You are the right candidate. Things are going to be fine.' "[1]

Laura spoke during opening night at the Republican National Convention. "You know I am completely objective when I say . . . you have made a GREAT choice," she began. TV viewers didn't get the chance to hear her speech because Andrew Heyward, president of CBS's news division, decided to preempt it with a *48 Hours* piece about pharmaceutical scams on the elderly.

After the convention Laura and her mother-in-law spent twenty days campaigning together through key states, aiming to capture female votes. Impressed by her toughness, Greg Grant, a horticulturist on the faculty of Stephen F. Austin State University in Texas, decided to create a lavender-pink hybrid petunia that he named Laura Bush. Meanwhile, the media largely ignored her.

Laura figured that her high school auto accident would eventually surface, and it did. The tabloid the *Star* broke the story in its March 7, 2000, issue, which came out in early March. Many of the details were wrong.

REVEALED! BUSH'S WIFE KILLED BOYFRIEND, the headline blared. In fact, Mike Douglas, the victim of the crash, was not a boyfriend. The story also said that after the accident, Laura stayed out of school for "a month or two." In fact, she went back on the next school day.

On March 3, the *Dallas Morning News* ran a story saying Laura confirmed reports about the accident.

"It was a very, very tragic accident that I was involved in when I was seventeen. . . . It was terrible for everyone involved," she said from a campaign stop in Providence, Rhode Island.

The Associated Press obtained the accident report and ran a story a day later. It said the police report stated that the weather was clear and neither driver had been drinking.

"As far as we know, no charges were filed," Midland city attorney Keith Stretcher was quoted as saying. "I don't think it's unusual that charges weren't filed."

After that, any story about Laura's upbringing mentioned the accident. While the stories listed Judy Dykes Hester as the only passenger in the car, none of them quoted her or indicated that an attempt had been made to find her. But the tragic event continued to haunt Judy for years afterward, as it did Laura and other close friends.

After high school, Hester did not keep in touch with Laura or other friends from high school, and they drifted apart. But Judy saw her at their twenty-fifth high school reunion in Midland in 1989. They all had breakfast the next day at the Midland Country Club, where Judy met George and the twins. In 1997, Laura held a reunion for Lee High and Midland High. The guests gathered in tents on the grounds of the governor's mansion. A rock-'n'-roll band played while it rained relentlessly. Judy remembered Regan Kimberlin Gammon's telling her that because Mike Douglas's mother's family was originally from the area, he was buried at Austin Memorial Park Cemetery not far from Regan's house. Regan's husband's family was also buried there, and Regan occasionally visited Mike's tombstone.

At the reunion, Laura was just as friendly as ever. When Bush was elected president, she invited Judy and her husband, Jay, an artist who lived with her in a small Texas town near San Antonio, to attend the inauguration. They did not go, but Laura continued to send Judy Christmas cards from the White House.

After the November 2000 election, as the Florida recount battle raged, Laura and George spent a lot of time at their new Crawford ranch. They stayed in the existing farmhouse while their new ranch house was being built. Laura was busy choosing furniture and interior decorations. She got support from friends like Nancy Weiss, Pamela Nelson, Regan Gammon, Debbie Francis, and Katharine Armstrong, who would drop in. If she felt the stress, she never showed it.

When Bush suffered a setback in the legal battle to win the presidency, Laura called Anne Johnson from the campaign plane flying into Austin and suggested they go out to a Chinese restaurant.

"I'm so upset, I can't go to a restaurant," Anne said.

So instead, Anne and Clay Johnson picked up Chinese food, which they ate with Laura and George at the home of Bush friends Timothy J. Herman, a lawyer, and his wife, Mary, the director of the Texas Book Festival.

"When we arrived, I asked George how he was," Anne said.

"I don't know," he said. "This thing is really getting to me."

He pointed to a boil on his face.

Bush took the oath of office as the forty-third president at a minute past noon on Saturday, January 20, 2001. After Chief Justice William H. Rehnquist administered the oath, Bush spoke of his love for his country and his desire to "work to build a single nation of justice and opportunity." He pledged to conduct himself with "compassion and character." In retrospect, his references to reclaiming America's schools, cutting taxes, building up the country's military capability, and confronting weapons of mass destruction seem especially significant.

That morning, Laura—code-named Tempo by the Secret Service—was a guest on NBC's *Today* show.

"You appear to be a very traditional woman," Katie Couric said. "Is that a fair characterization?"

According to a Nexis search, Laura herself had first used the word *traditional* in describing herself in the *Houston Chronicle* in 1997, leaving herself wide open to misinterpretations. "I've always done what really traditional women do, and I've always been very, very satisfied," she said.[2]

During the campaign, Laura tried to clarify her characterization of herself. Thus she said that as a teacher and librarian, she had had jobs that were "traditionally" for women. When Katie Couric asked the question on the morning of the inauguration, Laura tried again.

She said she did not think "traditional woman" was an entirely fair description.

"I've had traditional . . . jobs that were traditionally women's jobs," she said. "I've been a teacher. I've been a librarian. I had the luxury of staying home and raising my children when I had children. That was really what I wanted to do, was to be home with them. But I also think I've been a very contemporary woman in a lot of ways. I had a career for a number of years. I didn't marry George until I was in my thirties. I worked on issues always that are very, very important to me, whether working as a teacher or librarian or working as a volunteer or working as the first lady of my state. And so I think I'm both ways."

In enumerating the ways in which she was not traditional, Laura left out the fact that she hated to cook. In Dallas, "When she had to cook, she would go to the grocery store that day, just before dinner, because she wanted to postpone it as long as possible," said Anne Johnson.

Just before the Bushes' first Thanksgiving at Camp David, a reporter asked if she would be doing the cooking.

"This year, I will not be cooking the turkey," Laura said, laughing.

Asked why she was laughing, Laura said, "I haven't had to cook in a few years. It's been a great relief to my family."

Despite Laura's attempts at a more nuanced self-description, the "traditional" label stuck. For months, the first thing reporters asked was whether she considered herself a "traditional" wife and whether she would be a "traditional" first lady. Reporters compared her to Mamie Eisenhower, who once said that her job was to turn the lamb chops. They contrasted her with Hillary Clinton, who conceived of her role as first lady as a kind of copresident.

Laura would say that she did not want to be put in a box, that people are too complex to be labeled in such a way. In fact, she preferred not to be called first lady at all. Instead of "first lady's office," her office answered the phone "Mrs. Bush's office." When asked if she would be more like Hillary Clinton or Barbara Bush, she always said, "I think I'll just be Laura Bush." At one point, asked to describe the most important thing about being first lady, she answered facetiously, "Being married to the president."

Next, reporters tried to uncover the hidden differences between her personal political opinions and those of her husband. When asked whether women should have the right to an abortion, Laura would avoid the question by saying only that she agreed with the president that the number of abortions should be reduced by teaching abstinence and the need for responsibility. In fact, despite her more liberal views, abortion is the only major issue on which she disagrees with her husband.

Finally, reporters wanted to know if Laura gives her husband "advice." If they had asked whether she expressed her opinion, they might have elicited at least a snippet of useful information. *Advice* implies that she had special expertise or experience. Since she was perceived as being more liberal than her husband, the liberal media naturally thought that she was in a position to give advice since they assumed she must be right and he must be wrong. When Barbara Walters asked the stock question in an interview with both of them, Laura said, "We talk about issues," and added, "I don't think George wants a lot of advice from me."

"That's not true," Bush interjected.

"Well," his wife countered, "I don't want a lot of advice from him."

Despite her modest disclaimer, Laura's friends confirm George Bush's account. "He discusses a lot of stuff with her and has huge respect for her way of thinking," says Nancy Weiss. "But she would never demand or presume to think she was giving advice."[3]

The next favorite question from the media was whether Barbara Bush gave Laura advice. Laura would respond by mentioning how Barbara told her not to criticize her husband's speeches. Barbara

Bush would say, "I don't think you instruct Laura Bush very much," meaning she is her own person and needs no instruction.

In fact, early on, Laura occasionally asked Barbara questions.

"She called Barbara Bush about what she should take from Austin into the private quarters of the White House," Andi Ball, her chief of staff until Bush's second term as president, said. Laura asked if she needed to take any furniture. "You don't need to take any furniture because they take care of you in every way," Ball said. "She brought photos, books, her Christmas decorations, including ones the girls had made."

"Laura is confident and secure in her own self," said Doro Bush Koch. "But she will say to my mother, 'How did you handle this?' "

Laura did not consult her mother-in-law about larger issues or about how to handle herself.

Laura had never been comfortable giving interviews and agreed to them only out of necessity. She did not like being characterized as traditional, and she did not like sparring with the press about her role as an adviser to her husband. She was especially offended that some television correspondents, prima donnas that they are, would show up late for interviews with her. After a few months of this, Laura decided she had had enough.

"In May 2001, Andi Ball came to me and said, 'Mrs. Bush doesn't want to do any more interviews,' " said her press secretary, Noelia Rodriguez, a Democrat who had worked for Los Angeles mayor Dick Reardon.

Given that doing media interviews has been part of the job for modern first ladies, this was a shocking development. Rodriguez wondered what was the point of having a press secretary. Laura did not tell either woman what was behind her decision. That was part of what Pamela Nelson called the "mystery" of Laura Bush. It was not that she was trying to be secretive or that she did not know what her own motivations were. Rather, like her husband, she considered talking about herself and her own deliberations to be egotistical.

"Instead of taking it on as a battle, I thought I would address what might have prompted that message," Rodriguez said. "So I started doing things that would make her feel comfortable in interviews. We did role playing."

Rodriguez would pose hypothetical questions and suggest a few answers.

"I told her it's not the question they ask but the answer you want to give that we need to focus on and how to get there," Rodriguez said. "She was a dream principal. She looks wonderful and is so poised. She is charming and disarming. But for roughly a month, she didn't do interviews."[4]

"She was hesitant to do press," Andi Ball said. "She probably would have been happy not to do it. Noelia pushed her."

Israel J. "Izzy" Hernandez, a longtime Bush aide who is close to the family, thought Laura's hesitancy went beyond her feelings about the press.

"There are a lot of things that are important in her life," he said. "I think because her life was moving so quickly, I think she wanted to make sure those things that were important stayed important. The ability to go for a walk, to go out to a restaurant, how she spent her time, and the fact that some of her friends whom she would see almost daily were no longer close by, all played a role. She decided to slow things down, not be in the public eye, and find a balance between her public role and her personal life."

Slowly, Laura returned to doing press interviews. Ball said Laura brings a briefing book with her to these events, but she doesn't really need it.[5] The briefing material includes rundowns on policy points she wants to make about improving education, combating youth gangs, or enhancing the rights of women.

"She knows the material," Ball said. "Maybe a handful of times in all the time I worked for her has she said something wrong," perhaps citing a wrong figure. "But she catches it before we leave."

12

First Correspondent

A big part of any first lady's job is simply answering letters. She is in many ways the nation's "first correspondent." Every week, Laura receives hundreds of letters on subjects ranging from her husband's policies to a cancer victim's plight to questions about Barney, the first dog. Unless they are form letters, she reads and replies to each one, personally signing them. When reading over a draft of a reply prepared by the correspondence section, she will say, " 'You didn't answer this question in the letter. The third paragraph had a question,' " Andi Ball said. Traveling with her husband on *Air Force One*, Laura will pen notes in response to letters brought to her in a tote bag. In addition, Laura writes notes by hand to her friends.

Friends and aides e-mail Lindsey Lineweaver, her personal aide, who prints out the notes and gives them to Laura. Friends usually call the direct line to the residence, which George Bush delights in picking up, surprising friends trying to reach Laura.

Laura has twenty-one employees. It's not a lot to handle the onslaught of work, so they double up on certain jobs. Gordon Johndroe, who became Laura's press secretary in October 2002 after being press secretary at the Department of Homeland Security, often carried her cosmetics case on trips. Andi Ball carried Altoids, tissues, Sharpies, and a gel Laura uses to wash her hands. During the first presidential campaign, after Laura couldn't find her contacts before she was to give a speech, Lineweaver added an extra set to the huge bag she carries everywhere.

Laura's contacts are not tinted. Nor, contrary to some reports, has she had plastic surgery or Botox treatments.

"We saw a lady who had had injections to fill in the wrinkles in her lips," said Nancy Weiss. "I said to Laura jokingly, 'We ought to do that.' She said, 'Can you see me walking into a plastic surgeon's office and wanting to have something done?' Laura's point was that it would be all over the papers the next day. Laura and I have said to each other, 'Wouldn't it be fun to have this done or that done?' And we always end up saying, 'Why would we do that?' Then we start lifting our faces with our hands to see how it would look. Then we say, 'No, it probably wouldn't look better, and it might look a lot worse.' "

All first ladies adopt a favorite cause, and Laura's has been her long-standing concern and involvement with education and child welfare. "She brought her interests from Texas and added to them," said Anne Heiligenstein.

Laura supported the president's No Child Left Behind Act, which was intended to improve reading instruction in the schools by reintroducing phonics. Wherever she went, she cited the need to teach kids to sound out letters. She visited schools that were doing a good job to spotlight what they were doing right. When Democrats and teachers objected to the regular testing that the act requires as "gestapo-like" and warned that teachers would "teach to the test," Laura would weigh in with her own experience.

"If you're teaching to the test, you're teaching what you want children to know, what's part of the curriculum," Laura would say. "I'm not worried about it. Accountability is absolutely fundamental to making sure that schools are doing well, and not as a punitive test but as a way to correct, to find out where the problems are."

When test scores started improving after public schools began adopting phonics, Laura expressed pride in the accomplishment. Ironically, the toniest private schools never abandoned phonics in teaching reading. "Of course we teach phonics," Beth Tashlik, the head of the tony Collegiate School's lower school in New York, said. "You can't teach reading without it."

Laura promoted her initiatives without calling attention to herself. Unlike Teresa Heinz, she rarely referred to her own experiences. Laura was so averse to becoming the center of attention that she instructed Andi Ball never to give her a speech with the word *I* in it. It made speechwriting difficult, to say the least. In another example of her modesty, after Laura entered the White House, the Daughters of the American Revolution asked her to sign up. She joined the DAR in May 2001, according to Andi Ball. But Laura never told her friends, Bush family members, or the media. Because Laura thought the term "first lady" sounded too regal, Bush started jokingly calling her "Lady."

As part of her initiatives, Laura became active in cognitive-development projects and in supporting libraries. She organized a conference at Georgetown University on childhood cognitive development. She turned Ready to Read, Ready to Learn into a national program. She got the government, through the Department of Health and Human Services, to distribute magazines to parents of newborns on Medicaid.

"Sometimes my job is to go to schools a day before she arrives to talk with the kids and teachers about Mrs. Bush and what she might talk with them about," said Dr. Reid Lyon, who became Bush's reading adviser in the White House. Lyon said he tries to relax teachers and children before Laura's visit, but they are always on edge.

"Then, when she walks into the classroom, there is this magical transformation," Lyon said. "What had been anxiety turns into a glow you can see on their faces. She connects in such a warm and genuine fashion. I have seen even the most hyperactive kids transfixed, waiting for her next words. They listen to her, they like to hear her read, and they like to read to her. She inspires them, and she inspires their teachers."[1]

Beth Ann Bryan, who was Bush's first education policy director when he was governor, noticed the same phenomenon when Laura toured Rainbow Rooms, centers that provide donated books and clothes on an emergency basis for abused or neglected children who are about to go into foster care.

"As we came out of one of the centers, there were three little girls who were four or five," Bryan said. "Mrs. Bush stopped and walked over and started talking to them. She was so taken with those little children. They were so taken with her. It was like no one else was there."[2]

On top of her duties as first lady, Laura has somehow found time to read at least a book a week. If asked what she was reading, Laura has rattled off titles ranging from *Ship of Fools* by Katherine Anne Porter to *Music for Chameleons* by Truman Capote. But her favorite books are plague books, a genre that includes literature on the bubonic plague and other epidemics. "I love plague books," Laura said to Pamela Nelson.

"The first lady undoubtedly is the most literate person in President Bush's inner circle," *BusinessWeek*'s Thane Peterson wrote. "Jackie Kennedy seems like a dilettante by comparison." Peterson cited an interview Laura did with Susan Stamberg of National Public Radio. "Stamberg asks her to read a few lines, and the first lady thumbs through a well-worn copy of *The Brothers Karamazov* held together with a rubber band. As she reads and they talk, it's quite clear she knows the dense and difficult eighty-page Grand Inquisitor section of the novel and its surrounding chapters almost by heart. You get the impression she would just as soon dispense with the small talk and keep on reading. I doubt that many literature professors know it as well."

In the Grand Inquisitor chapter, Christ appears at church and is sent away for being too radical. "Why did You come here, to interfere and make things difficult for us?" the Grand Inquisitor says as he sentences Jesus to be burned at the stake as a heretic. He then decides to banish him. Yet there is an ambiguity to the chapter, and when asked about it, Laura has said, "It's about life, and it's about death, and it's about Christ. I find it really reassuring."

In Debbie Stapleton's view, reading is the way Laura refreshes and revitalizes herself. Every morning, the Bushes wake up at 5:30. Bush turns on a coffeemaker set up by White House residence staff and brings Laura a cup of coffee, just as he did before they entered public life. They read the papers together. He glances at the headlines but mainly reads the sports pages. She reads a wide variety of newspapers and magazines and brings items to his attention. Or, based on what she has read, she takes action herself.

"She will read something, and all of a sudden, we have a whole new initiative we are working on, or we write a letter to someone," Andi Ball said. "It's very hard to keep ahead of her. I think I've read the paper, and she'll ask if I had seen this article or that article that I had not noticed. We are working on women's health issues, and in the midst of it, she has read an article about someone who is seeding native grasses, and we are calling the policy shop in the West Wing to get more information. She is extremely hands-on. She makes changes to her speeches in pencil right up until she is about to give them."

Laura took on breast-cancer awareness as an issue both because her mother had breast cancer and because of her long friendship with Nancy Brinker. Brinker got to know Laura and George through her then husband, Norman Brinker, who started Bennigan's, Chili's, and other restaurant chains. In 1982, Brinker started the Susan G. Komen

Breast Cancer Foundation after her sister contracted breast cancer. Working through affiliates in 15,000 communities worldwide, the foundation has raised more than $750 million for breast-cancer research and education and sponsors Race for the Cure events.

"Laura would come to the early Komen [foundation] events when she was first lady in Texas," Nancy said. "I gotta tell you, they were really long. You know how volunteers can be sometimes. A lot of people in public positions would come for five minutes, make the cameo. But Laura would stay for the entire meeting. I thought, 'This is a real person. She is not bolting out the door.' "[3]

Early on, Nancy asked Laura if she could hold a Race for the Cure survivors event in the White House. On June 1, 2001, Laura did just that, and brought along the president and Jenna Welch, who had a successful cancer operation in 1999.

"I have never asked her to do something when she did not respond and help," said Brinker, who later became ambassador to Hungary. "If she is your friend, she is a real friend. If they took me and said you have to take six friends with you in a spaceship and you're going to land on Mars, Laura would be one of my first choices because she is not just intelligent but steady. She wouldn't panic if she met a Martian. She would figure out how to deal with it. I would be hysterical."

More than anything, Laura's love of reading has been the centerpiece of her role as first lady. With more than a million dollars from private donations, Laura and the Library of Congress hosted the first National Book Festival on the East Lawn of the Capitol on September 7, 8, and 9, 2001. During the three-day event, some 25,000 people moved from book signings to author presentations and readings to booths promoting literacy programs.

Asked by a reporter what she was reading, Laura said that Nathaniel Philbrick's *In the Heart of the Sea* was on her bedside table. She hoped to delve into David McCullough's biography of John Adams.

"The president just read it," she said.

Laura had first broached the idea of a national book festival to Dr. James H. Billington, the librarian of Congress, on the evening before Bush's inauguration. As part of the inauguration festivities, Laura had asked a half-dozen authors to read from their works to help launch a national campaign to promote reading by children.

"Literate children become literate adults," she said.

Among the authors were Stephen Ambrose, Mary Higgins Clark, and several writers of children's books. At a reception that night in the great hall of the Library of Congress, Laura chatted with Dr. Billington.

"She wanted to know about the library," Dr. Billington said. "As a professional librarian herself, I just remember how sensible her questions were. They reflected a professional interest in libraries and also how libraries relate to education. She said that in Texas, she had these book festivals, and they were one of the more successful things she had done. She wondered if it would be possible to do something like that on a national scale. I said, 'That's a wonderful idea.'"[4]

At the Coolidge Auditorium in the Library of Congress, Billington introduced Laura as "the first professional librarian ever to live in the White House." Laura welcomed everyone and invited them to "revel in the joy of the written word."

The president was with her.

"The band wanted to play 'Hail to the Chief,'" Dr. Billington said. "But the president said he wanted to be seen just as a spouse that evening."

Offstage, Texas writer Kinky Friedman, dressed in black hat, black jeans, and black boots, puffed on a cigar. "Laura's a big cheerleader for books," Friedman said. Asked if he voted for Bush, he said, "I don't vote."

After the success of the first book festival, the Library of Congress continued to hold it each year. Because of its popularity, it had to be moved to the Mall. Eventually, 85,000 people attended.

Because they shared a love of reading, Laura invited Ludmila Putina, the wife of Russian president Vladimir Putin, to open the second festival with her in a Rose Garden ceremony. The following year, Mrs. Putin held her own book festival in Moscow, and Laura attended.

In 2001, the Community Foundation for the National Capital Region established the Laura Bush Foundation for America's Libraries. J. W. Marriott Jr. led the fund-raising effort. The foundation, of which she is honorary chair, gives books to libraries of schools in low-income areas. So far, it has distributed more than $2 million worth of books.

"When you give just five thousand dollars to a school for library books, that can quadruple the book budget they have," according to Beth Ann Bryan, who became executive director of the foundation.

"It's not her nature to talk about herself," said Laura's friend Pam Willeford, the first executive director of the Laura Bush Foundation. "She does it by example. But she cares deeply and passionately about the issues she has been involved in."[5]

13

A PRIVATE MOMENT

When the Bush people took over, they found that the Clinton administration had operated the White House like a fraternity house. Aides attended meetings in T-shirts and jeans. As in a college debating society, business was conducted late into the night and all weekend. Carpets and upholstered furniture were fraying, and empty pizza cartons were scattered about in offices. Because the president was almost always late, the Secret Service often made jokes about CST—Clinton Standard Time.

Bush looked at the White House as a symbol of America, like the Washington Monument.

Anne Johnson would never forget the afternoon she and her husband, Clay, were flying from Camp David to Washington on *Marine One*.

"The president, very emotionally, said, 'Annie, look at that,'" Johnson said. "I looked out the window and saw the Washington Monument. Even before 9/11, you could tell that this was a man who dearly loved this country and took seriously all that it stood for."

Joshua B. Bolten, who was White House deputy chief of staff for policy and later became director of the Office of Management and Budget, recalled that early on, Logan Walters, Bush's personal aide, told him that even on weekends, the president expected men to wear jackets in the Oval Office.

"The president communicates a respect for the White House," Bolten said. "That this is a national treasure that should be nurtured. I think *reverence* is not too strong a word for his attitude. We are here for a limited time and are obliged, like good fiduciaries, to turn it over in better shape than we received it." Laura upholds the same standard, according to Bolten.

"In the chief of staff's suite, my office was directly across from Andy Card's," Bolten recalled. "We were working all hours. My assistant had piles of papers piled up. Mrs. Bush communicated that this was not proper decorum for the White House. We cleaned it up and rearranged things. At some point she had floated through and noticed it."[1]

"She brings grace and dignity and stature to the White House," said Pam Willeford, Laura's friend who was in Regan Gammon's book club with Laura in Austin and later became ambassador to Switzerland.

Bill Clinton used the White House as a partisan fund-raising instrument, putting up political supporters in the Lincoln Bedroom and holding large receptions for them. While some overnight guests of the Bushes at the White House and Camp David have given campaign contributions, all have been dignitaries, family, or real friends going back years.

"Marvin and I are the family members who are local in the Washington area," said Doro Bush Koch. "When the president came into office, he said to us, 'I just want you to know that every time we go to Camp David, you're invited.' From then on, every time he goes, his office will call to invite us."[2]

With a few exceptions, the same people who were listed as the Bushes' overnight guests at the governor's mansion in Austin have appeared as their guests at Camp David. One such couple is Alphonso and Marcia Jackson. Bush got to know Alphonso when he headed the Dallas Housing Authority. The two couples began to socialize, and their kids went to the movies together. Laura invited Marcia to join her on the board of Child Protective Services Community Partners, which supports social workers.

"Laura stood out as a person who wanted to bring a diverse face to Dallas," said Marcia Jackson, who is African American. Shortly after George became governor, she said, "Laura invited us to stay overnight at the governor's mansion. We stayed in the Sam Houston Room. I'm not even sure if any African-Americans had ever stayed in Sam Houston's bed previously."[3]

Before the reception after Bush's second inauguration as governor, Marcia sprained her ankle and had to stay in their hotel room.

"George and Laura asked Alphonso where I was," Marcia said. "When he told them, Laura said, 'Do I need to go up and see her?' Now this is inaugural night. That is how thoughtful she is."

When Bush became president, he named Alphonso Jackson secretary of housing and urban development.

"There are many whites who interact with blacks at work, but in their private lives, they don't," Marcia said. "I think that [their socializing with blacks] says a lot about them as people."

When the Bushes moved into the White House, the Secret Service and residence staff were overjoyed. The Clintons treated agents and household help with disdain. "With Bush, there was an instant change," a former Secret Service agent said. "He was punctual. Clinton was never on time for anything. Bush and his wife treated you normally, decently. They had conversations with us. Everyone got a morale boost with Bush. He was the complete opposite of Clinton."

According to those who work with them, the Bushes treat everyone around them with consideration.

"The president and Mrs. Bush are very respectful of the fact that we, too, have families," said Anne Heiligenstein. "They rise early and have dinner at a reasonable time. That allows the residence staff to have some certainty in scheduling. The same for Secret Service agents. The Bushes feel strongly that if you are late, that is rudeness. If there is a rule in the White House, it is be on time. If the staff meeting is called for ten, you are there at ten."

Those who have seen Laura and George in unguarded moments have also been touched by their genuine love for each other.

"We were at the president's birthday party on July 4, 2004, on the Truman Balcony in the White House," said Rebecca Turner "Becky" Gonzales, wife of Attorney General Alberto R. Gonzales. "He holds it on July 4 instead of his actual birthday, July 6. It's intimate, and just their closest friends are there. They have a dinner with the president's favorite foods, generally picnic food like fried chicken and corn on the cob."

At one point, Becky needed to go to the restroom.

"I was walking down the great hall of the White House when I realized I was walking toward the president and Mrs. Bush, who were down by the elevator," she said. "He kind of swung her around, as if they were dancing, and he nuzzled into her neck. I'd clearly walked into a private moment and wasn't sure what to say. I finally said, 'Great party!' "

Bush smiled at her. "You could see his happiness," she said.

At a previous party, given by Clay and Anne Johnson for Karen Hughes when she left her post as White House communications director, Gonzales was talking with one group of people while her husband, then White House counsel, was talking with another group.

"I hadn't seen Al much during the daylight hours," Becky said. "Even though we were talking to different groups, sort of with our backs to each other, we reached out and were holding hands."

Bush took note of what they were doing.

"It was like being caught in a tender moment, but he grinned knowingly and was being supportive," she said. "They both have been so encouraging and have set such a good example, both with their manner with the staff and with their marriage. Because of that, during the hard times when we have felt the pressure because of all our spouses have been through in the White House, watching the two of them and how they stay so connected has made it easier."[4]

When they came to Washington, the Bushes brought Maria Galvan, their housekeeper at the governor's mansion, to be their personal housekeeper in the White House. Galvan took care of Laura's clothes, pressing them and packing for her. Laura included Galvan in her own social events, such as a luncheon for friends and family at the new National Museum of the American Indian on Laura's birthday on November 4, 2004.

Laura's friend Adair Margo and her husband, Dee, had a similar relationship with their housekeeper, Adela Gonzalez. When Adela's daughter Monica graduated from Baylor University, Laura, then first lady of Texas, hired her as an aide. When Adair and her husband stayed at the White House for a week, Laura invited Adela to stay with them.

"Adela and I were being taken up to the third floor on the White House elevator by Harold W. Hancock," Adair recalled. "He was a White House doorman and elevator operator. Laura got off first on the second floor. Mr. Hancock turned to us and said, 'I love these people. They're so courteous. The previous inhabitants never knew my name.' "[5]

Bush would chat with Hancock in the elevator about baseball and first dog Barney. In October 2002, Hancock died at the age of seventy-two of bone cancer. Laura and George took time out from their duties to attend his funeral. Most of the residence staff attended as well.

The next day, a *New York Times* story on Hancock's death quoted Hillary Clinton as saying, "He [Hancock] always cheered me up, because he was always so upbeat and positive and nice." She added, "He was so gracious and such a gentleman."[6]

When Adair saw the story, she asked Adela, "Didn't Mr. Hancock say they never knew his name?"

"Yes," Adela said.

Because of the extensive Secret Service preparations that precede his trips outside the White House, Bush prefers not to go to restaurants. At one point, he told Laura he didn't like to be stared at while he was eating. Laura laughed and said, "Well, maybe you shouldn't have run for president."

In contrast to her husband, Laura regularly slips out of the White House to have lunch with friends at places like Café Deluxe, Zola, or the Old Ebbitt Grill. Her Secret Service detail sits at nearby tables.

The Bushes are required to pay for the incremental cost of their personal meals and personal parties—the cost of a lamb chop, for example. The White House or the State Department pays for official entertaining. The Republican National Committee pays for Christmas parties and Christmas cards. In their first four years in the White House, the Bushes gave only four state dinners. Instead, several times a week, Laura and George would have friends over. Or they would go to dinner at the home of friends like Anne and Clay Johnson.

Robert McCleskey, the accountant who manages the Bushes' investments, also paid nearly all their bills. A slow-talking Midlander, McCleskey went to first grade with Laura at North Elementary and played baseball with George in grade school. He lived five blocks from Laura's house and dated her a few times in high school. Laura's mother was his Sunday school teacher.

Now McCleskey, who wears black cowboy boots and a white cowboy hat, keeps George's baseball-card collection in a bank vault. Any mail addressed to "George W. Bush, Midland, Texas" is delivered to McCleskey. (One writer requested a $30,000 loan from daughter Barbara.) Sometimes several times a week, the president or his secretary will call him. Because of frequent urgent calls from the White House, McCleskey had to break down and get a cell phone.

When the Bushes are away, he keeps tabs on their Crawford ranch, visiting to "check up on things." McCleskey pays the bills with checks that he signs and that list Bush as the account holder.

"Even though it has my signature, some people when you send them a check with 'George W. Bush' on it won't deposit it," McCleskey said. "We have to call them to get them to run it through."

McCleskey is Jenna Welch's accountant as well. He joked that George hired him because he was the cheapest accountant he could find.

Back in high school, McCleskey was a "kicker," said Pamela Nelson. She defined that as someone with a pickup truck who wears boots and knows about ranching. "He comes up from Midland and tells them stories about Midland in the White House or at the ranch," Nelson said. "The president wants to know who is going to Johnny's Barbecue now."

McCleskey was the trustee for the trust Bush set up when he became governor. He was also trustee of the two trusts set up for the twins that paid for their college educations. When Jenna decided she wanted to become a teacher in Washington, McCleskey approved her request for enough money to buy a Saab. Jenna needed a car to go to work, McCleskey decided. Barbara, on the other hand, didn't need a car.

"Being president is expensive," McCleskey said. "You can't make much money on your investments, and a whole lot of expenses that go along with being president come out of his pocket, such as entertaining guests or buying a gown from Oscar de la Renta."[7]

On their 2004 federal income tax return, the Bushes listed $784,219 in adjusted gross income, including his salary as president of $400,000 a year. They paid federal taxes of $207,307. They contributed $77,785, about 10 percent of their income, to charities.

———

Besides responding to letters and giving her opinion when appropriate about administration appointments and policy, Laura is in charge of redecorating in the White House.

As a rule, first ladies confine their decorative touches to the residence and public portions of the White House, but the Bushes were appalled by the shabby condition of the West Wing, and Laura took charge of refurbishing that as well.

Laura has always had a knack for interior decorating, a talent she applies when visiting her friends. When she spotted a Biedermeier table from Czechoslovakia off in a corner of the Greenwich, Connecticut, home of Craig and Debbie Stapleton, she suggested they move it to a prominent spot in the center of their living room.

"When I showed her the plans to our house, she said it would make more sense to add this or move that," Debbie said. "I don't think in the past ten years I've done any remodeling without showing her the designs. She has an incredible sense of interior design, space, and how it should be used."

Laura should have been an architect, Craig Stapleton said.

"There's nothing she likes more than to organize the design of houses both in the construction phase and also in terms of interior finishes," Craig said. "She knows the nuts and bolts of construction. You have a private time with her, and you have a roll of plans under your arm, she is thrilled."

When Laura goes to antiques shops, she scopes out items for her friends.

"She has a complete recall of all her friends' houses," said Kenneth Blasingame, the interior designer Laura met through Anne Johnson's sister Betty Sewell. "She will see something and say, 'This would be great for Regan in her upstairs bedroom beside the bed.' "[8]

On December 18, 2000, just after the Supreme Court ruled on the election, Hillary Clinton gave Laura a tour of the White House, and they had coffee together. Laura was no stranger to the mansion. Back when her father-in-law was president, she had slept in the Lincoln

Bedroom and the Queen's Bedroom. Now she was quietly dismayed at what she saw. Not only were carpets and furnishings fraying and in disrepair in the West Wing and public areas, the Oval Office was done in loud colors—red, blue, and gold. The Lincoln Bedroom looked worn because it hadn't been decorated in so long. The East Wing was cut up into small offices and had exposed electrical conduits. Many of the furnishings looked dated.

Despite her opinion of the decor, Laura never said anything critical about Hillary.

"I said something negative to Laura about Hillary in the solarium," Pamela Nelson said. "Laura said, 'I'm just surprised that her book is selling so well.' But I could tell she didn't want me to say anything. By her demeanor, she will say, 'Let's not go down that road.' She won't even roll her eyes."

Bush is the same way, quietly praying for Peter Jennings, whose broadcasts were often critical of him, after the ABC anchor was stricken with lung cancer.

During the first week after the inauguration, Laura toured the White House with Ken Blasingame and James Powell, an Austin antiques dealer who is an expert on period furnishings. Nancy Weiss was staying with Laura at the White House and went along with them.

Laura preferred an open, airy, comfortable appearance and light, neutral colors. As the blue carpets in the West Wing needed replacing, she had camel-colored carpets installed. Instead of a generic white, she chose sandstone for the walls. Besides redecorating the Oval Office, she redid the Cabinet Room. She had the six gold sconces that were created for the room in 1934 when Franklin Roosevelt was president reinstalled. The White House Historical Association offered to replace the carpet that had been there for thirty-five years. Blasingame and a National Park Service expert designed a wool rug featuring a red field spangled with gold stars.

Throughout, Laura drew on historic furnishings from the White

House storage facility in Beltsville, Maryland, which holds more than 30,000 items used in previous administrations.

"She is very respectful of history and tradition and the fact that this is a very special place," Andy Card said. "Their attitude is they will be here for a short time. While they are here, they should respect what happened before they got here, and leave a legacy that will be respected by future presidents."

Laura's influence extends to Camp David. When a head of state from the Middle East was visiting, she noticed that the bathroom was the first thing people saw when entering Dogwood Lodge. Equidistant from Aspen Lodge, which is the president's cabin, Dogwood and Birch are the two cabins where dignitaries stay. She had the bathroom door moved.

"Some presidents have used Camp David as a retreat that they didn't share with others," Card observed. "Some presidents didn't invite foreign visitors to Camp David. This president shares Camp David with staff and friends, and they also use it as a way to show special respect for foreign leaders. Because of that," he said, "she paid particular attention to what Camp David is like for the guests who stay there."

14

CALL 911

Ever since Bush's tenure as governor, Laura had always asked the media to respect the twins' privacy and not take photos or write about them. She wanted Jenna and Barbara to feel as much like normal teenagers as possible, and the media in Texas went along with her wishes. But the twins turned out to be so normal that they engaged in underage drinking and—in the case of Jenna—produced someone else's driver's license in order to be served at Chuy's in Austin. When the incidents became court cases, the national media could no longer reasonably be expected to ignore them.

By now, Jenna, the blonde, was a sophomore at the University of Texas at Austin. Barbara, the brunette, was going to Yale. They were nineteen.

Collister "Terry" Johnson Jr., one of Bush's roommates at Yale, remembered when he was staying at the Bushes' country home on Rainbo Lake near Athens, Texas. Laura told Barbara and Jenna, who were twelve, to "say good night to Uncle Terry."

"Barbara comes up and gives me a peck on the cheek," Terry Johnson said. "Jenna comes up, grabs me by the shoulders, plants a kiss on my lips, and says, 'Good night, T.J.' That captures the difference in their personalities."[1]

"I think Jenna wanted to go to the University of Texas because she was so connected in Austin, and she wanted to have her friends and not lose them," said Pamela Nelson, who gave the twins art lessons for two years. "Barbara was a little more adventurous. She had done a semester in Rome in high school. I think she went to Yale for the adventure. Her father and her grandfather went there. I suspect her grades were better, but Jenna made pretty good grades."

Good grades or not, on May 29, 2001, Austin police officer Clay Crabb was dispatched to Chuy's after restaurant manager Mia Lawrence called 911 at 10:34 P.M. Crabb later wrote in his report that when he arrived at the restaurant on Barton Springs Road, Lawrence told him the subject of her call was a blonde wearing a pink halter top who was seated in the bar area with her back to the wall.

Crabb and another officer "were about to go in and talk to the girl Mia pointed out when I was tapped on the shoulder by a subject identifying himself as a member of the Secret Service," Crabb wrote. By then, the officers knew that the alleged offender was Jenna Bush, and they explained to the agents that they were checking into an allegation that she had used fake identification to buy a drink.

The Secret Service agents did not interfere. Instead, Michael Bolton, a Secret Service supervisor, told Jenna and Barbara what was happening and then told the police the girls were going to leave. Two days later, the Austin police issued tickets to both girls for class-C misdemeanor violations. Jenna was cited for misrepresentation of age by a minor, Barbara for possession of alcohol by a minor.

The episode began when a waitress became suspicious of the driver's license Jenna had handed her. The waitress showed it to Lawrence, who noted that the license had someone else's name on it. In addition, the photo looked "slightly off." Lawrence told Jenna she would not be served.

"Whatever," Jenna said, according to the police report.

Apparently thinking Barbara was older than Jenna, the waitress brought her and two friends three margaritas and three tequila shots. The bartender kept watch to make sure Jenna drank none of them. After other patrons pointed out that Barbara was the same age as Jenna, Lawrence called 911. By the time officers arrived, the tequila shots were gone. Each of the margaritas was at least "partially consumed," the police report said. When officer Clifford Rogers asked Jenna for the identification she had used, she handed it over and started to cry.

"She then stated that I do not have any idea what it is like to be a college student and not be able to do anything that other students get to do," Rogers wrote.

Another officer asked restaurant manager Lawrence what she wanted the police to do with the girls.

"I want them to get into big trouble," Lawrence said.[2]

Left unsaid in the report was that Austin is a liberal, university town that is generally anti-Bush. Police Chief Stan Knee told the *Austin-American Statesman* that what was unusual about the incident was not the way the police handled it but that they were involved at all.

"Most business establishments usually handle those things themselves," the chief said. "Once we were notified of the crime, or the potential crime, we felt obligated to make as thorough a report as possible."

In fact, court records showed that only one person that year had been given a class-C citation for attempting to use fake identification to buy alcohol. Ironically, when he was governor, Bush had signed into law a toughened, zero-tolerance version of the statute.

For Barbara, it was a first offense. But on May 16, Jenna had pleaded no contest to a charge of possession of alcohol at Cheers Shot Bar on Sixth Street in Austin. In response to the new charge, Jenna, on July 6, pleaded no contest to misrepresenting her age. Her driver's license was suspended for a month. She paid a $600 fine for the infraction at Chuy's and for the previous charge. She also got three months of deferred adjudication, a form of probation, plus thirty-six hours of community service. She was required to attend an alcohol awareness class. Barbara also pleaded no contest and was sentenced to deferred adjudication. She had to attend alcohol awareness class as well.

After the incident at Chuy's, Mike Young and John Zapp, the owners of the restaurant, apologized. "Usually, we wouldn't have handled it the way it was handled," Young said.

In Washington, a reporter demanded that the White House say something about the incidents because, after all, the press had reported it. But press spokesman Ari Fleischer refused to take the bait. Exasperated, the press finally resorted to demanding that the White House critique the media's coverage of the episode.

"Can you tell us if you believe that coverage of the episode yesterday is a legitimate occupation for the press?" a TV correspondent implored.

"I am not going to deem [sic] to tell the press at this juncture what the press should or shouldn't do," Fleischer said. "I think that's why you're here." But *People* magazine, having just named Laura one of the fifty most beautiful people in the world, put the girls on the cover of its June 18, 2001, issue.

"We tried to dissuade them from doing it," said Noelia Rodriguez, Laura's press secretary at the time. "What we objected to wasn't mentioning the drinking incidents but focusing on the twins so much by putting them on the cover. We had given them tremendous access, but after that, Mrs. Bush stopped doing interviews with *People* for more than six months."

Washington Post reporter Ann Gerhart, in her book *The Perfect Wife*, put the blame squarely on Laura. "These girls have all the *noblesse*, and none of the *oblige*," Gerhart wrote. In addition to the drinking incidents, Gerhart claimed that the girls did not treat their Secret Service detail with "respect." Based on a report in a Yale magazine, she said that Barbara gave the "slip" to her Secret Service detail when she and some fellow students drove to Manhattan for a World Wrestling Federation match.

"Using an electronic pass to go through a tollbooth, the car in which Barbara was riding then speeded up and left the agents, who were paying their toll in cash, behind," Gerhart wrote.

The story was absurd on the face of it. Besides the fact that Secret Service agents use electronic toll passes, they could, as part of their official duties, have turned on their sirens and bypassed any toll.

"After the alleged incident was reported, I was with Barbara and Laura in New York, along with my daughter Lara," Regan Gammon said. "We were laughing about it. It was ridiculous."[3]

While the girls initially did not like having Secret Service protection, Secret Service sources say both girls developed excellent relationships with their agents. Laura did not cooperate on Gerhart's book, and Gerhart had no way of knowing how the girls had been brought up.

"George is the disciplinarian, but Laura is so close to those girls," said Anne Lund Stewart. "I can't tell you how much she communes with them and counsels them."

No one was in a better position to see how the girls were brought up than Israel J. "Izzy" Hernandez. After graduating from the University of Texas, he became an aide to Bush when he was managing partner of the Texas Rangers. When Bush started his race for governor, Hernandez became his personal aide. Except for two years spent pursuing a master's degree, Hernandez continued as an aide until Bush entered the White House. Then he became deputy assistant to the president and assistant to Karl Rove. He has remained close to the Bush family and has been a frequent guest at Camp David.

During Bush's first run for governor, Hernandez's home was broken into. George and Laura invited him to stay with them. He lived in their guesthouse for a year. Besides eating breakfast and dinner with them almost daily, Hernandez went out to restaurants and baseball games with the family.

Just twelve years older than the girls, Hernandez was like an older brother to them, carpooling and keeping tabs on them. When Laura, as first lady, took Jenna on her European trip, Izzy Man, as Bush called him, went along.

When Barbara and Jenna were in grade school, they'd had temporary Secret Service protection because their grandfather was president and the country was engaged in the Gulf War. "They would sometimes leave the classroom at the end of the day and go home with their friends without telling the agents, who had no girls to take home," said Hernandez. "As they got older, they understood the need for protection. While they still weren't happy about having agents around, they developed good relationships with them and treated them with respect."[4]

Like most teenagers, when the girls were in junior high, they had a love-hate relationship with their parents, Hernandez said.

"They went through a phase when, if you said to them, 'How was school?' they would say, 'Why are you always asking me how school was!' Laura would get mad when they were trying to see what they could get away with. Laura would say, 'Jenna, you're not going to put that one by me.' Then Barbara would say, 'But why?' Barbara would come in with an analysis of why Jenna was right."

For Laura, "The most important thing in her life was her family," Hernandez said. "Even when the campaigns started, she always tried to time everything so she was there when the girls were there and when the president came back from trips. She would make sure they all ate together and spent time together."

Like his father, George said he believed in unconditional love in bringing up their two daughters, meaning he would support them no matter what. That did not mean he would not discipline them. When Barbara Bush was fifteen, they were all going to go to a football game in Austin.

"The girls were quite trendy and artistic," Anne Johnson said. "I think they get that from Laura. She has a great eye. Back when girls started wearing short tops with their middles showing, Barbara came down to go to the game. Her midriff was showing."

"You're wearing that to the football game?" Bush asked.

"Yes, I am," Barbara said.

"You will have to go put on a shirt," he said.

"I'm not doing that," she said.

"You're not going to the game like that. I'm sorry," Bush told her.

"So," Anne recalled, "she went upstairs, put on a shirt, and came down in tears."

Like most teenagers, the girls were embarrassed to acknowledge that they had parents. They made their father wait in the car when he came to pick them up at parties. They would come out; he was not allowed to go in.

One night, while the Johnsons were having dinner with the Bushes in Austin, Barbara came into the dining room with a date.

"When are you going to be back?" Bush asked.

"When I get back," she said.

"See how much respect I get?" Bush said to Anne and Clay Johnson.

"The daughters are like their parents, complete opposites," Anne Johnson said. "Barbara is just like her mother: quiet, studious, more introverted. I think she looks like President 41," the term inside the Bush camp for former president George H. W. Bush. "Jenna is gregarious, always on, likes to be the center of attention. Jenna looks like her mother but acts like her father and vice versa with Barbara. Bar [their grandmother] said, 'If you could integrate them, you would have a very happy person.' Jenna has always had a serious boyfriend. Barbara has one now. Jenna has had a string of them."

After the episode at Chuy's, both girls graduated from college without further incident.

"Laura has two free-spirited kids who have grown to be incredibly independent and sassy," Craig Stapleton said. "She has given them their independence and self-confidence. She has managed it beautifully. When the girls began campaigning, they became public figures.

But they have come out as very natural, unassuming kids. There is no arrogance in those kids at all. There is no sense of entitlement. They just want to be normal kids. A lot of that goes back to their mom."[5]

Jenna decided to go into teaching inner-city children, as her mother had done. Barbara planned to help people afflicted with AIDS.

"What the girls want to do reflects who they are and what they have learned at home," Anne Johnson said. "These people are sincere. They walk the walk."

During Bush's second inauguration as president, Anne and Clay Johnson sat just behind the first lady and the twins.

"As a mother of twins, there was the most special moment during the ceremony," Anne Johnson said. "I looked at the girls, who were directly in front two rows forward. I noticed, even when they were not talking, that their heads were about a foot from one another."[6]

"Occasionally, they would say something to each other and not even have to lean over," Johnson continued. "I think it's pretty remarkable that these fraternal twins are really as close as identical twins. Usually, there's some competition between fraternal twins, but there is none with Barbara and Jenna. They adore each other. I think that speaks to the support and love that they have from the parents."

15

COMFORTER-IN-CHIEF

Two days after the first National Book Festival, Laura was scheduled to testify before the Senate Health, Education, Labor and Pensions Committee about the need to improve reading instruction. Andi Ball and Margaret Spellings, then Bush's domestic policy adviser, were with her.

As the first lady was getting in a Secret Service car for the trip to the Capitol, an agent told her that a plane had flown into the World Trade Center. By the time she arrived at the Rayburn Office Building, she was told that a second plane had hit. Clearly, it was a terrorist attack.

"Senator [Edward M.] Kennedy met us as we drove up," Andi Ball recalled. "Instead of going to the hearing room, we went to his office, where the TV was on. As we were going in, she said to me, 'He has had so many tragedies in his life. He would have more understanding of a tragedy like this.'"

Kennedy was cordial and gave Laura a painting he had done. Lawrence McQuillen of *USA Today* asked Laura, "Mrs. Bush, you know, children are kind of struck by all this. Is there a message you could tell to the nation's—"

"Well," Laura said, looking a bit tense, "parents need to reassure their children everywhere in our country that they're safe."

At that point, Laura became the comforter-in-chief, calmly reassuring the nation and dispensing advice on how parents should deal with the tragedy.

"As we were leaving and walking down the corridor to get in an elevator to get back to the cars to go back to the White House, the agents said we can't go right now," Andi Ball said. "They said we need to go back and wait a few minutes. By then, the Pentagon had been hit. Our agents thought another plane was coming toward Washington. The Capitol was being evacuated."[1]

They went to Senator Judd Gregg's office, where Ball asked Laura if she wanted to call her mother.

"We got her mother on the line," Ball said. "The agents said the girls were okay. They were at their respective colleges and had been taken to secure locations. She spoke with the president."

The agents said they were going to take everyone to a secure location, which turned out to be the basement of Secret Service headquarters on New York Avenue. Andi Ball asked if they could bring their advance people, who had arrived on their own. At the time, Laura traveled with only two cars and four agents. The agents called for additional cars and backup. After 9/11, the number of agents on Laura's detail was more than doubled.

"We were sitting on each other in the backseat," Ball said. "Everyone had a cell phone up to their ears. I tried to call our office. I couldn't find our staff. The traffic was so bad that everything was stopped. Later, an agent said a car had sideswiped them. We knew the White House had been evacuated. There was a rumor Camp David had been attacked. It was chaos."

They watched TV in horror as they saw the towers fall.

"I think we all wept. It was just so unbelievable," Andi said.

Later in the day, they were told Bush was returning to the White House, and Laura could meet him.

"Mrs. Bush was worried about Maria Galvan, their housekeeper," Andi Ball said. "The Secret Service tracked her down. She was staying with someone from the White House flower shop."

Bush returned to the White House at 5:30 P.M., and Laura met him in the Emergency Operations Center, a bunker of rooms deep underground. That night, at eleven-thirty, they were sleeping in their bedroom on the second floor when a Secret Service agent, breathing heavily from running, woke them up.

"Mr. President! Mr. President!" the agent said. "There's an unidentified aircraft heading toward the White House!"

Wearing bathrobes, the Bushes went back to the underground bunker, where an aide pointed out a roll-out bed. Then the word came that it had been a false alarm. The plane was a friendly.

"George had to literally lead her to go downstairs," Nancy Weiss said. "She can't even find the bathroom without her contacts. She is very, very blind. She wears hard lenses because the correction is so much better."

When Ball returned to the White House the next day, it was surrounded by agents in black shirts with submachine guns. Many members of Laura's staff were frightened. One young woman couldn't stop weeping.

Laura met with the staff to try to comfort them. She asked Andy Card's wife, Kathleene, who is associate pastor at Trinity United Methodist Church in McLean, Virginia, if she would talk with them. She immediately drove to the White House.

"What I did was to begin a conversation that we could all have together," Kathi Card said. "I think it's important in a situation like that for people to know that no matter what chaos is going on outside of you, God is with you."[2]

Laura also tried to comfort her staff, but Kathi Card never saw fear in her. "Someone with a strong faith is not a fearful person," Card said.

In the next couple of weeks, Laura spoke at a memorial service in

Stonycreek Township, Pennsylvania, near the site where United Airlines Flight 93 crashed on September 11. She talked mainly about how to help children.

"After 9/11, we did all the morning shows, black radio, *Oprah*, Telemundo, Univision," said Noelia Rodriguez. "They all described her as a former teacher. All of a sudden, she had become much more visible. In fact, the world was listening to her more."

On NBC's *Today* show, Laura told Katie Couric that parents should read to their children. After 9/11, "more than ever, a bedtime story is appropriate," she said. "Children love the reassurance of their parents' own voice."

Because the White House remained a prime terrorist target, simply entering was an act of courage. Yet neither Bush nor Laura wavered. Laura's close friend Debbie Francis talked with Laura on the morning after 9/11.

"She was remarkably calm but serious," Francis said.

That calmness reassured a nation on edge. On *Oprah*, Laura said parents needed to hug their children and give them physical comfort, and they needed to talk to them as well as to listen to them.

"Children take their emotional cues from their parents," she said, smiling reassuringly. "They need a very calm and relaxed atmosphere at home. Of course, we can't explain terrorism. We really can't. It's just a horrible, evil thing, but one good thing out of this is we've seen so much good," Laura said. "Americans are strong. They are very resilient. We see that every single day."

Laura's lack of artifice came across to viewers. In contrast to that, Hillary Clinton told NBC's Jane Pauley that when the two hijacked airplanes hit the World Trade Center, Chelsea was at Battery Park near the towers. Dramatically, Hillary claimed that Chelsea heard the rumble and saw the smoke. It was a great yarn, but Chelsea later wrote in *Talk* that when the planes hit, she was in a friend's apartment on Park Avenue South. She watched the events unfold on TV.

Now, instead of resenting press interviews because they focused attention on her and her thoughts, Laura welcomed them as a way to further a cause—helping out in the War on Terror.

In October 2002, Rodriguez left as Laura's press secretary, a year and a half after Laura had said she didn't want to do any more media interviews. Rodriguez was proud that she had gotten Laura to go on *60 Minutes* and *Meet the Press*. Laura thanked her for pushing her to do "things I might otherwise not have done."

"She's never going to be the kind of person who calls the press secretary and says, 'I want to be on *Meet the Press* next week,'" Rodriguez said. "But she doesn't shy away from it anymore. September 11 was a turning point. Instead of thinking about whether to do it, she knew in her heart this was an important way for her to connect with the American people who wanted to hear that everything will be okay."

"I don't think Laura was hardwired for any of this," said Laura's friend Katharine Armstrong.[3] "She wasn't a political animal. But Laura rolls up her sleeves, and she rises to the occasion. She is just a lady in every way."

After 9/11, Bush became the CEO of the War on Terror. He recognized that the failure to catch the hijackers was systemic. The government had never taken the threat from Al Qaeda seriously enough. Instead of assigning blame and pointing a finger, Bush began taking steps to correct the problems. He made it clear that lack of cooperation between the FBI and the CIA would not be tolerated. He asked Congress for billions in additional funds for the CIA. He met daily with his FBI and CIA directors, focusing them, pressuring, and giving them support. He also came up with approaches to combating a new kind of threat, including the Patriot Act and the doctrine that held that any country harboring terrorists would be considered a terrorist country.

On the weekend of October 8 and 9, 2001, Nancy and Mike Weiss were with Bush and Laura at Camp David.

"At dinner, someone would bring a note in to him," Nancy Weiss recalled. "He or Andy Card or Condi Rice would scrawl something on it and send it back. Mike and I had no idea what was happening. Then on Sunday, we got on the helicopter and landed north of Baltimore for the annual National Fallen Firefighters tribute. When we took off again, George started to practice his speech."

"You can surmise that we started bombing Afghanistan," Bush told the Weisses.[4]

"When we got to the White House, it was obvious the weight of what was happening was on Laura," Weiss said. "She wanted us with her while he was making the speech. We watched it on TV from their bedroom."

Weiss remembered that ten years earlier, Laura had read a book about the plight of Saudi women, who were not allowed even to drive a car. Back then, she expressed dismay to Nancy, and in the aftermath of 9/11, Laura was focusing on the far more severe plight of Afghan women.

"She was concerned about the plight of women in Afghanistan. She fully supported him," Nancy said.

On November 17, 2001, Laura took over the president's weekly radio address to talk about women in Afghanistan. Giving the address was a first for a first lady. As her husband had done, she carefully distinguished between Muslims and terrorists.

"The severe repression and brutality against women in Afghanistan is not a matter of legitimate religious practice," Laura said. "Muslims around the world have condemned the brutal degradation of women and children by the Taliban regime. The poverty, poor health, and illiteracy that the terrorists and the Taliban have imposed on women in Afghanistan do not conform with the treatment of women in most of the Islamic world, where women make important contributions in their societies."

Dr. Condoleezza Rice, who was then national security adviser, confirmed that 9/11 was a turning point for Laura, when she became more involved in foreign policy. It was Laura's idea, Rice explained, to "fully and completely expose what the Taliban regime was doing to women, emphasizing violations of women's rights prior to the U.S. invasion of Afghanistan. When you think about it, it's a natural for the United States to do, but very often things that seem perfectly logical after you think of them don't come to you prior to that. And it turned out to be hugely important for us in terms of broadening the base of support for the war, in terms of really vivifying for people what this regime was like."[5]

Despite cries from the administration's critics that the United States would be bogged down in a quagmire, by early December, it was almost over. The Taliban had abandoned Kandahar, their last stronghold. On December 13, the Bush administration released a videotape of Osama bin Laden chatting with followers. Recovered in Afghanistan, the videotape showed that bin Laden had had prior knowledge of the attacks. He gloated over the roughly 3,000 deaths.

"We calculated in advance the number of casualties" that would result when two airliners crashed into the World Trade Center, bin Laden said. "I was the most optimistic of all" in predicting how many would be killed.

In August 2001, Laura was discussing plans for the traditional White House Christmas parties with Catherine S. Fenton, her social secretary, who had worked for Nancy Reagan and Barbara Bush in the White House.

"She said we never had a Hanukkah party," Fenton said. "So we incorporated it in the plans for the traditional Christmas parties."

The idea flowed naturally from Laura's innate sense of inclusiveness. Jews were a rarity in Midland, and Laura had no close Jewish friends back then. But when working as a librarian in Austin, she had briefly dated Jeffrey Weinberger, a Jewish friend of Peggy Weiss's husband, Ron. In 1975, with the Weisses, Weinberger would found Jeffrey's Restaurant in Austin.

At 5 P.M. on December 10, 2001, the White House held the first Hanukkah candlelighting and celebration in its history.

"We brought a menorah in from a synagogue and lit the lights with the president and Mrs. Bush," Fenton said. The lighting was in an area that is the entrance to the residence from the East Wing. "We followed that with a cocktail reception with a holiday buffet for four hundred guests on the State Floor," Fenton said.[6]

Besides holding the first Hanukkah candlelighting and party, Laura served the first entirely kosher meal in the White House. It was for guests invited to a ceremony at the Holocaust Museum to open the first U.S. exhibition of Anne Frank's writings, including pages from her diary.

Joshua Bolten, who is Jewish, had noticed Laura's interest in Judaism when he began working as policy director for the first campaign in March 1999. "I would have dinner with the family at the governor's mansion or at the ranch," Bolten said. While not Orthodox, Bolten did not eat shellfish and ate meat only when it was served in a kosher home or restaurant. "I didn't make a big deal of it, but she noticed that I would just pass on certain items of food. She was sensitive to that."[7]

Laura would make sure to include a vegetarian alternative like a grilled portobello mushroom with cheese melted on it.

"She doesn't pepper you with questions, but she would ask interesting questions about the Jewish holidays or the meaning of the rituals," Bolten said. "Whenever I was over for a meal, they would say grace. They would ask me to say grace in Hebrew and ask for the translation."

When Bush became president, he and Laura sometimes invited Bolten to stay over at Camp David. Laura remembered a prayer

Bolten had said at meals back in Texas. Called the "Shehecheyanu," it begins, "Blessed are you, Lord, our God, King of the Universe, Who has kept us alive, sustained us, and enabled us to reach this season." The prayer is said on a blessed occasion, such as the first day of a holiday. At Camp David, Laura would ask Bolten to say the blessing on a joyful event. Prior to such events as the lighting of the Hanukkah candles, Laura would consult with Bolten or other senior Jewish staffers on Jewish sensitivities and customs.

On April 18, 2001, on the eve of Holocaust Remembrance Day, Laura and George toured the U.S. Holocaust Memorial Museum. It was the first of several visits by Laura.

Fred S. Zeidman, the chairman of the museum's governing council, had been a friend of the Bushes' from Houston for more than fifteen years. But it was not until 2005 that he learned that Laura's father had been a liberator of the Mittelbau-Dora concentration camp in Nordhausen, Germany. Laura had mentioned the fact in her August 31, 2004, speech to the Republican National Convention, but the media never picked up on it. Few of Laura's close friends had even heard about it. Nancy Weiss knew of it only because Laura's mother mentioned it when George and Laura lived in Midland. Harold never spoke of it.

For Bush, the lessons of the Holocaust now took on special meaning.

"The president has said to me several times since 9/11," Zeidman said, "that almost every day he gets up and thinks about what he learned during his tour of the Holocaust Memorial Museum. It's given him the resolve during the tough times involving Iraq and the War on Terror, because he knows that it's the right thing to do to prevent further loss of life and to protect America."[8]

On the morning of the second Hanukkah candlelighting and party, on December 4, 2002, Bush met with Jewish leaders in the Roosevelt Room. Jay Lefkowitz, an observant Jew who was chief of the president's Domestic Policy Council, remembered that one participant stood up and said that some sixty years earlier, his father had been part of a delegation of Jewish leaders who sought to meet with President Franklin D. Roosevelt to urge bombings at least of railroad tracks to thwart the Nazis' ability to kill Jews in concentration camps. The Jewish leaders were never granted this meeting, and Roosevelt never took action to thwart Hitler's genocide. He said it would divert resources from the effort to win the war.

"Mr. President," the man said to Bush, "I think I can speak for everyone in this room when I say that if you had been president, there would be millions more of us alive today."

On May 15, 2002, Laura flew to Europe for her first solo visit abroad as first lady. The goal was to rally support for the reconstruction of Afghanistan. She took along daughter Jenna.

In Budapest, Laura's second stop after Paris, reporters asked if she had discussed with her husband claims that he had failed to act on intelligence reports that had predicted the attacks. (In fact, on his videotape, bin Laden said the plot was so well planned that few within his own organization were aware of it. The hijackers themselves did not know they were to fly into the World Trade Center until just before they boarded the planes.) Laura said they hadn't discussed the issue much, but she firmly rebutted the assertion, explaining that the reports were so vague that no action could have been taken based upon them.

"I know my husband," she said, "and all Americans know he has acted in Afghanistan and in the War on Terror. I think, really, we need to put this in perspective, and I think it's sad to play upon the emotions of people as if there were something we could have done to stop" the suicide attacks.

Noelia Rodriguez thought it was the first time Laura had expressed her true feelings about the criticism, much of it unfair, that was just beginning to be aimed at her husband.

"She was resolute and firm," Rodriguez said. "She defended her husband, and no doubt about it. In other words, she was saying, 'Don't ask me about it again.' I thought it was the real Laura Bush coming out. I had seen it behind the scenes."

"She has just enough feistiness not to let the media totally run over her," Regan Gammon noted. "She is very smart, so she recognizes where they are coming from and where they are going before they get there."

In Budapest, Laura visited the National Institute of Oncology with her friend Nancy Brinker, who was now ambassador to Hungary, and talked with patients there. Brinker, the creator of the Race for the Cure, had been interested in becoming ambassador to Hungary in part because the country has one of the highest cancer rates in Europe. After the events, "We kicked off our shoes and talked as girlfriends," Brinker said.

Laura flew on to Prague in the Czech Republic, where the Bushes' friend Craig Stapleton was ambassador. She was going to talk to the Afghan people on Radio Free Europe/Radio Liberty. Stapleton had proposed to her advance people that she accompany him to a ceremony on May 19 commemorating the liberation of a concentration camp in Terezin. Some 33,000 people had died there, and another 87,000 were transported from Terezin to Auschwitz and other Nazi death camps. Laura's advance people had rejected the idea, saying it would be a "downer."

"On Sunday afternoon, we were sitting around with Jenna," Stapleton recalled. "Laura asked what we were doing that day. I said that I was going to the memorial service at Terezin, the staging ground for the Jews who were going to be transferred to Auschwitz to be killed."

Laura asked Debbie Stapleton what she was doing. She said she was going to a little church in Prague.

"Laura said she would like to go with me to Terezin," Craig Stapleton said. "So, unannounced, she went to the ceremony."

Miloš Zeman, the Czech prime minister, and other political leaders were "amazed," Stapleton said, "because she didn't do it as a news event but as a personal gesture."[9]

The ambassador presented a large wreath of purple and white carnations on behalf of the American people. Looking stricken, Laura silently placed her small spray of flowers nearby.

16

Culture Wars

On February 13, 2003, Dana Gioia was sworn in as the ninth chairman of the National Endowment for the Arts (NEA). Gioia (pronounced JOY-uh) is of Mexican and Italian descent and was the first member of his family to attend college. An accomplished poet and writer, he has an MA in comparative literature from Harvard University as well as an MBA from Stanford University. He is also a musician who has reviewed classical music for *San Francisco* magazine.

In 1991, Gioia wrote a controversial *Atlantic Monthly* article entitled "Can Poetry Matter?" In the piece, he said that poets today write for themselves instead of for the public. Like George Bush, who has no use for the elitism of the academic world, Gioia took aim at academics. Fifty years ago, Gioia said, there were no teaching posts for poets, and they had to get involved in real life. Today, rather than engaging in "coded discourse" with university colleagues, they need to communicate directly to their readers.

Gioia wrote that "the explosion of academic writing programs, the proliferation of subsidized magazines and presses, the emergence of a creative-writing career track, and the migration of American literary culture to the university have unwittingly contributed to [poetry's] disappearance from public view." Like subsidized farming that grows food no one wants, he said, "a poetry industry has been created to serve the interests of the producers and not the consumers. And in the process, the integrity of the art has been betrayed."

Gioia was well aware of the culture wars that had swirled around the NEA, and at first he wanted no part of them. Grants to controversial artists like Karen Finley, Andres Serrano, and Robert Mapplethorpe had produced a conservative backlash, and in 1996, the Republican-led Congress cut the NEA's budget by 39 percent, from $162.5 million to $99.5 million. Congress voted to phase out funding the agency over two years. Eventually, the NEA had to let go of half its staff.

"When I got a call from White House personnel saying the president was interested in nominating me as chairman of the National Endowment for the Arts, I said I wasn't interested," Gioia said. "Somehow, the first lady had read some of my books and liked them. The president liked the fact that although I was a well-known writer, I had been in the business world and had an MBA. They pestered me until I agreed to be interviewed. I told them the reasons I didn't want the job."[1]

After another interview with Anne Heiligenstein, Laura's policy director, Gioia said he would take the job if he received assurances that he would not be presiding over a "moribund institution." He said he wanted to rebuild the endowment as an agency that Americans could be proud of. Gioia not only got those assurances, but on the day he was sworn in, George and Laura invited him to dinner at the White House.

"I had never met the president or first lady until I was sworn in," Gioia said. "He said his objectives were artistic excellence and education. I said that is what my priorities were."

Gioia sat next to Laura, who "clearly knew a lot about me," Gioia said. She asked if he would travel with her the next week through the South and Southwest, where she was making a series of speeches.

Unless she is with the president on *Air Force One*, Laura usually travels on a sixteen-seat Gulfstream jet. Whichever plane she is on is designated Executive One Foxtrot. On the plane with Gioia, she was reading Winfried Georg Sebald's *Austerlitz*.

"We talked about books, theater, painting," Gioia said.

Gioia accompanied Laura to a dedication at the Modern Art Museum of Fort Worth, a new facility that had mounted a new exhibition.

"To my surprise, she was completely conversant with contemporary art," Gioia said. "She knew far more about it than many professional art advocates do. She knew the painters, she knew their backgrounds, she recognized the works. She knew the schools of art."

They then went on to the Cowgirl Hall of Fame.

"I was the only man traveling with this entourage," Gioia said. "I realized my ultimate job was to amuse them. There was a mechanical bucking bronco. They wanted me to get on."

Gioia said he really didn't want to do this.

"With a smile, Mrs. Bush said she really wanted me to," he said. "So I got on and whooped it up. The pictures of this created no end of amusement in the East Wing."

The night before, Laura stayed at the home of her close friends Debbie and James B. Francis Jr. in the tony village of Highland Park within Dallas. During Bush's first presidential campaign, Jim Francis, who owns an investment company, headed the Bush Pioneers, whose members each committed themselves to raising at least $100,000 for the campaign. Jim had known George since 1970, and Debbie first met Laura in the Dallas hospital where she was waiting to have her twins. After Laura and George moved to Dallas, Debbie and Laura participated in an exercise class together and talked on the phone at least once a day. The couples spent weekends together at Rainbo Lake near Athens, Texas, where both families had rustic weekend homes.

When Laura was preparing to give her first speech during George's first run for governor, she told Debbie that she hoped there would be a podium to stand behind. Debbie mentioned it to the woman in charge of the event, given by the Park Cities Republican Women's Club.

"Absolutely, we'll have a podium for her," the woman said.

"It turned out to be clear plastic," Debbie Francis said. "If you were concerned about your knees shaking, that would not help."

In the spring of 2004, George decided to build a separate office for himself on his ranch. Laura wanted to buy the bathroom fixtures.

"So we ran out to HomeExpo in Dallas," Debbie Francis said. "She had a small Secret Service detail with her. A lot of people wanted to talk with her, but it was a little intimidating to talk to the first lady as she looked at toilets."

The night before Laura was scheduled to speak at the art museum in Fort Worth, Jim Francis got up at about 5 A.M. to go to the bathroom. He slipped on a book he had been reading the night before and fell on the floor with a crunch.

"Jim was lying there in agony," Debbie said. "I said, 'Gosh, Jim, maybe I need to call an ambulance.' "

"No," Jim said. "The whole block knows Laura's here. If an ambulance comes at five A.M. with sirens, people will think something happened to her. It will be on CNN."

Jim lay quietly until 7:30 A.M., when Laura got up. When Debbie told her about the fall, Laura offered to have her private nurse take a look at him. When the nurse arrived at eight, she said Jim might have broken a rib. So while Debbie went to the art museum with Laura, the Francises' son Jimmy took his father to a doctor. Jim was in such pain he could hardly stand.

"I think I've broken a rib," Jim said.

"Why do you think that?" the doctor asked.

"Well, a nurse examined me this morning," Jim said.

The doctor wanted to know how he was able to see a nurse so early in the morning.

"Laura Bush is staying with us, and the nurse travels with her," Jim said.

"Have you been drinking?" the doctor said.

Jim's son assured the doctor that Laura Bush really was staying at their house.

At the hospital, Jim Francis learned he had broken five ribs.

The day before Dana Gioia was sworn in as head of the NEA, Laura was scheduled to hold a symposium for poets. But she canceled the event after one of the invited writers—Sam Hamill, author of thirteen books of verse—sent out thousands of e-mails requesting poems opposing the impending invasion of Iraq. Almost 3,500 poets responded to his plea, sending them to a Web site called Poets Against the War.

"I was overcome by a kind of nausea," Hamill wrote after finding the invitation to "Poetry and the American Voice" in the mail. Laura's cancellation of the conference "confirms my suspicion" that the Bush administration was not interested in poetry when it "refuses to remain in the ivory tower," said former poet laureate Rita Dove.

Of course, the range of antiwar and antiestablishment poets invited by Laura only confirmed that Laura had not applied a political litmus test to the guest list. Her staff had consulted the NEA, the Library of Congress, and other experts to compile a list of distinguished poets with no thought to their political views. Nor, as even the left-wing *Nation* magazine noted, had the subjects of the symposium— Emily Dickinson, Langston Hughes, and Walt Whitman—exactly been country-club Republicans. Whitman's *Leaves of Grass* had been considered so subversive that the Interior Department, where he'd held a job, fired him. Hughes wrote pro-Communist works that got him hauled before Senator Joseph McCarthy's subcommittee on subversive activities.

Still, said Stanley Kunitz, another former poet laureate, "I think there was a general feeling that the current administration is not really a friend of the poetic community and that its program of attacking Iraq is contrary to the humanitarian position that is at the center of the poetic impulse."

None of the 13,500 poems eventually posted on the poets' Web site mentioned the 300,000 people executed by Saddam Hussein, the men and women whose ears and limbs had been cut off, or the gang rapes of women as their husbands and families were forced to watch.

"While Mrs. Bush respects and believes in the right of all Americans to express their opinions," her office said in a statement announcing the "postponement" of the symposium, "she, too, has opinions and believes that it would be inappropriate to turn what is intended to be a literary event into a political forum."

Unknown to the public, Laura loved poetry and would sometimes read a poem aloud to a friend. She was aware that poetry was not exactly a growth industry, that a book of poetry was never going to be a bestseller. So she relished the chance to put the stamp of the White House on poetry, welcoming poets whose work was so unappreciated. Now some of them had essentially slapped her in the face, using her generous gesture to push their own political agenda. While the White House projected a stiff upper lip, the truth was that Laura was hurt. For her, it was a lesson in how, when one is first lady, an innocent gesture can be twisted into something ugly. Looking back, Andi Ball thought that naively inviting the poets was the one misstep she and Laura had made.

Ironically, while the poets were up in arms, Dana Gioia was having dinner with the Bushes every few months and finding that their support of culture and the arts was "steadfast and unwavering." Their goals and Gioia's were the same.

"What they are interested in is artistic excellence and education," Gioia said. "Instead of funding the work of individual artists, we want to focus on things of unquestionable excellence and make them more broadly available than ever before."

With Jack Valenti, Laura agreed to be honorary co-chair of Shakespeare in America's Communities, which combines sending touring companies to all fifty states to perform Shakespeare's plays with providing tool kits to introduce high school students to Shakespeare. Gioia announced the program—which includes performances at military bases—on Shakespeare's 439th birthday.

Many in the media pooh-poohed the effort. "Gioia's aspirations are likely to be blocked not by direct opposition but by Bush's tax cuts—by the gradual reduction of fiscal oxygen to which so many government programs will succumb," wrote Fred Hiatt, editorial-page editor of the *Washington Post*. "By the time Shakespeare turns 449, the NEA may be lucky to afford a cake."

In fact, because of Laura, funds for cultural programs have been increased. On January 29, 2004, she visited the NEA on Pennsylvania Avenue, the first time a first lady had visited the agency. Laura announced that the White House was proposing to Congress an $18 million increase, or 15 percent, for each of the next three years. The increase—which Congress eventually cut to $2 million in the first year—would have been the largest in twenty years.

With the additional funding, Laura said, the NEA could help support the American Masterpieces program, which sends American orchestras and other musical ensembles, theater groups, and collections of paintings to communities and military bases around the country. The paintings represented a variety of genres, including American impressionism, the Hudson River School, works by Latino and Native American artists, and the art of the American West.

"For many people in the Tipton Housing Authority in Georgia, this is their first opportunity to see live theater," Laura said of the program. "High school students in neighboring counties of Waycross and Blackshear were so excited about the program that they declared a day in October William Shakespeare Day."

Along with poets and artists, librarians also became foes of the Bush administration as the American Civil Liberties Union whipped them into hysteria about the Patriot Act. The organization claimed that the FBI now could use "sneak and peek" tactics in libraries to probe the reading habits of sinless grandmothers without informing the targets until after the search. But the FBI was not interested in people's reading habits, and it could conduct a search only with a judge's order. If terrorists were about to unleash a biological-weapons attack that could kill ten thousand people, would anyone want the FBI to inform a suspect that agents, in an effort to catch other plotters before it was too late, were searching his computer? In any case, four years after the enactment of the Patriot Act, the FBI had conducted no searches at libraries under the business-records provision of the new act.

The fact that Laura was the first librarian to live in the White House made no impression on librarians, who, on their Web sites, berated her for being married to George Bush. The Progressive Librarians Guild, for example, scolded Laura for engaging in "censorship" by canceling the White House poetry symposium, which "would have included anti-war poets." Additionally, "Mrs. Bush publicly represents, first and foremost, her husband's administration, which is responsible for massive cuts in all spheres of public service." The guild conceded that "some libraries have benefited somewhat during the present Bush administration," but dismissed this as having "more to do with political publicity rather than public policy since, with Mrs. Bush, a former librarian, the administration has an eager front person."

The truth was that because of Laura's support—and despite this kind of reflexive opposition—funds distributed by the Institute for Museum and Library Services to libraries and museums increased 25 percent, from $193 million to $240.6 million, in the first four years of the Bush administration. At a time when almost all domestic programs except homeland security and intelligence were being cut,

Bush asked for an increase of $21.5 million for fiscal 2006. Indeed, because of Laura, the entire spectrum of cultural agencies either received budget increases or were spared cuts. Nonetheless, liberals and the media found a way to turn Laura's announcement of a budget increase for the NEA against her.

"That silence resounding through the arts community is the stunned kind," wrote Linda Winer of *Newsday*. "The sound you might detect, if you are attuned to the audiology of incredulity, is the mass dropping of jaws in response to President George W. Bush's proposal to increase spending on the National Endowment for the Arts by 15 percent."

By the end of her piece, Winer had brought in Halliburton—a company that Dick Cheney had long ago given up any financial interest in and that had nothing to do with the arts. She wrote that while she was trying to process the "credibility" of Laura Bush supporting culture, she thought of Tony Kushner's play *Only We Who Guard the Mystery Shall Be Unhappy*, which portrayed Laura reading to Iraqi children from *The Brothers Karamazov*.

"I'm sorry you're dead," Kushner quotes the first lady as saying to them, "but all children love books. . . ." Even if a child is dead, if a parent reads to that child, the "child will learn to love books, and that is so, so important."

Winer concluded, "I worry that the attention suddenly lavished on the NEA will turn out to be just as realistic."

Thus, through one device or another, liberals discounted the evidence before them that George and Laura Bush were strong supporters of the arts and cultural endeavors. While theoretically Laura could enlist her husband to order increases in budget proposals, in practice there was no need for her to do so.

"If it's a particular interest of the first lady, we will pay attention to the funding for those programs, and they will always prevail," said Clay Johnson, Bush's Yale roommate who became deputy director of the Office of Management and Budget.[2] But Johnson said Laura's influence extends beyond budgets. OMB routinely asks for her opinion or suggestions on appointments and on issues affecting agencies that deal with subjects of interest to her, such as education, the arts, women's rights, juveniles with social problems, AIDS, libraries, and the humanities.

Bush himself also bounces a range of policy questions off Laura. "I don't believe he sits down with her and says, 'I have six policy items I want to go over with you,' " Johnson said. "Rather, issues come up in informal conversation. She is very smart and very wise and can give him an objective, big-picture perspective that after an hour or so with the policy people, he may have lost. As an example, the president will talk to her about civil-service reform issues. She will say, 'Do you really want to do that, or do you really want to make a change in leadership at a time like this?' "

In that case, Laura is not trying to challenge or influence a decision but making sure Bush has thought it out.

"If he doesn't have a good answer for her question, he will go back and ask more questions or perhaps change his mind," Johnson said. "They are very similar, but yet she is the still water that runs deep. He is the whirling dervish. Neither is a threat to [the] other. They are really partners."

"She's always been a very positive influence on me," Bush once said, "in terms of forcing me to ask the right questions."

At a Super Bowl dinner at the White House on February 6, 2005, Laura asked Clay Johnson, after Bush had gone to bed, how the cultural programs would fare in the administration's budget proposal. Johnson said not to worry. OMB was very aware of the priorities of the first lady.

"She didn't even need to make a phone call," Anne Johnson said.

Two days later, the *Washington Post* ran a story headlined FEDERAL CULTURAL PROGRAMS SUFFER LITTLE PAIN FROM BUSH BUDGET. The story noted that while Bush's proposed 2006 budget slashed "hundreds" of domestic programs, "cultural groups did relatively well."

Besides the NEA, the institutions getting a boost included the U.S. Holocaust Museum, the Smithsonian Institution, and the National Archives.

The article did not mention Laura. In contrast to some first ladies like Hillary Clinton, she preferred to keep her influence quiet.

Henry Moran, executive director of the President's Committee on the Arts and the Humanities, credited Laura with putting an end to the culture wars that had brought the NEA to its knees and distracted the country from the appreciation of real artistic achievement. Moran compared Laura's leadership in the arts to Jackie Kennedy's. But while Jackie spotlighted museums and artistic venues, Laura emphasized bringing art and culture to all Americans.

"I think of Laura Bush as expanding access and availability of artistic and creative experiences for families and enlarging cultural opportunities across the country," Moran said. "She is one of the two first ladies who will go down in history as contributing the most to the cultural life of the country."[3]

17

INVASION

When Pamela Nelson arrived at the White House for her monthly visit on March 19, 2001, the invasion of Iraq was imminent. The day before, after months of playing cat and mouse with United Nations weapons inspectors, Saddam Hussein had defiantly rejected Bush's ultimatum to leave the country within forty-eight hours. At the White House, workers were applying a plastic coating to the windows so, in case of attack, they wouldn't shatter.

Nelson was apprehensive, but when Laura saw her, she gave her a big hug. She was solemn but reassured her high school friend that the invasion would not occur that day. Pamela went to the meeting of the Commission on Fine Arts she had planned to attend. During the afternoon, information came in to the White House from the CIA that Saddam Hussein would be at a compound called Dora Farms in Baghdad later that night. By late afternoon, George Tenet, Donald Rumsfeld, Richard B. Myers, Colin Powell, Dick Cheney, Condoleezza Rice, and Andy Card had convened in the Oval Office to discuss the risks of starting the invasion of Iraq by bombing Saddam.

Calling the rejection of his ultimatum Saddam's final mistake, the president, at 7:15 P.M., said, "Go!" He walked to the residence and told Laura and Nelson of his decision.

"We both kind of gasped," Nelson said. "I just was scared, frankly. This was going to be such a big step. She seemed a lot steadier. She had a sense of the enormity of it, the gravity of it. But there was no hand-wringing. She had seen him wrestle with it."[1]

Dinner was at 7:30 P.M.

"George was very somber," Nelson said. "He had just been in four hours of meetings being briefed. He said, 'Maybe we'll get lucky, but it's not going to be easy like the last one,' " referring to the invasion of Afghanistan. "We held hands, and the president said a prayer asking for strength and wisdom."

Bush said he would be making the announcement on television later that night. He asked Pamela not to tell her husband, Bill, back in Dallas.

At 10:16 P.M., Bush said from the Oval Office, "My fellow citizens, at this hour, American and coalition forces are in the early stages of military operations to disarm Iraq, to free its people, and to defend the world from grave danger."

Daughter Barbara was visiting, working on a design for a dress. She, Laura, and Nelson—along with Barney—watched the address in Bush's office in the Treaty Room on the second floor. After Bush's announcement, cable-TV shows began running alerts at the bottom of the screen stating that Bush and the first lady had gone to sleep. Bush was still in the Oval Office.

"We better go to bed because the crawl is saying we're asleep," Laura said.

"George came upstairs," Nelson recalled. "Barbara tried to make him laugh. He went to bed. Laura and I stayed in the Treaty Room waiting for Tony Blair to go on TV. There were sirens in Washington. The elevator stayed on floor two when the president was there in the residence so he could be hustled to the bunker. I had a gas mask in my closet. I hoped I could sleep."

Before dinner the next night, "George told us of the horrible torture that happened to the Iraqi people," Nelson said. "Tongues cut out, horrible rapes. He talked about it a lot."

At dinner, Laura read a letter George's father had faxed to him. His father said that his son "had much more on his watch than any president since Lincoln," Nelson said. "And he knew it was a very hard decision to make. He said, 'I love you more than tongue can tell,' as Robin used to say."

The comparison with Lincoln was apt, not just because of the challenges Bush faced in pursuing the War on Terror but because of the ridicule he endured from the media and critics. "There is a cowardly imbecile at the head of our government," one newspaper said of Lincoln. A *New York Times* story on his first inaugural address said Lincoln was lucky that "it was not the constitution of the English language and the laws of English grammar that he was called upon to support."

The letter from Bush's father "made me weep," Nelson said, and the president "remarked that I was pretty weepy." He said his father writes beautifully.

"The apple doesn't fall very far from the tree," Nelson said.

"I'm certainly not the writer he is," George said.

"You're a very good writer," Laura said.

Probably half of Laura's friends were Democrats, as Laura once was, and some opposed the war, quietly or openly. Laura's friend JaneAnn Fontenot, a nurse midwife, declined to be interviewed for this book because, she said, "My politics are opposed to the Bush administration in many ways, and for that reason I would not feel comfortable being interviewed at this time. It has not affected my friendship with Laura or my opinion of her, which says a lot about both of us."[2]

According to Regan Gammon, "If Laura knew her response, she would probably say, 'I know the war makes her feel conflicted and feel bad.' Instead of saying, 'What do you mean she doesn't agree with George?' "[3]

Each of Laura's friends lost at least one friend or had to put up with venomous attacks from a friend or relative over the bitter controversy surrounding the war. But to quote Saint Jerome, "The friendship that can cease has never been real." Nancy Weiss, for example, was friends with a drama professor who was reared as a Quaker. "He wrote the most bitter e-mails to all of us," Weiss said. "He said George was 'a liar and a cheat.' I wrote back and said, 'I totally understand your disagreement with the war, but I can tell you this: I have known this man for twenty-seven years, and I can tell you that his heart and soul are good and that he wants to do what's right for this world and this country.' "

Nancy mentioned the friend's reaction to Laura.

"What about all those people who were killed by Saddam?" Laura asked.

"She understood all along why I was making decisions I was making," Bush told NBC's Tom Brokaw. "She understood the threat that Iraq posed. She understood that Iraq was a part of the War on Terror. And she's like a lot of people, she was nervous about war."

In assessing whether Iraq had really been a threat, commentators would later rarely mention that even Saddam's generals thought they had chemical weapons they were supposed to use during a U.S. invasion. It would take two years after Saddam was gone to determine that he'd been bluffing.

Without any publicity, Laura and George often visited the families of fallen soldiers.

"They meet with thirty, forty, or fifty families in a row," Craig Stapleton said. "The president and Laura go from one family to another in different waiting rooms over the course of several hours. I can't imagine a more excruciating experience. I don't think he could get through that without her there."[4]

"I find it extremely hard to thank a soldier or a Marine for the sacrifices they have made for us," Andy Card said. "Or to see a parent or a spouse or a child and say thank you for the sacrifice that your son or dad made for us. But as hard as it is for me, it's harder for the president. Laura is a great strength to the president when he meets that duty. Her own life experiences have shown her pain that she doesn't want to see anybody else experience."[5]

One of Laura's antiwar friends was Cathie Blackaller. Cathie had lived next door to Laura in Midland, and they became friends in junior high. Blackaller had been one of the prettiest girls in Laura's class at Lee High School. She was named Miss Personality and Senior Class Favorite. A vegetarian, Blackaller went to India to study with the Dalai Lama. She became a counselor at Bluebonnet Elementary School in Austin. During the ten years that followed Cathie's diagnosis of breast cancer, Laura kept in touch with her, visiting her in the hospital, inviting her to the inaugurations, putting her in touch with specialists in Houston, and going to a birthday party for her with Regan Gammon and Pamela Nelson at Peggy Weiss's home in Austin.

"I don't know why Laura keeps inviting me to all these happenings," Cathie said to her sister-in-law Victoria "Vicki" Wilson, who had gone to Lee High. "I really don't fit in with these rich people."

In fact, Laura had friends whose financial situations ranged from just scraping by to $100 million or more. As an artist, Pamela Nelson described herself as a friend of modest means. As a gift one Father's Day, she gave the president a pair of socks.

"It's not much of a present," she said to Bush.

"It makes a statement," the president replied.

In 2004, Laura invited Cathie Blackaller to the White House for Valentine's Day. "[Cathie] mentally labored over going to the White

House," Vicki Wilson said. "She was so much against the war. Then she said she didn't have the right clothes. Of course, she didn't have any hair. I said, 'Take your wig. With your luck, you'll end up sitting beside the president.' "[6]

In the end, Cathie decided to attend the festivity and stayed at the White House in Jenna's bedroom. Laura also invited some of Cathie's high school friends from Midland: Robert McCleskey and his wife, Barbara; Bill and Kitty Sallee; Mike and Barbara Proctor; Mike and Betty Jones; Regan Gammon; and Peggy and Ron Weiss. Ron, who had known Laura for thirty years, was struck by the fact that she "seems to have a lot going on in her mind all the time, but she is not likely to share that because I think she is a very unselfish person. She is more likely to ask others what they think and doesn't feel a need to talk all the time."

The following Saturday, Laura took the women for a tour of the Holocaust Museum. The guys "hung out with George and gave him a hard time," McCleskey said. Susie Evans, who lived in Washington, came over for dinner at the White House on the second night. As her sister-in-law had predicted, Cathie sat next to the president.

A little over two months later, on April 22, 2004, Cathie Blackaller died. The night before, Regan and Peggy Weiss had gone to see her.

"Cathie's politics were definitely not in line with the Bush administration," Peggy Weiss said. "But she put that aside. At the end, she said going to the White House was one of the biggest events in her life."[7]

By the summer of 2003, the mainstream media had abandoned any pretense of fairness to Bush. By mischaracterizing what he had said or downplaying or ignoring the other side, the media created a cartoon character of the president as monster or buffoon.

Thus the media hammered Bush over his statement in his State of the Union address that the "British government has learned that Saddam Hussein recently sought significant quantities of uranium from Africa." Each day brought new headlines insinuating that Bush had lied. In fact, not only did the British intelligence service MI6 believe that Saddam had sought uranium from Niger, both a British and a Senate intelligence committee investigation later concluded that the MI6 report had been well founded. Yet the story reporting the British House of Commons Intelligence and Security Committee's conclusion appeared in the United States as a separate story in only one paper—the *Wall Street Journal*. The *Washington Post* devoted one paragraph to the conclusion near the end of a twenty-two-paragraph story. The *New York Times*, which by then had run fifty-six stories mentioning the infamous sixteen words in Bush's State of the Union address, had no story on the British Parliament report.

When the 9/11 Commission reported that it had found no "collaborative relationship" between Iraq and Al Qaeda, the *Washington Post* said in its lead that the conclusion challenged "one of the Bush administration's main justifications for the war in Iraq." Yet Bush had never said that Saddam and Al Qaeda were working together as partners. He said there had been many contacts between them, a fact that the 9/11 Commission confirmed. But the *Post* story mentioned that point in the fourth paragraph under the headline AL QAEDA–HUSSEIN LINK IS DISMISSED. Taking a similar approach, the *New York Times* buried the mention of contacts between Al Qaeda and Saddam in the eighth paragraph of its story. When Dan Rather and CBS received bogus documents questioning Bush's National Guard service, they ran them on *60 Minutes Wednesday* even though their own experts told the producers before the broadcast that they were probably fake. Yet it did not require an expert to determine that the proportional spacing used in the supposedly typewritten documents did not exist in the early 1970s when they were dated.

When Kitty Kelley came out with her book *The Family*, it was taken seriously by most media outlets, including NBC's *Today*, which focused on the book in three back-to-back segments. Kelley not only accused Laura of being the "go-to" for bags of marijuana in college, she said George had used cocaine at Camp David when his father was president. According to Secret Service sources, the only first-family member who clearly took any drugs was James Earl "Chip" Carter III, one of Jimmy Carter's sons, who smoked marijuana. At one point, Rosalynn Carter told the press that all three of her sons had "experimented" with marijuana.

Laura tried to make light of the media war against her husband.

"She mostly shrugs about the media," Pamela Nelson said. "In September 2004, I said, 'How are you doing?' She said, 'Well, it's the Kitty Kelley book and Dan Rather this week.' I said, 'It sounds like a pretty bad week.' She laughed it off and went on to something else. Neither [she nor the president] gets obsessed about it or they would drive themselves crazy."

"It's painful for her to see members of her family and friends get unfairly chopped up by the media," Katharine Armstrong said. "She is very realistic. She understands that that is part of the deal. She does not wear her emotions on her sleeve, although she is human, and you might see it in her eyes. She is a strong, dignified woman who never complains."

Despite the attacks on Bush in the media, "In private, they don't criticize their opponents or their friends, which is comforting because I know they are not criticizing me," Anne Johnson said. "They are so vilified at times by the press, but the girls don't hear 'Oh, that so and so.' They just don't do that."

But occasionally, Laura has revealed her feelings.

"I remember she said she watched TV once during the 2004 campaign," said her friend Sandy Langdon. "She said, 'I had to turn it off. I couldn't stand it. Now I know why I wasn't watching it. So many negative things.' "[8]

"She torments herself by reading the *Washington Post* and the *New York Times*," Nancy Weiss said. "She sometimes gets her feelings hurt. Based on Ann Gerhart's book, a *Texas Monthly* article said she is a 'bad mom.' She handles it calmly, but I can tell things like that do upset her."

18

"HURRY UP, BUSHIE!"

During the autumn of 2003, Bush and a few top administration officials were informally discussing a quandary over dinner at the White House residence. While they were not seeking her advice, Laura gave her opinions freely, and they were taken seriously.

They were talking about whether a well-connected political appointee had been deceitful with the Bush administration about a personal matter. The cabinet officer whose agency was involved leaned toward letting the matter go. But Laura saw things differently.

"I don't think so," she said simply when the issue was raised. The appointee never took his post.

"In a small percentage of times, she will be against the potential nominee," Andy Card said. "We try to ask her early enough in the process so it's not a rejection. Her view is then a suggestion."

Only two examples of Laura's counseling her husband have come out. The first occurred soon after 9/11, when Bush said bin Laden was "wanted dead or alive." Sidling up to him later, she gently gibed, "Bushie, you gonna git 'im?" The president got the point. For days, he told people that Laura hadn't "approved" of his choice of words.

"She didn't want to see me become too bellicose, react with

bloodlust," Bush explained. "I'll tell you this: She's not a shrinking violet. I mean, if I do something she thinks needs to be toned down or something, she'll tell me."

The second example occurred in July 2003, when Bush said, "Bring them on," referring to those who would attack American forces in Iraq.

"Whoa, Bushie!" Laura said to him afterward.

But while these examples are known by the public, privately, the Bushes, like most spouses who respect each other, influence each other on a daily basis. For Laura, that means coming out from behind her books and having an impact on the world stage. For George, it has been her help in smoothing out his rough edges, giving him more discipline and balance, and widening his intellectual horizons.

"He's produced for her a life that she never expected to have," Craig Stapleton said. "She wakes up every day with a big smile and says, 'What are we going to do today?' She thinks of herself as incredibly fortunate to have this life, doing interesting things, meeting interesting people."

Laura, in turn, has influenced her husband, often by simply rolling her turquoise eyes or cracking a joke. More than anyone, she understands the burden of being president.

"She makes sure he is in the right emotional, spiritual, and mental spot to carry the burden," Card said. "She has a good sense of when the president needs to laugh or be in a quiet place. Or maybe to escape in a book or with a puzzle or a conversation."[1]

Laura evaluates the people who work closely with the president.

"She can help him when he hires them, and she can help explain and develop their relationship so he gets to know them better," Craig Stapleton said. "She makes sure she knows the cabinet members and their spouses." Laura thinks well of most people, he said, "So if you are not getting a favorable rating from Laura, that would be of note. There is no one in the White House who doesn't respect her views on whatever she is interested in," Stapleton said. "And that's not because she asserts herself. It's just because she is right all the time."

Laura has become more forceful, Stapleton said, as time goes on. "She knows a lot about public policy and people," he said. "She has strong views. She talks about issues with the president. He wants to know, 'What do you think of this guy or this policy?' She came back from Africa and saw firsthand what AIDS was doing. . . . Her opinion, like Colin Powell's, was we have to do more. This is not acceptable. And that's what the president did."

Laura has also taught Bush to be a better listener, Stapleton said. "Even on subjects where he knows more than you do, he listens very carefully now to what people have to say."

Much of the communication between Bush and Laura is through humor.

"They tease each other all the time," Stapleton said. "But it always has an element of truth. She definitely doesn't have a problem saying, 'Hey, you missed that one.' She tells him almost always in a teasing way, rather than a reprimand, when he goes over the edge. She says, 'Come on, Bushie!' That is a standard retort to a whole bunch of comments. When he's relaxed, he can be over-the-top sometimes. She says, 'Hey, wait a sec. You didn't mean to say that.' And usually, he didn't."

They have a loving relationship that is respectful of the other, Debbie Stapleton said. "They communicate with humor. They have this wonderful rapport. It's like a hidden language. They understand the inside jokes."

When Laura criticizes Bush, "It's done so nicely that he doesn't even realize it," Andi Ball said.

"I've seen her give him the greasy eyeball over a flippant or inconsiderate remark or when he failed to show the right kind of courtesy or attention to someone," their friend Donald B. Ensenat said. "She doesn't need to verbalize with him. It registers."

Having lived with the Bushes for a year, Izzy Hernandez regularly saw Laura try to "rein in" George.

"If he said bin Laden was wanted 'dead or alive,' she would say, 'Bushie, that's a bad phrase. You need to say it in a better way,' " Hernandez said. "He would say, 'What do you mean! That's exactly what I mean to say: dead or alive.' They'll have an exchange, and he might get snappy, but she would put her foot down. He may not say, 'You are right,' " Hernandez continued. Instead, "He'll listen and digest it. He might go away pouting, in a joking way. Then he'll change. He'll just do it."[2]

At times, Laura reminds him of points he wants to make or suggests that he not gesture so much with his hands during a public appearance.

"At Pope John Paul II's funeral, she said, the TV footage kept showing her leaning over and whispering to him," Pamela Nelson said. "She said, 'I was saying that his dad said this pope was associated with lots of miracles, and so pray for a miracle. So I leaned over and reminded him about the miracles.' "[3]

One evening, Terry Johnson had dinner at the White House with his wife, Liz; Laura and George; Robert J. "Rob" Dieter and his wife, Gwynneth; and Anne and Clay Johnson. Afterward, Laura wanted to see a movie. Terry was expecting light entertainment. Instead, Laura chose Siddiq Barmak's *Osama*. Based on a true story, the film was the first produced in Afghanistan after the fall of the Taliban, and it depicted the suffering of women under that regime. In the movie, a mother decides that the only way to avoid starvation is to force her beautiful twelve-year-old daughter to pretend to be a boy. Under the Taliban, women could not go out in public alone, obtain an education, or work for a living, and the family had no male breadwinner.

"But if the Taliban recognize me, they will kill me," the terrified girl says.

When the Taliban discover that she is not a boy, they imprison her, and she meets a gloomy fate. Terry thought Laura wanted to impress upon the president that removing the Taliban was not just a strategic part of the war on terror but also a liberation of women living under oppression.

If Laura does become annoyed, it is fleeting, Craig Stapleton said. "She will tell you what is bothering her," he said. "She doesn't go away and worry about it. It will be over right there. Laura doesn't let him be grouchy very long, either. He'll go into a very short grouchy period, where he barks a little bit. It's a slight reaction to cumulative pressures of his job."

"When he is hungry, he is really grumpy," Nancy Weiss said. "He'll come back to the residence late in the afternoon and say jokingly, 'Who are you talking to on the phone? Get off the phone!' He says that a lot. He probably wants attention. Isn't that a male trait?"

The needling cuts both ways. Debbie Francis remembered how, once, when Laura wanted to see her husband, she tucked a message inside Barney's collar and sent him trotting into the Oval Office.

"There was no serious business going on," Francis said. "He was in there with a friend. Then we heard the laughter."

The note said: "Hurry up, Bushie!"

No one can imagine the kind of pressure being president of the U.S. imposes on an individual and how easily a president can be corrupted by power. To be in command of the most powerful country on earth, to be able to fly anywhere at a moment's notice, to be able to grant almost any wish, to take action that affects the lives of millions, is such a heady, intoxicating experience that only people with the most stable personalities and well-developed value systems can handle it. Simply inviting a friend to a White House party or having a secretary place a call from the White House has such a profound effect that presidents and their aides must constantly remind themselves that they are mortal.

"The White House is a character crucible," according to Bertram S. Brown, M.D., a psychiatrist who formerly headed the National Institute of Mental Health and was an aide to President John F. Kennedy. "It either creates or distorts character. Even if an individual is balanced, once someone becomes president, how does one solve the conundrum of staying real and somewhat humble when one is surrounded by the most powerful office in the land, and from becoming overwhelmed by an at-times pathological environment that treats you every day as an emperor? Here is where the true strength of the character of the person, not his past accomplishments, will determine whether his presidency ends in accomplishment or failure."

Steeped in Midland values, Bush sees himself as a humble servant of God. The character traits he brings to the office keep him from falling victim to the arrogance that commonly afflicts both presidents and their aides and that has brought about so many of the scandals and misjudgments of the past. The fact that the Bushes continue to be friends with the same people who were their friends in grade school is an indication of these traits.

"When you are president, people are programming you," Don Evans said. "There has to be somebody around who is making sure your life is fully balanced. Part of that for them is staying connected with their friends they have been close to throughout their lives. She is particularly good at opening their time to friends. It's all part of continuing to lead this remarkably well-balanced life and keeping it all in perspective as much as anybody can do."[4]

If Bush ever starts to veer off course, Laura is there to keep him grounded.

"One time I was sitting in the Treaty Room with the president and Laura," Laura's friend Adair Margo said. "He was smoking a cigar and called Condi Rice to tell her she had done a great job on a speech she had given that day. He then told Laura about a speech he had given that same afternoon and how he had had lots to say, talking for about forty minutes. She listened and then said, 'Did you have a little bit of Clintonitis?' "[5]

Above all, Laura gives her husband support.

"He gets mad at himself when he publicly says the opposite of what he means," Pamela Nelson said. "I was there when he made a speech and said exactly the opposite of what he meant. He came upstairs to the residence and told Laura. She said, 'Well, that was just one sentence. Everything else was powerful and inspiring.' "

"She's affirming but without being in any way cloying," said Condoleezza Rice, who spent almost every weekend with them at the ranch or at Camp David when she was national security adviser. "I think the reason their relationship is so wonderful is that it's clearly emotionally close, but it's also kind of on an intellectual level. They discuss things. If she disagrees, she might roll her eyes or say, 'You don't really think that, do you?' It's soft. It's not harsh."[6]

Sometimes, Rice has seen them holding hands. Other friends have seen him pat her behind.

"It's a remarkable relationship," Rice said. "And I still think they look like high school sweethearts when they're together."

19

TLC

After Bush had been in office three years, the *Los Angeles Times* ran a piece saying that the Georgetown set considered him a "party pooper" because he was not interested in going to their soirees. Because of Bush, "Washington's social life has come to a screeching halt," Sally Quinn was quoted as saying. "Since there's no social life at the White House, and no social life in the city, Washington as we know it is over."

What members of establishment Washington did not get was that the Bushes socialized constantly—but not necessarily with them. Instead, the Bushes maintained close ties to their friends from every stage of their lives.

On May 30, 2003, Bush held a reception for 500 of his Yale classmates as part of the thirty-fifth reunion of the Class of '68. It was supposed to take place on the South Lawn of the White House, but rain forced it inside.

Guests were amazed at George's recall.

"In the receiving line, Laura was ahead of George," said Becky Curtis, the wife of Bush's classmate Phillip H. Curtis. "Laura asked the person in front of me where he was from."

"Washington, D.C.," the man said.

"Oh, did you grow up here?" she asked.

"No, he's from Huntsville, Alabama," George said before the man could answer.

"The guy was clearly startled that he remembered that," Curtis said.[1]

Before heading over to the White House, Peter Akwai, a classmate from Hawaii who had a sex-change operation in 2002, realized that the event would probably have to be moved inside because of rain. Figuring that would require dressing up more, Leilani Akwai, as she is now known, took the precaution of wearing a purple satin evening gown to the White House. Not knowing how former classmates would react to the momentous change, and feeling the need for some extra protection, she also wore a talisman around her neck given to her by a friend—a raccoon penis bone. As it turned out, Akwai said, "The raccoon bone must have worked its magic, for the president greeted me in the receiving line with warmth and sincerity.

"I said, 'Hello, George, I guess the last time we spoke to each other, I was still living as a man,'" Akwai said.[2] "And he looked me right in the eye, smiled with a slight suggestion of a conspiratorial wink, grasped my hand firmly, and said, 'And now you're you!'"

Usually, George leaves parties to go to sleep by 9:30 P.M. Laura often continues to socialize. But the night of the class-reunion reception, Bush stayed up way past his bedtime, making his exit at 11 P.M. Because they were from out of town, Bush invited seven of his Yale friends and their wives to stay over at the White House. The guests illustrated the diversity of Bush's friends. One of them, lawyer Roland W. Betts, is a Democrat who married Lois Phifer, an African American teacher Betts met when he was an assistant principal at a public school in central Harlem. When Bush wanted to take over the Texas Rangers, Betts became the club's largest investor.

Donald Etra, another guest, is a lawyer in Los Angeles whose clients have included actors Eddie Murphy and Fran Drescher. An Orthodox Jew, Etra is a liberal Democrat. As a criminal-defense lawyer, Etra is opposed to many of the provisions of the Patriot Act. Several times since 9/11, he has discussed his reservations with Bush. Etra said he thought that, rather than authorizing the FBI to wiretap an individual at any phone, a judge should have to approve each telephone number to be tapped.

"He listens carefully, and we agree to disagree," Etra said. "That doesn't inhibit our friendship. I'm a liberal Democrat. I was a Nader's Raider. But he's never held that against me."[3]

As for the other guests, Rob Dieter then was a professor at the University of Colorado Law School and is a former Democrat. Muhammed Saleh, a Timex vice president, is a Muslim from Jordan.

Laura's friends are just as diverse. "I think people underestimate how much they include people from all backgrounds," said Debbie Stapleton. "They understand that the fabric of life in America is made up of a lot of ethnic and cultural diversity. It's not phony, it's not fake. It's genuine."[4]

While Bill Clinton would parade Vernon Jordan around, Bush and Laura considered their friendships private.

One of Laura's Washington friends is Winton Holladay, a native Washingtonian who met Laura when the Bushes were working for George Senior's campaign. Holladay's mother-in-law, Wilhelmina, founded the National Museum of Women in the Arts in Washington. In May 2005, Winton co-chaired a fund-raising event for the women's museum with Anne Johnson, a member of the board of the John F. Kennedy Center for the Performing Arts.

Holladay keeps a low profile and does not like to see her name in the paper. She is careful about telling people of her friendship with the first lady. But when Holladay turned fifty, "Some friends of mine gave me a luncheon party, and I invited Laura," she said. "I didn't tell any of my friends she was coming. In fact, I didn't tell the hostess because I knew this friend of mine would have gotten so undone if she knew Laura was coming. I forgot the Secret Service would have to make a check."[5]

Two days before the luncheon, Holladay called her friend.

"Connie," Holladay said, "there is one guest who is coming that I didn't tell you about."

"My friend got so flustered," Holladay said. "She said, 'My driveway is all torn up, and there's plywood all over the driveway.' "

"Connie," Holladay said. "Laura Bush has seen plywood before. She's very normal. She's just like one of us."

On May 29, 2004, Bush dedicated the National World War II Memorial on the Mall. Laura had invited Pamela Nelson's mother, Lanell, and her father, Charles Hudson, who had participated in the D-day invasion at Normandy, to stay at the White House. She had known them when she was growing up.

"She had a luncheon for my parents," Pamela said. "They are both very elderly. My mother—who has since died—had dementia. So it was quite an effort."

Laura kept checking with Pamela about the menu and how she could make her mother comfortable.

"She thought about what my mother could eat and not spill on herself and not be embarrassed," Nelson said. "She called about when would be the very best time for them to get up and get dressed and be there."

During the luncheon, Laura focused the conversation on Nelson's parents.

"Tell me more about when you were at D-day," she said. "Tell me more about your letters home."

"She had peach roses on the table, my mother's favorite color," Nelson said. "She had the calligraphers draw a little picture of the memorial on the menus that they could keep. She had the White House photographer come and take all these pictures of them in almost every room in the White House. I cried. It was huge. She understands that it's special to go to the White House. It was like, okay, now we've done it all."[6]

Almost every day that Andy Card has seen her, Laura has asked him about his wife, his daughter, or what is going on in his life. "She doesn't have to ask," Card said. "That says a lot."

Laura's friends are always amazed that when they call or see her at the White House, she seems to have nothing else to do but visit with them. She seems to remember everything from their last conversation.

"People get short when they are in public life and get pushed and pulled constantly," Craig Stapleton said. "She never gets like that. She may have dozens of Christmas parties to go to, but she has enough time for you so that you feel you are glad you called her. You don't feel that she is real busy. I won't call her for a month. Then, when I call, we talk, and she says, 'Let's talk again tomorrow night.' "

When Laura's friend Katharine Armstrong, whose parents own the 50,000-acre Armstrong Ranch in Texas, was going through a divorce in the fall of 2002, Laura helped move her into a house she rented next to Regan Gammon. "It was a low point in my life, but she doesn't forget her friends," Armstrong said. "She came over with Regan, and we decided where to place my furniture. We moved things around and hung pictures."

When she was first lady of Texas, Laura became friends with Alice Carrington, the owner of an art gallery in San Antonio. When Alice's husband, Claiborne, a Bush Pioneer, died in 2002, "The president called from Italy, and Mrs. Bush embraced me," she said. "She helped me stay busy and involved in things. That has meant so much to me. I can't believe how they have cared for me when they are trying to care for the whole country."[7]

On September 24, 2004, the mother of Laura's close friend Penny Royall died.

"Laura called and says, 'What are you doing Saturday? Can you come over and work out?'" Royall said. "I said, 'Sure.' She said, 'Stay for lunch. By the way, my hairdresser is coming. Do you want her to do your hair?' She made a day for me where she totally took care of me. We had a wonderful workout. Then a wonderful lunch. We watched a movie with Jenna. We had supper."

The visit was on October 2, in the heat of the campaign.

"Things didn't look particularly wonderful then," Royall said. "She was going to three or four states in a day. But in spite of that, my friend was able to focus on my loss and give me a day of TLC. That is who she is."[8]

Two days later, Laura was talking with Nancy Weiss about Penny Royall's loss.

"Do you know," Laura said to Weiss, "as sad as she was, Penny spent the whole day with me."[9]

If Laura draws strength from her friends, they also help and support each other. Having gotten to know each other at the Bushes' gatherings, they became buddies and began to socialize and go on vacations together. While diverse in many ways, they have certain qualities in common. They are extremely smart and positive. They keep up on current events and American history. They are direct and good at telling anecdotes. While many have the soft touch of southern charm, they have inner strength as well. No one can push them around.

"Clay won't keep a gun in the house for that very reason," Anne Johnson joked.

Like Laura, almost every one of her friends at some point in their lives experienced a tragedy or had to deal with a major personal problem. One friend had breast cancer. Another had a son who, at age two, became brain damaged after nearly drowning in her swim-

L aura disregarded her advance team and accompanied her friend Craig Stapleton, ambassador to the Czech Republic, to a ceremony on May 19, 2002, to remember the Jews who died at a concentration camp in Terezin. Laura held the first Hanukkah candle-lighting and celebration in the White House and served the first entirely kosher meal there. (*AP/Wide World*)

L aura has broad influence on her husband and his administration, and in some cases has suggested strategy. According to Secretary of State Condoleezza Rice, it was Laura's "initiative and her idea to really fully and completely expose what the Taliban regime was doing to women." On July 16, 2003, Laura and Dr. Rice met with the U.S.–Afghan Women's Council. (*White House Photo*)

D r. G. Reid Lyon, Bush's reading adviser, often traveled with Laura as they pushed for reintroducing phonics into reading instruction. (*Courtesy of G. Reid Lyon*)

RIGHT: Dana Gioia, chairman of the National Endowment for the Arts, was surprised by Laura's knowledge of contemporary art. Because of Laura, Bush asked for an increase of $21.5 million in the NEA's budget and boosted funding for other cultural agencies. (*AP/Wide World*)

BOTTOM: Unknown to the public, Laura and the president constantly visited injured American troops and families of fallen American soldiers. (*White House Photo*)

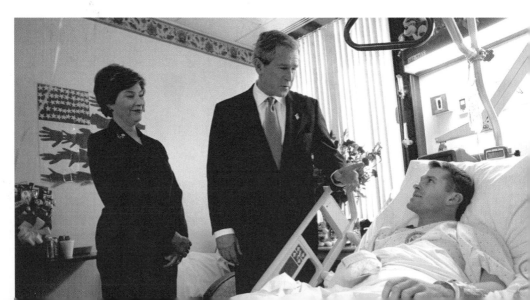

During a visit of Laura's friend Debbie Francis, Laura wanted to see her husband, so she tucked a message inside Barney's collar and sent him trotting into the Oval Office. The note said: "Hurry up, Bushie!" (*White House Photo*)

Vygaudas Ušackas, the Lithuanian ambassador to the United States, found Laura had a deep appreciation of the history of his country and its subjugation by the Soviets. At right is the ambassador's wife, Loreta. (*White House Photo*)

RIGHT: Laura and the president gave a state dinner for Kenya's president, Mwai Kibaki, on October 6, 2003. In private, they entertain a diverse circle of friends in the White House, at Camp David, and at their Crawford ranch. (*White House Photo*)

At Sea Island, Georgia, on June 9, 2004, Laura walked with, from left, Cherie Blair, Bernadette Chirac, and Ludmila Putina. (*White House Photo*)

At George and Laura's wedding, future president George H. W. Bush asked George's friend Donald Ensenat, "What do you think?" about the quiet former librarian. But "President 41" soon became one of Laura's biggest fans. (*White House Photo*)

Laura decided to campaign hard i the second presidential election because she wanted her husband to carry on the work he started and because she hoped for validation of achievements in the face of so much criticism. (*White House Photo*)

Laura spoke at the Republican National Convention in New York City on August 31, 2004. Bush said if he had told her before they were married that she would be doing this, she would have called off the wedding. (*White House Photo*)

Jenna, at left, and Barbara are best friends. Watching them from two rows back at Bush's second presidential inauguration, Anne Johnson, one of Laura's friends, noticed that their heads remained barely a foot apart, even when the twins were not talking to each other. (*White House Photo*)

BOTTOM: On the night of the November 2, 2004, election, Laura's attitude was "What will be, will be. We gave it our best shot," according to her friend Craig Stapleton. From left are Sam LeBlond, Doro Bush Koch's son; Jenna Bush; President Bush; Barbara Bush; Laura Bush; President 41; former first lady Barbara Bush; Bush's sister Doro Bush Koch; and Bush's brother Neil Bush and his wife, Maria. Sitting in a chair at right is Laura's friend Lois Betts. (*AP/Wide World*)

L aura's friends and relatives attended a birthday luncheon
she gave on November 4, 2004, at the new National
Museum of the American Indian. Gathered in the White
House before the luncheon are, left to right, sister-in-law
Margaret Bush, Nancy Weiss, Anne Johnson, Jan O'Neill,
Debbie Francis, Sandy Langdon, Marcia Jackson, longtime
chief of staff Andrea G. "Andi" Ball, Rebecca Turner "Becky"
Gonzales, Barbara Bush, Jenna Bush, a friend of the twins,
Taylor Ensenat, sister-in-law Doro Bush Koch, Liz Johnson, and
the Reverend Kathleene Card. Seated are Lois Betts, Laura
Bush, Winton Holladay, and Gaby Reynolds. Lynne Cheney
also attended. (*White House Photo*)

RIGHT: For Laura's fifty-eighth birthday in November 2004,
the president gave the first lady Miss Beazley. (*White House
Photo*)

BOTTOM: When sick children asked to see Barney, Laura
tried to oblige. Here she visited Children's National Medical
Center in Washington. (*White House Photo*)

When George Bush saw men cleaning up after horses during the second inaugural parade on January 20, 2005, he saluted them and gave them a big smile. (*White House Photo*)

Instead of going to inaugural balls in January 2005, thirty-seven friends of George and Laura went to the "un-ball" at the Red Sage restaurant in Washington. From left are Nancy Weiss, Regan Gammon, and Pamela Nelson. (*Courtesy of Nancy Weiss*)

With his Yale friends and their wives, President Bush jokingly appointed Clay Johnson III and his wife, Anne Johnson, to imaginary posts at the wedding party he and Laura gave at the White House on January 27, 2005, for Collister "Terry" Johnson Jr.'s son Coddy. From left are Ambassador Robert J. "Rob" Dieter, Gwynneth Dieter, Lois Betts, Roland W. Betts, Ambassador Clark "Sandy" Randt Jr., Sarah Randt, President Bush, Laura Bush, Liz Johnson, Terry Johnson, Taylor Ensenat, and Ambassador Donald B. Ensenat. (*White House Photo*)

As part of her Helping America's Youth initiative, Laura visited boys participating in the Passport to Manhood program, which promotes responsibility, at the Germantown Boys and Girls Club in Philadelphia (*White House Photo*)

Laura's influence as counselor to her husband was one reason Bush put $15 billion over five years into fighting AIDS in Africa. On July 12, 2005, Laura visited women involved with the Mothers to Mothers-to-Be program in Cape Town, South Africa, which provides counseling, education, and support to pregnant women infected with AIDS. (*White House Photo*)

Telling the president she was tired of his old jokes, Laura stole the show at the White House Correspondents' Association dinner on April 30, 2005. (*White House Photo*)

ming pool. A third had a daughter who was mentally retarded. In each case, Laura offered support and did what she could.

Like Laura, none of the friends has lost the sense of wonder each shares with her about being in the White House and seeing history unfold. When Laura held the first National Book Festival, Pamela Nelson was staying in the White House and slept in the Lincoln Bedroom.

"I really couldn't sleep that night," she said.

Besides getting used to referring to George as "the president" and Laura as "Mrs. Bush" in front of others, the friends operate under certain ground rules. The most important is that unless they get clearance, they do not talk to the media. For security reasons, they are careful not to mention the Bushes' impending visits to their homes. They also understand that their role is not to be policy advisers. In the case of the president, "I think it helps him to unwind to see friends," Dr. Charles Younger said. "He is a very disciplined guy, and he has his routine. But after work, before he goes to bed, he likes to have a good time and not think about work. I think he likes having people around who aren't going to discuss policy or ask him to do things."[10]

Each of the friends has had to deal with constant requests for special favors. "Hardly a week goes by when I don't have a call asking, 'Do you think you could call and ask Mrs. Bush to do this?' " Debbie Francis said. "I have to tell them, 'Here's the process, but I can't do it myself.' "

"One acquaintance asked me to call the president's scheduler and tell her not to plan anything in Texas with Governor [Rick] Perry on a certain date because she wanted Perry to speak to a charity group for her, and she didn't want the president to interfere," Anne Johnson said. "Someone wanted to know if we could help get a friend out of jail. On another occasion, someone wanted help obtaining a visa for a housekeeper. These are things that we just cannot help with. There are times when we can connect people or point someone in the right direction, but some people who ask just have no idea how busy the president is or that there are legal limitations on what even he can do."

Even when a request has been legitimate, the friends do not always get what they want. As a board member of the Kennedy Center, Anne Johnson once wanted to arrange for the president to meet with a particular performing artist.

"Karl Rove and I are close personal friends, and he was ignoring me about a meeting I wanted to have in the Oval Office for the Kennedy Center," Johnson said. "I told Laura about it, and she did not intervene."[11]

20

Sex and the City

On August 31, 2004, Jenna and Barbara Bush introduced their father at the Republican National Convention in Madison Square Garden in New York City. After nearly a year of partisan attacks from the Democratic primary field, it was the long-awaited kickoff of the president's counteroffensive.

"We spent the last four years trying to stay out of the spotlight," Jenna said. "Sometimes, we did a little better job than others."

Referring to their grandmother, Jenna said, "Gammie, we love you dearly, but you're just not very hip." She added, "She thinks *Sex and the City* is something married people do but never talk about."

While the twins, at age twenty-two, were knockout gorgeous and outrageously charming, their remarks, written by Karen Hughes and Bush media adviser Mark McKinnon, made some people wince.

"I cringed at the reference to Barbara Bush," Nancy Weiss said.

In a September 4, 2004, column, Robert D. Novak blamed the comment on Andi Ball, who, as Laura's chief of staff, supposedly had approved the speech. But Ball had never seen it. Laura had read it and shown it to a few friends. No one questioned it.

"She tends to leave things like that up to someone like Karen," Weiss said. "She trusts her."

Knowing Laura likes to dance, Clay Johnson had jokingly suggested before the first convention that she walk onstage to a song with the lyrics "She's the bad mamma jamma; just as foxy as can be. . . ." Bush pointed out that if he had told Laura before they married that she would be speaking at the Republican National Convention, she would have called off the wedding.

At the second convention, Laura talked about George's commitment to education and national security.

"These are times that require an especially strong and determined leader," Laura said in a speech written by Karen Hughes with input from Condi Rice, Gordon Johndroe, and others. "And I'm proud that my husband is that kind of leader."

The next morning, Laura ate breakfast with seven of her friends in her suite at the Waldorf. Later that day, Anne Johnson was having lunch at Kennebunkport with President 41 and Barbara Bush. Anne said she thought Barbara had said the most quotable line at the convention.

"What was it?" Bar asked.

"I heard that in response to the girls' comment about you not knowing what *Sex and the City* was, you told a reporter, 'Well, it is the same as sex in the country, isn't it?' "

Bar laughed and said she had not said this.

"President 41 sort of cringed when I was telling the story, but I think he forgave me," Anne Johnson said.

Laura turned out to be an immense asset to the campaign, softening the president's image, explaining his policies, and drawing in contributions of more than $5 million. During the first campaign, she had mainly attended small fund-raisers. This time, she was a big draw and addressed large rallies. The idea for participating far more than before was her own. She wanted to continue the work she and her husband had started. Especially in light of all the unfair criticism, she also wanted to increase people's awareness of the work Bush had done and affirm Bush's record with a win at the polls. Karl Rove and Ken Mehlman, who headed the campaign, were more than happy to oblige. Whenever they suggested a campaign appearance, Laura accepted. In all, she barnstormed in twenty states.

"At first, everybody wanted her to campaign with the president because she was so much fun, and the president was having a better time if she was around," Craig Stapleton said. "But she was so good at politics and raising funds that they had to use her separately."

Stapleton had lunch with Laura during the campaign and asked why she wanted to put so much effort into it.

"It's a lot better than losing," she said.

"During the first election, the country did not really know her," said Jim Francis, who headed the Bush Pioneers in the 2000 election. "Laura had a larger impact on the second election. The public knew her, and there was an affectionate relationship between them."[1]

Laura shocked her friends when she publicly took on his critics. Early on, she told the Associated Press that she thought the issue surrounding her husband's National Guard service was a "witch hunt, actually, on the part of the Democrats."

Less than a week after CBS unleashed bogus documents about Bush's Guard service, Laura became the first person from the White House to say the documents were likely forgeries. "You know they are probably altered," she told Radio Iowa in Des Moines. "And they probably are forgeries, and I think that's terrible, really."

Wading into the debate about embryonic-stem-cell research, Laura said that opponents of her husband's ban on federal funding for research on new lines of stem cells were giving "false hope" to many.

"I hope that stem-cell research will yield cures," she told the Pennsylvania Medical Society. "But I know that embryonic-stem-cell research is very preliminary right now, and the implication that cures for Alzheimer's are around the corner is just not right, and it's really not fair to people who are watching a loved one suffer with this disease." She also said that her father had died of Alzheimer's in 1995, and she pointed out that Bush had been the first president to approve any federal funding for research on the affliction.

Meanwhile, the two Bush daughters were like rock stars on the campaign trail, attracting younger voters and contributing their wit and pizzazz. When *People* asked the twins what three things Bush would take if he were sent away to a desert island, Jenna asked, "He couldn't bring Barney?"

"He would bring a picture of Barney," Barbara said.

"Running shoes," Jenna said.

"And the Bible," Barbara said.

Asked about their mother, Jenna said, "Some Windex, maybe."

On A&E, Barbara said that her father always joked that when he first married Laura, he would "take off his shoes to walk on the carpet, because he didn't want to mess up, like, the vacuum lines on the carpet."

There were a few glitches along the way. "Our next stop is SY-ox City," Jenna said in Iowa at one point, referring to Sioux City. From her car, Jenna stuck out her tongue at reporters in St. Louis, prompting Laura to tell her, "Maybe you should work on your issues of impulsiveness, or something."

On the campaign trail, as in the rest of Laura's life as first lady, everything was planned down to the minute. Before each event, Laura received a briefing book with sketches of as many as thirty people she might meet. But on the morning of April 23, 2004, she was in Memphis at Snowden Elementary, an inner-city school that turned sixth graders who couldn't read into proficient readers by giving them extra help with phonics. Bush was asking Congress for a $100 million appropriation to expand the extra-help program—called Striving Readers—to schools throughout the country.

Before taking media questions at 11:12 A.M., Laura stood for photos with local law enforcement officers and firefighters. Gordon Johndroe, her press secretary, was waiting for her in a hold room. After the photo op, Laura joined him there.

"Her eyes were huge, and she had this look on her face as if she had just seen a ghost," Johndroe said. "She was in shock."

Laura told Johndroe that she had just seen Harvey Kennedy, whom she had dated for two years in high school and not seen since. He was in the photo op.

"Should I call the president?" Johndroe joked.

After graduating from Midland High, Kennedy had gone to the University of Texas at El Paso. Hearing of Laura's accident through Regan Gammon, he had visited her in Midland just before Thanksgiving in 1963. That was the last time they had seen each other. After graduating from college, Kennedy joined the navy. In 1993, he retired as a captain. He later became chief administrative officer for Shelby County sheriff Mark H. Luttrell Jr. in Memphis. Because it "sounds like such a story," Kennedy had told only his wife and a few others that he had gone steady with the first lady.[2]

One of those Kennedy told was the sheriff, who was a friend. When a local Secret Service agent offered Luttrell a photo op with Laura, the sheriff asked Kennedy if he wanted to go in his place.

"Of course, I couldn't turn that down after not seeing her for forty years," Kennedy said. "I told the local Secret Service agent that I knew her a number of years ago, and that I knew her pretty well. I said, 'I think she'll remember me.' "

When it was his turn for a photo to be taken, Kennedy introduced himself.

"She was kind of flabbergasted," he said. "She was momentarily at a loss for words, but she recovered nicely. She said, 'What are you doing here?' I gave her a fifteen-second synopsis of my life. We had the photo taken, and I left."

To the media, Laura talked about the need to teach children to sound out letters and assess how they were doing through regular testing. While she gave her usual flawless delivery in complete sentences and paragraphs, she was preoccupied. At a fund-raiser later that day, she met County Commissioner Bruce Thompson. Saying she was a bit shaken by the day's events, she mentioned Kennedy and learned more about what he did for the county. Then, from her plane, Laura called Andi Ball.

"You won't believe this," she said, and told her what had happened.

"She said he looked older, but she recognized him," Andi Ball said. "Our advance team was shocked. They were calling me and saying, 'We're sorry; we didn't know.' But how could anybody know? She wasn't upset. It was fun for her that it happened this way."

In many ways, Bush is an antipolitician. To be sure, he loves being with people, he loves campaigning, and he loves to win. But like Harry Truman, he has an aversion to the acting and pretense of politics.

"He dislikes snobs, hypocrites, the glitterati, and the so-called intelligentsia," Terry Johnson said. "He dislikes all that stuff because he thinks it's phony."[3]

In Clay Johnson's opinion, it is Bush's distaste for pretense that motivates his trademark smirks or half smiles, expressions that many have interpreted as arrogance. When responding to loaded questions from reporters, Bush was signaling, ever so subtly, what he was really thinking. The smirk is not a sign of arrogance but rather an effort to convey his feeling that he is participating in a charade.

"He's a bad actor, a bad pretender," Johnson said. "He doesn't get up and say, 'One and one is two' unless he really knows it's two. What you see is what you get. So when you see him working that lip or showing discomfort, he can't act that away. It means he's bored or perturbed. A real actor would not show that."[4]

Bush saw the debates as part of the phoniness of politics. Whether one candidate could outsmart the other with clever words is not what makes a good leader. Actions and track record are what count.

"My observation of the president was he didn't really want to be at the first debate," Andy Card said. "It was a show or a volley of sound bites rather than an exchange of knowledge. I don't think he was as relaxed in that setting as he came to be during the second debate."

"After the first debate, he was quite taken aback by people's comments that he had not done well," Clay Johnson said. "And then when he saw the tapes and saw what the American people saw, he changed his assessment of his performance."

Through it all, Laura was her usual calm, supportive self.

"Under fire, whether it's 9/11 or political debates, we've never seen her get edgy," said Craig Stapleton, who was with Laura during the second and third debates. "She smiles and laughs, and you think you're going to the movies."

"Laura said some friends said they were so nervous they couldn't look at him or peeked out of their covers from their beds," Pamela Nelson said. "She said, 'I couldn't believe everyone was so nervous.'"

When John Kerry began his quest for the presidency, pundits said he needed to define himself. In the final days before the election, they were still saying it. As Jay Leno joked, even Kerry's favorite sport, windsurfing, depended on which way the wind was blowing.

What Kerry had going for him, cutting into Bush's margin, was the support of the mainstream media. On the TV program *Inside Washington*, *Newsweek*'s assistant managing editor Evan Thomas said the media "want Kerry to win." Relentlessly, the liberal media distorted coverage of Bush and his White House, giving only one side on critical issues, ignoring successes, and creating a mythological figure of Bush as puppet, religious fanatic, or bigot. The final effort to drive Bush from office came on October 25, when the *New York Times* ran a page-one story saying that 380 tons of explosives had vanished from an Iraq facility called Al Quaqaa "sometime after the American-led invasion last year." The story suggested that poor security had led to the disappearance, but despite the lead, the paper had no evidence of whether the explosives disappeared before or after the U.S. invasion.

As with her husband, reporters tried to put Laura on the defensive, asking, "What do you tell the wives and children of American soldiers who have died?"

"As we do the hard work of confronting terror, we can be proud that fifty million more men, women, and children live in freedom thanks to the United States of America and our allies," Laura would say. "After years of being treated as virtual prisoners in their homes by the Taliban, the women of Afghanistan are now able to walk outside their doors without a male escort. And the little girls in Afghanistan, who were forbidden to be educated, are now in school. And because we acted, the people of Iraq are free from the torture and the tyranny of Saddam Hussein."

Wherever she spoke, Laura never failed to thank the military for their patriotism and their courage and to express sympathy for those who lost their loved ones. In private, Laura was the same way.

"My older sister's son went to West Point and went to Iraq," Laura's friend Sandy Langdon said. "There was never a day when I saw Laura that she didn't ask about Cliff."[5]

One day, when Langdon was hosting a luncheon at her house, she asked her sister Wendy Kazmarek to give the blessing.

"When she gave it," Langdon said, "Laura continued it."

"I want to bless all our servicemen and women in this war," Laura said. "I hope they all come home safely."

Everyone had tears in their eyes.

2 1

VICTORY

On the afternoon of November 2, 2004, exit polls were giving John Kerry a clear win. Doro Bush Koch, who had campaigned for her brother in fifteen states, called her mother, Barbara, at the White House. She said she didn't feel up to joining the friends and family whom George and Laura had invited over to watch the election results.

Not known for mincing words, the former first lady said, "You come down here right now! We need you."[1]

"She had that voice like in my childhood," Doro said.

A chastened Doro and her husband, Bobbie, drove to the White House from suburban Maryland and arrived just before 7 P.M. "It was intense," Doro said. "My mom and I would go off in a corner. We didn't want to feel the tension."

The only bright spot was Karl Rove, who confidently predicted that the president would win.

"At three-thirty P.M., Karl Rove phoned me because a mutual friend who had come for the election results landed in the hospital when a drunk driver hit his cab on the way to the Willard Hotel," Anne Johnson said. "In closing, I asked Karl how it looked to him.

He replied, 'Close but clear,' which is pretty much how it ended up. This is when the Kerry exit-poll results were reaching a high pitch."[2]

Anne and Clay Johnson were having an election-night party at their home in Spring Valley. In attendance were Texas senator John Cornyn and his wife, Sandy, and what Clay called the "lifers"—Texans like White House counsel Al Gonzales, soon to be attorney general; Domestic Policy Adviser Margaret Spellings, who would become education secretary; Alphonso Jackson, the future secretary of housing and urban development—along with other key White House aides and friends of Laura and George's. The party was called for 7:30 P.M.

"Al Gonzales arrived half an hour early, chose his seat in front of the upstairs TV, and mapped out every possible scenario," Anne Johnson said. "He only moved from his chair once in five hours, to get a bowl of chili." Along with the chili, Anne Johnson served tamales imported from Rosie's Tamale House in Austin.

Back at the White House, Rove was manning what he jokingly called his "bat cave," an operations center in the old family dining room on the State Floor. With him were White House aides Israel J. Hernandez, Ashley Estes, Susan Ralston, and Brett M. Kavanaugh. They compared current and previous absentee-ballot returns with Republican National Committee counts of voters turning out in each county and extrapolated the results. In the Roosevelt Room, senior staff like Andy Card and Condi Rice were watching the returns come in. On the second and third floors, the friends and family watched Fox with the sound turned down.

"George was uncharacteristically quiet," Nancy Weiss said. "I think the first exit-poll results took the wind out of us."

"He always approached things with big ideas and objectives," Don Evans said. "Find the best people you can to pursue those goals. Lead them in that direction. Give them leadership through your trust in them, your determination, your courage. You commit yourself to it a hundred percent. And when it's over, it's over, and you move on.

That's where he was at that moment. I felt that as in the 2000 election, while people were anxious, he felt at peace about the effort."[3]

"Everyone was nervous, jumping on phones," Craig Stapleton said. "But Laura was very calm. Her attitude was 'What will be, will be. We gave it our best shot.' "

For two hours, Stapleton sat between Bush and his father. "We were keeping score, talking to people in the field, talking to Karl Rove," Stapleton said. "His dad was more nervous. He wasn't even eating, he was so nervous."

"By ten-thirty or eleven, we knew that statistically, Kerry couldn't win," Jan O'Neill said.

Photographers were brought in to take photos of the entire family looking happy. To give reporters some descriptive color, the press office said the guests had a buffet dinner. The names of the invited friends were not given.

Some of the residence staff were quietly expressing joy that Bush was winning. No one forgot how nasty the previous occupants of the White House had been. Hillary Clinton had fired a White House usher for returning two calls from Barbara Bush. Back when she was still in the White House, Christopher B. Emery had taught her how to use her laptop computer. In a panic, she had sought his help again. After Hillary fired Emery, the father of four could not find a job for a year.

Rove kept phoning the networks to get them to call the all-important Ohio for Bush.

"By late afternoon, Karl was saying the exit polls were not right," said Israel Hernandez, who was now working as Rove's assistant. "He called the networks and explained why their methodology was wrong."[4]

Finally, at 12:41 A.M. on November 3, Fox broke ranks with the other networks and projected Bush the winner in Ohio.

Late in the evening, when it appeared Bush might make a victory speech at the Ronald Reagan Building, Dick and Lynne Cheney came over with their family, including their granddaughter Kate Perry, age ten. President 41 seemed to be relieving the tension by having a twenty-minute "grandfatherly conversation" with her, Debbie Francis recalled. The elder Bush thought Kate said her teacher had seventy instead of seventeen cats.

"They went on and on," Nancy Weiss said. "I got up and moved around, and I looked over, and he was still engaged with her."

When it became clear that Kerry was not going to concede that night, Rove told Bush he should wait until later in the morning to declare victory.

"We started going to bed," Regan Gammon said. "I went to my room at three A.M."

On Wednesday at 3:08 P.M., Bush delivered a victory speech at the Ronald Reagan Building. Calling for the nation to come together, he said, "We are entering a season of hope."

As it turned out, Bush won a second term by more than three and a half million votes. No Democratic presidential candidate since 1964 had received as high a percentage—51 percent—of the popular vote.

In Karl Rove's view, it all came down to character.

"The public wants a president with convictions and the courage to act on them," Rove said nine days after the election. "They want a leader who is steady and firm, who can withstand strong political headwinds and won't be blown about by events."[5]

Especially after 9/11, the public wanted to know how a president would react in a crisis.

"Does he have not only the mind but also the heart that allows that individual to remain strong and sure in the face of supreme challenges?" said Rove, who became deputy chief of staff in the second term. "Since we can't possibly anticipate everything that will arise, we need to make a judgment about the qualities and character of the person running for office. In 2004, when events in Iraq and elsewhere often seemed to conspire against us, the president's character shone through to the American people. So did John Kerry's. And that's a large part of the reason the voters returned President Bush to office."

On November 4, 2004, two days after the election, Laura had a luncheon at the new National Museum of the American Indian for two dozen of her friends to celebrate her fifty-eighth birthday. The event included a tour of the museum with its director, Rick West.

In a private dining room, daughters Jenna and Barbara were at one table holding forth. "They said the first lady is trying to get them to straighten up their rooms at the White House," said Anne Johnson. "Maria Galvan, the housekeeper, was sitting with us and said they were just about out of things to straighten up."

Jenna said that when her mother was little, she would line up her dolls in a certain order before she went to bed. She could not sleep unless every one of them was in its proper place. According to Jenna, the president said, "Laura, I wish you had told me about this before I married you."

The following weekend, Barbara was going to visit her boyfriend Jay Blount, who was a year behind her at Yale. Blount and several of Jenna's boyfriends had stayed at the White House in separate bedrooms. At the lunch, "Maria was rating the boyfriends in front of the girls," Anne Johnson said. "She liked the ones who insisted on washing their own clothes when they were staying at the White House and also the ones who were friendliest to her. I could tell the girls were listening. Barbara's beau got the highest marks."

Along with a pair of antique pillowcases, Anne gave Laura a card. "Happy Birthday from All of Us!" it said. "You know, the ones who helped age you faster than normal." It was signed by Katie Couric, Matt Lauer, Barbra Streisand, Bruce Springsteen, and George Bush.

As his birthday present, Bush gave Laura a Scottish terrier. Barney had also been a birthday present to Laura, but he had turned out to be a one-person dog, totally devoted to the president and oblivious to everyone else.

The new dog, Miss Beazley, was born on October 28 in the same New Jersey kennel as Barney. (Her father is Barney's half brother.) Beazley, as Laura called her, was named after a dinosaur character in Oliver Butterworth's children's book *The Enormous Egg*.

On Friday, November 12, the Bushes had dinner at the home of Anne and Clay Johnson.

"At about 6:52 P.M., the fifteen-vehicle motorcade left the White House in a steady rain, headed up the Whitehurst Freeway in very light commuter traffic, and up Foxhall Road to Johnson's home near American University," the White House pool report said. "The pool never actually saw Bush and was unable to learn who else, if anyone, dined with the men and what, if anything, was eaten. The pool was confined to quarters—read, the vans—throughout. The motorcade left to return around 9:10 P.M., returning to the White House around 9:28 P.M."

In addition to the first couple, the guests included Yale friend Roland W. Betts and FBI director Robert S. Mueller III and his wife, Ann. The Secret Service set up a command post in the basement. Anne Johnson had insisted that the agents bring dogs to sniff for explosives, prompting Mueller to suggest she join the FBI.

Rodney Scruggs, the chef from the American University's president's residence, made filet mignon, potatoes au gratin, and white asparagus. Bush took his sauce on the side and ate all his vegetables. Anne Johnson made guacamole.

At the dinner, Laura said she had been "stunned" when the exit polls showed Kerry winning. "The crowds were so much more jubilant during the campaign than they were four years ago, and it didn't make sense," she said. "I wondered," she joked, "if the campaign had been transporting the same people from stop to stop to be in the rope lines."

Laura said both she and Bush were elated when the second round of exit-poll numbers came in. "Can you imagine how the Kerry side felt, after thinking at first they were winning?" she said.

Anne mentioned that her sister Betty Sewell had received an e-mail from a friend in California saying that she and Clay had "sold out to the rich and the powerful." Anne said, "I don't think that she meant Michael Moore." Anne said that she had suggested Betty reply "in the Laura Bush fashion," as Laura had done when Teresa Heinz made her nasty remark. "Betty got a nice note back from her friend, and the understanding approach completely defused the situation," she told Laura. "Turning the other cheek does seem to work—except for the Taliban, of course."

The Johnsons' Peruvian housekeeper had asked if she could bring a first grader and a third grader from her family to meet the president. So just before dinner, Anne asked Bush if he would say hello to Pierre and Gabriela Yliquin.

"He practically ran into the family room," Anne said. "Pierre had his hair standing on end with a lot of gel, which I'm sure it took him some time to apply. Gabriela had on some pretty jewelry. When GWB entered the room, Pierre said, 'Oh, I don't think I can breathe.' Gabriela said she couldn't breathe, either."

Anne assured them they were going to be just fine, and the president started a conversation with them.

"He excitedly called Laura in, and [the children] talked about their family and their school," Anne said. "This is a first couple who no longer had to look for votes."

―――――――

When Pamela Nelson arrived on November 17 for her monthly visit, Laura and George were getting ready to fly to Little Rock for the dedication of the Clinton Library, then to Santiago, Chile, for the Asia-Pacific Economic Cooperation leaders' meeting.

"Laura asked the president how long the trip to Arkansas would take and then how long to Chile," Nelson said. She said she had gotten a "briefing," but this information wasn't part of it.

"Now you're showing off," Bush joked.

Laura had just dedicated a redesigned Pennsylvania Avenue in front of the White House, a project she personally helped direct. Concrete barriers had been replaced by an inviting expanse more secure than before.

John V. Cogbill III, the chairman of the National Capital Planning Commission, which was in charge of the project, remembered that the first time he'd met with Laura in her office in the East Wing, the Bushes' dog Spot, who has since died, flopped down at Laura's feet and fell asleep. "Our designer was talking about putting down crushed granite as in the Tuileries Gardens in Paris," Cogbill said. Obviously unimpressed by this reference, Laura responded, "We have that down at Crawford. It gets all over your shoes. I think we want something better than that."

Around the time of Pamela Nelson's visit, Washington was buzzing about who would keep their post in the administration. As usual, almost all the speculation turned out to be wrong. Above all, the Bush administration excelled at keeping secrets.

"They were talking about the appointment of Condoleezza Rice as secretary of state," Nelson said. "And I was thinking about whether I would be reappointed to my small arts commission."[6]

At the dinner table, Jenna said she wanted a car so she could drive to the charter school where she would be teaching. Robert McCleskey duly authorized a payment from Jenna's trust fund. George knew that Barbara and her boyfriend Jay Blount had temporarily broken up.

"Are you divorced now?" Bush teased.

"They were talking a lot about Miss Beazley," Nelson said. "They got a picture [of the newborn puppy] with [its] eyes open. The girls said, 'Mommy, you'll have to hold her constantly.' "

The day before Thanksgiving, the Bushes planned to entertain King Juan Carlos and Queen Sofia of Spain in Crawford at a luncheon of turkey and bass. So Pamela brought chocolate-covered almonds from Spain as a present. On Thanksgiving, Laura and George would have turkey leftovers with President 41 and Barbara Bush and Laura's mother, Jenna Welch. Jenna was staying with them for a month. For a scrapbook she planned to give her mother, Laura was collecting all the photos, place cards, and invitations for the events she would attend.

A year earlier, Robert McCleskey had seen Jenna Welch driving the wrong way down the one-way street where he had his office in Midland. McCleskey told Laura, who had noticed that her mother was starting to have short-term-memory problems. Jenna agreed to try a retirement home into which several of her friends were about to move. She liked it so much she immediately sold her house for $131,000.

Barbara Bush said to her, "Why don't you just move into the White House? You wouldn't have anything to do. Everyone would take care of you."

"That's just the point," Jenna said. "I wouldn't have anything to do."

Shortly after moving into the retirement home, Jenna was visiting Laura's cousin Mary Mark Welch in Dallas. Jenna noticed a copy of Christopher Andersen's *George and Laura: Portrait of an American Marriage* on a bookshelf. Thumbing through it, she came across a quote attributed to Laura. According to the book, Laura had said to George, "Rein it in, Bubba."

"Now, can you imagine Laura ever saying, 'Rein it in, Bubba?' " an incredulous Jenna asked.[7]

The new owners of the house at 2500 Humble Avenue where

Laura grew up were Texans Jamie and Delaney McCaghren. They found that a cat named Henry came along with the property. Technically, Henry belonged to W. B. "Trey" Robbins III and his wife, Kathy, across the street. But the three Robbins boys were a handful, and Henry had long ago decided to spend most of his time with Harold and Jenna.

"Henry divorced us and took up with them," Kathy Robbins said.[8]

According to the new owners of Jenna's house, Henry never watched television. But the night of the November 2 election, Henry stayed up into the early-morning hours watching the election returns with them in their bedroom.

"We thought Henry must have been used to watching Bush election returns with Mrs. Welch," Jamie McCaghren said.[9]

Invigorated by their victory, Laura and George held fifteen different holiday celebrations at the White House for a total of 6,500 guests. They sent out 2 million Christmas cards, up from 1.3 million in 2003, 1 million in 2002, and 875,000 in 2001. Paid for by the Republican National Committee, the postage alone totaled $600,000. The Christmas decorations included 155,500 lights on forty-one trees. Pastry chef Thaddeus R. DuBois baked 24,000 cookies, 200 fruitcakes, and a 300-pound gingerbread White House for the State Dining Room.

Diplomats invited to the receptions were surprised at the difference between how the media portrayed the first couple and what they were really like. Bush was funny, knowledgeable, and interested in what others had to say. Laura was outspoken and up-to-date on policy issues.

Vygaudas Ušackas, the Lithuanian ambassador to the U.S., remembered that at one reception, he was explaining to Bush and

Laura that his president, Valdas Adamkus, would not be going to Moscow to commemorate the end of World War II, since the Soviets' victory resulted in Lithuania's subjugation.

"The first lady had a deep knowledge of the history and expressed genuine sympathy toward our small captive nation, which was kept under the oppression of the Soviets for more than fifty years," the ambassador said.[10]

"She's always extremely well informed," said Condi Rice. "She really does her homework. I've watched her on trips, and she's read the briefing books cover to cover. She's taken the time to know a little bit about the history of the country or some particular struggle that the country is particularly proud of.

"I'll never forget when Jiang Zemin, then president of China, came to the ranch," Rice said. "[He and his wife are] both quite elderly, and his wife moves very slowly. And you would just always see that the first lady was making sure not to walk ahead of her or to just sort of make sure that she was comfortable and not put her in a position that was embarrassing because she was somewhat slow. Heads of state and their families love being around her, so that's a real asset."[11]

Visiting dignitaries appreciate not only her manners but her interest in substantive matters.

After one Christmas party, Laura's friend Deedie Rose stayed overnight at the White House and attended a coffee the next morning with Sehba Musharraf, the wife of the president of Pakistan, and a few other wives.

"We were all making small talk," Rose said. "We asked Mrs. Musharraf how long her trip had taken. But Laura asked about her role in empowering women in Pakistan through educational and economic opportunities. Real information was being exchanged rather than small talk."[12]

"Laura really likes it when there's only one conversation at a table," Pamela Nelson said. "When she sets up White House functions and decides where people will sit, she likes round tables because she wants everyone at a table to be in on one conversation. She likes talking about ideas rather than just petty stuff or chitchat."

In one incident, which he related ruefully to Anne Johnson, Jeff Eubank, deputy U.S. chief of protocol at the State Department, was rushing between floors at the Waldorf for a United Nations General Assembly session when he suddenly found himself face-to-face with the first lady coming out of an elevator. Eubank was taking Prime Minister Junichiro Koizumi of Japan down to another floor and picking up Hamid Karzai, the president of Afghanistan. In the rush, Eubank, who had been general counsel to Al Gonzales when Gonzales was Bush's secretary of state in Texas, inadvertently introduced Koizumi as Karzai.

Without missing a beat, the first lady said, "Well, yes, of course, I know Prime Minister Koizumi." As Eubank whisked off the prime minister of Japan, Laura said, "Thank you, Jeff."

"Jeff was mortified," Anne said. "He is such a pro. I'm sure the mix-up would have haunted him had she not been so gracious."

As part of the holiday celebrations, Laura gave what became known as a slumber party for her friends from Southern Methodist University. It actually consisted of a luncheon and a sleepover at the White House.

"When we had a college reunion, Laura was the one who had everyone to lunch at her house," sorority sister Janet Heyne said. "She still does that."

At the luncheon on December 1, 2004, Laura mentioned that she had been in touch with a Kappa Alpha Theta sorority sister who had been expelled because she repeatedly ignored curfews, staying with her boyfriend.

"At that time, what the girl did was a huge no-no," Heyne recalled. "Finally, she got kicked out of the sorority. They took her pin. We were all upset about it. We liked her so much."[13]

Almost forty years later, a few of the sorority sisters were still disapproving, saying the girl "put us in an embarrassing position with her behavior." But "Laura was a friend of hers, so she got in touch with her," Anne Stewart said.

The luncheon was notable for one comic mishap.

For dessert, the pastry chef made individual crème brûlées in the shape of a candle. "Sharon Dodson was trying to figure out how to eat it," Stewart said. "Laura said, 'Push it so it lies on its side and cut into it.'"

Sharon did as she was told.

"She cut into this hard chocolate candle, and the cream filling squirted right across Laura's chest," Stewart said. "Laura had just done TV with the networks and had on a red dress."

"Well, I'm not going to be invited back," Dodson said.[14]

After the luncheon, Laura and her friends walked through the Oval Office to take a tour of the Rose Garden. Bush was away having lunch with Dick Cheney. When the women returned to the Oval Office, the president was sitting at his desk. Janet Heyne recalled their exchange as an example of how the first couple "play fight."

"Get out of here," Bush said. "This is my office."

"I have to go through to get back in," the first lady said.

"Well, hurry," Bush said. "I have an important meeting."

For New Year's Eve, Laura and George invited Nancy and Mike Weiss, Ron and Peggy Weiss, and Regan and Billy Gammon for dinner and champagne at the ranch. They arrived the day before and stayed for the weekend. Pamela Nelson came for an overnight stay, arriving the same day the Bushes did. Pamela brought a gift of bean tamales, and Billy Gammon gave Laura a copy of *The Essays of E. B.*

White. Laura mentioned White's commentary, referring to the "joy of complexity."

"She just loved that," Nelson said. "Then she quoted [White] as saying, 'I love the world.' Laura said, 'I think all writers and artists love the world, and that's why they're so curious.' "[15]

Pamela led the women in a yoga session. Her mother, Lanell Hudson, had just died. The session helped relieve the stress. Then Laura and Pamela took a long walk.

"She said it was the perfect time for my mother to go, that my mother is happy now," Pamela said.

Pamela and Nancy worked an Elms wood jigsaw puzzle. As a frequent visitor to the ranch, Condi Rice found that working a puzzle and chopping wood were the main activities. Since she made it clear she had no desire to chop wood, she became expert at working puzzles with Laura and the president.

"This isn't something that we did in Birmingham, Alabama," Rice said. "So I was a very poor puzzler at first. You can't take a piece and try and see if it fits. That's cheating."

What if a piece doesn't fit?

"Well, then," she answered, laughing, "you sort of sneak the piece back and pretend you didn't try to make it fit."

After dinner on the evening before New Year's Eve, Laura put on CDs of Texas singers like Roy Orbison and Buddy Holly. "The Midland girls—Laura, Regan, and I, and Nancy from Lubbock—danced," Pamela said.

The next day, Bush and Billy Gammon went off to cut wood.

"Billy loves to do the chain saw with the president," Regan said. "He brings his own chain saw. They cut cedar, the bad ones. They pile them all up. They burn them or whatever they do."[16]

Later, Ron Weiss went fishing with the president and Barney on the Bushes' eleven-acre, man-made lake stocked with black bass, bluegill, and perch. Peggy and Ron, partners in Jeffrey's restaurant in

Austin, brought two bottles of Veuve Clicquot Rosé for New Year's Eve. Laura supplied Dom Pérignon as well.

"We were all in bed by ten-thirty P.M.," Nancy Weiss said.

Meanwhile, back in Washington, Clay and Anne Johnson were celebrating New Year's at their home with several Bush friends.

"Let's call down to Crawford and wish the Bushes a Happy New Year," Anne said. She couldn't find the number of the ranch. "Well, I'll call the White House," she said.

"Hello, this is Anne Johnson, and we'd like to be transferred to Crawford and wish the Bushes a Happy New Year," she said.

In the past, White House operators had recognized her voice and put her through to Camp David. This time, she got a polite turn-down. Anne went and told Clay.

"Anne," Clay said to his wife, "do me a favor. Next time you give a message like that, don't give your name."

Just after the 2004 election, Bush's friend Terry Johnson and his wife, Liz, invited the Bushes to the wedding of their son Coddy, who had been the national field director of the Bush–Cheney '04 campaign. Bush called Terry and said he would hate to disrupt the wedding. Guests would need to pass through metal detectors, and the first couple would draw attention away from the bride and groom. Instead, Bush said he and Laura would like to throw a party for them at the White House. They invited all 110 people who were going to the rehearsal dinner.

In a toast to the Bushes, Terry joked at the event on January 27, 2005, that when Bush, Clay Johnson, Rob Dieter, and he wound up as roommates at Yale, they decided one of them should run for president. They drew straws, and Bush won. "The next four years were spent preparing the winner for the Oval Office," Johnson deadpanned. "The dirty clothes piled in the corner on the floor actually concealed secret plans. The napping in the library was a decoy to make everyone think we were not up to anything."

As Terry finished, Laura, sitting next to him, had a twinkle in her eye. From a corner of the room, a dozen young men emerged and began singing. They were the Baker's Dozen, an a cappella group from Yale of which Coddy had once been a member. Secretly, Laura had arranged for them to come down from New Haven to entertain the guests.

22

THE UN-BALL

For the second inauguration, Laura wore a winter-white day suit and coat from Oscar de la Renta.

"The color suggests a certain chic understanding that restraint can be the most powerful form of expression," cooed fashion writer Robin Givhan in the *Washington Post*. De la Renta claimed that the first lady could wear any color. But warmer colors like red went better with her skin tone. In fact, Laura thought she had ordered a warmer off-white. "She was a bit surprised when she saw it," Anne Johnson said.

More impressive was what *People* hailed as Laura's "new look," a slimmed-down first lady who in recent months had gone from a size eight to a size six. *People* said she had started working out two years earlier, but actually exercising dated back to the beginning of her days in the White House. With her latest personal trainer, Amy Alberson, she often worked out with Margaret Bush, wife of Bush's brother Marvin. An actor, Margaret performed in plays in northern Virginia. Laura often attended them with her daughters.

"She calls Margaret 'my darling sister-in-law,'" Anne Johnson said.

What made a difference in Laura's weight was the campaign and "not being in places where it was easy to eat," Nancy Weiss said. For breakfast, Laura continued to eat oatmeal or cold cereal with raisins and prunes.

"Laura, you're cooking again," Pamela Nelson said to her one morning at breakfast as she noticed the first lady's bowl.

After the campaign Laura tried simply to eat less at lunch and dinner and cut down on high-caloric Tex-Mex food. She preferred food that the president could "identify" over some of the creations of White House executive chef Walter Scheib III. Laura had inherited Scheib from Hillary Clinton, who'd hired him from the Greenbrier Resort in White Sulphur Springs, West Virginia.

On many occasions, Laura wished to serve elegant food. For example, for a luncheon for a charity that Oscar de la Renta supported, she served a lobster entrée followed by a green salad and sorbet. But she also wanted a chef who understood how to make comfort food. The menu at Café Deluxe, one of her favorite lunch spots, included meat loaf and roasted lamb shank as well as steak with french fries, lump crab cake, and pan-roasted shrimp and scallops.

Anne Stewart remembered when Scheib faxed Laura at the ranch a proposed menu for a White House dinner with some good ol' boys from East Texas.

"Look at this menu," the first lady said. "It's a mélange of wild mushrooms and organic flowers. How do I tell him I want grits? Pretty soon you don't know what you're eating."

Friends noticed that no matter what cuisine was served, the food was always julienned and presented in a pyramid. The first lady was not pleased.

"It wasn't just French or American or Mexican food or Texas food that wasn't right," Gordon Johndroe said. "It could be Chesapeake Bay–style cooking. It might be softshell crabs in a soup where something wouldn't be right."[1]

"From day one, she wanted to have her own person as chef," said Taylor Ensenat, a friend of Laura's who is married to Bush's friend from Yale Donald Ensenat. "[Scheib] only wanted to do French food. When [George and Laura] eat by themselves, they get tired of having a production made of every meal. They wanted a simple meal, and it never was."[2]

While Laura likes a range of dishes, Bush prefers food made by Matty Wendell, an Austin caterer who joined the White House advance staff and cooked at the ranch. Bush likes hamburgers and egg-salad sandwiches. Most of all, he relishes peanut butter—creamy, not chunky—and jelly sandwiches. At the White House, he prefers lunch from the navy mess in the basement of the West Wing.

"George is grilled cheese and hamburgers," Anne Stewart said. "If it's anything other than that, he doesn't know what it is. He is also speedy. This guy can clear a plate before you've even finished your hors d'oeuvres. We were there for the National Book Festival. He cleaned his plate and looked up at Laura and said, 'Laura, what did I just eat?' "[3]

In addition to working out, Laura likes to take long walks at the ranch and on the Mall near the White House. In the summer, she goes hiking with her Midland friends Peggy Weiss, Regan Gammon, JaneAnn Fontenot, and Marge Petty.

"Every year when Laura was first lady of Texas, they entered a lottery to be able to camp at Yosemite National Park," said Andi Ball. "They never won. When she got to Washington, she said to me, 'We're going to Yosemite because we won the lottery!' "

"You did?" Andi Ball said.

"Yes!" the first lady said, smiling mischievously.

The National Park Service had said it wanted the first lady to enjoy Yosemite and would open the campgrounds a day early for her and her friends. For the annual hiking trips, Secret Service agents who like to hike volunteer to go along. Usually, the women stay in tents set up for the summer. There is no publicity.

"She would wake up and put on her contacts, build a fire," Regan Gammon said about these trips. "She was a very good fire builder.

She and I would share a tent. JaneAnn and Margie and Peggy would share another tent. Sometimes Laura would go and build their fire."[4]

Despite the emphasis she places on good health, Laura has been known to occasionally sneak a cigarette with friends. In 1994 and 1995, she totally quit a lifelong smoking habit. When asked by the media, she has honestly said that it was "difficult" to quit. But after 1995, Laura went back to bumming cigarettes from friends, though never in front of George or her staff. At the White House, she might step outside on the Truman Balcony to take a few puffs. At the ranch, she might occasionally light up on the porch.

"She is a stress smoker," said Anne Stewart. "She still bums a cigarette."

"If she is sitting around with some friends and they are smoking, she may smoke," Dr. Charles Younger said. "She wouldn't tell you she never does it, but it's not an image she would like to promote as a healthy habit from the first lady who is supposed to be perfect."[5]

George Bush took the oath of office at the snow-covered Capitol at noon on January 20, 2005. It was the first inauguration since the attacks of 9/11, and the fifty-eight-year-old president looked far grayer than he had four years earlier.

"My most solemn duty is to protect this nation and its people from further attacks and emerging threats," Bush said as 13,000 police officers and soldiers maintained security around the Capitol and the parade route. "Some have unwisely chosen to test America's resolve, and have found it firm.

"The survival of liberty in our land increasingly depends on the success of liberty in other lands," the president said. "All who live in tyranny and hopelessness can know: The United States will not ignore your oppression or excuse your oppressors," Bush continued. "When you stand for your liberty, we will stand with you."

Like Ronald Reagan's "tear down that wall" address, which marked the beginning of the end of the Cold War, Bush's message was iconoclastic and powerful.

After the swearing-in, Bush and Laura watched the inaugural parade along Pennsylvania Avenue for two hours. Whenever pooper-scoopers came by to clean up after the horses, the president saluted them and gave them a big smile. They did a little jig in response.

"When I saw the pooper-scoopers, I said to my son, 'Watch the president,' " said Penny Royall, who sat with other Bush friends near Laura during the swearing-in. " 'He's going to be nice to these guys. He understands what it is to be a human being and not have the greatest job in the world.' "

That evening, Laura and George dropped in to inaugural balls. Their daughters wore gowns by Badgley Mischka. Laura wore a silver-and-blue embroidered de la Renta gown. At the wholesale prices charged by the designers, the gowns cost $3,000 and up.

Until the girls went on public display, Laura had not let them spend lavishly on clothes. Anne Stewart remembered shopping with Barbara and Laura in New York as George was announcing his first run for president.

"Barbara wanted this wonderful outfit," Anne Stewart said. "The blouse was a hundred and eighty dollars, and the skirt was two-twenty. Laura looked at the outfit and said, 'No, too expensive.' My daughter would have been lying down on the ground, screaming and crying. George and the two girls will get nose to nose and argue like two bulldogs. But with Laura, when she says no, the girls say 'okay.' "

"I would say splurging on the girls is a very recent phenomenon," Craig Stapleton said. "The president is the least materialistic person I can think of. He really doesn't care about things. Laura is more interested in things, but she is not possessive either. When the Rangers deal closed, he didn't have to worry about money anymore. But he wasn't thinking about beach houses, fast cars, or Palm Beach. He is not Palm Beach material."[6]

"On [inauguration] night, a bunch of us said, 'Who wants to go to the balls?' Nobody, nobody," Regan Gammon said. "We decided we would just have dinner somewhere. Roland Betts turned to me and said, 'You make it happen.'"

Instead of attending the inaugural balls, thirty-seven Bush friends went to the "un-ball," a dinner at Red Sage, which features Southwest cuisine. Regan chose Red Sage after the concierge at the Mayflower Hotel, where 400 Bush friends and family members were staying, showed her menus from local restaurants. Her husband, Billy, had once been there. At the dinner, Don Evans toasted the president, and Regan toasted the first lady.

"If it were not for her, a lot of us wouldn't have been here in this room," Regan said.

The next day, friends and family attended a luncheon at the White House. Laura's former boyfriend Ralph Ellis and his wife, Mary, chatted with Jenna Welch and later with Laura. Because Regan Gammon and Marge Petty had to go to the airport, Regan got Laura's assistant Lindsey Lineweaver to let them cut in line to have their photos taken with the first couple.

"She's not usually this rude," Bush yelled out to the next person in line.

Because Jim Francis was going to the Alfalfa Club dinner the next night with Bush, Debbie and Jim Francis, along with close Bush-family members, spent the weekend at the White House. Breeder Bill Berry had just delivered Miss Beazley. When Laura and the president introduced the puppy to the media on the South Lawn, the puppy ran for the bushes and disappeared through a hole in a hedge.

"It's her first day at the White House," Gordon Johndroe said. "We will get her some media training."

With Jim and Debbie Francis, both Laura and George were getting down on the floor at the White House to play with the new puppy.

"Barney acted so bored by Miss Beazley," Debbie Francis said. "Miss Beazley wanted to play and tumble. Barney acted like an old man. But then he would run in the snow, chasing balls and doing flips."[7]

After the grueling inaugural week, Bush was as energetic as ever, telling Jim Francis, "I'm not dragging." After the Alfalfa Club dinner, the Bushes and Francises sat in the Treaty Room. "Snow was on the big magnolia trees outside the window," Debbie Francis said. "The Washington Monument was lit up. I would catch myself and say, 'I can't believe I'm here.' "

With her husband in office for another four years, Laura began announcing staff changes as well as a new program initiative. When Andi Ball, her chief of staff, came to Washington, she agreed to stay for a year. Her husband, Lonnie, a geothermal-heating and air-conditioning contractor, had remained in Austin. After 9/11, Ball had felt she couldn't leave her post, so she remained chief of staff for the entire first term. Now she was returning to Austin. On the Sunday after the inauguration, Laura gave a dinner for her in the residence.

"The president said how great it was having me there the last four years," Andi Ball said, referring to her time in the White House but not her previous years working for Laura in the governor's mansion. "Laura Bush said, 'Ten.' And he said, 'Four years that seemed like ten.' "

Andi Ball wept, and Laura said to her, "Did I tell you that George wept so hard when he toasted me at our wedding that he couldn't say anything? Everyone said, 'Sit down, sit down!' "

Ball suggested as her successor Anita McBride, who was director of White House personnel during the Reagan and George H. W. Bush administrations and later became senior adviser in the State Department's Bureau of International Organizations. After interviewing her and several other people, Laura offered McBride the job. Gordon Johndroe announced the appointment along with that of a new social secretary, Lea Berman. Berman had served in the campaign and was social secretary and then chief of staff to Lynne Cheney, who recommended her to Laura. Berman and her husband, Wayne, entertained extensively in the enormous Embassy Row mansion that was their home in Washington.

Johndroe wanted to move on to the State Department as a spokesman for Condi Rice. For her new press secretary, Laura chose Susan Whitson, who had been an FBI spokesperson and then deputy communications director for the campaign. Chef Walter Scheib was also leaving and made no secret of why.

"We've been trying to find a way to satisfy the first lady's stylistic requirements, and it has been difficult," Scheib told the *New York Times*. "Basically, I was not successful in my attempt." He went on to complain that while it is "an honor to serve the first family, it is the same thing, night in and night out, over an extended period. And it's time for me to be exploring all of my creative abilities and not limiting myself."

"Laura was not happy with him but didn't want a confrontation," Anne Stewart said. "I don't think he acceded to their wishes. Finally, it got to the point where she couldn't quite handle it."

In part, Laura had put off making a change because she had more pressing matters on her mind. She had read about a program in Dallas that helped teach juvenile boys responsibility by giving them dogs to care for. She was also inspired by a *New York Times Magazine* story about a young Milwaukee father, a former pimp and drug dealer, who struggled to give his son the father he himself never had. With those stories as a trigger, Laura began thinking about her own experience teaching inner-city children in Houston and Dallas.

Rather than promoting an existing program, she conceived one of her own, one that focused on the constellation of problems that young boys may have. Her primary goal, like her husband's, was to improve reading skills.

"In the earlier stages of the campaign," Condi Rice said, "I remember her mentioning the overwhelming sadness of what was happening to young men, particularly African American young men, and wanting to do something about that."

Called Helping America's Youth, the program consisted of existing administration initiatives that received increased funding and a new one—a $150 million, three-year mentoring effort to keep young people from joining gangs by giving them positive role models. Equally important, by visiting programs that were successful, Laura highlighted initiatives that could be adopted throughout the country. In Baltimore, for example, she visited George Washington Elementary School. There, she said, "Boys often begin to fall behind girls in elementary school, and they are more likely than girls to be arrested for crimes."

Laura highlighted the Good Behavior Game, a program that has been in effect at some Baltimore schools for twenty years. It divides students into teams and rewards them with points for staying on task in school. Inappropriate behavior is discouraged by awarding points to the opposing team. Students in the program are less likely to drop out than similar students in other schools.

In the middle of launching her new initiative, Laura helped Jenna move into an apartment she had rented with some friends in the Adams Morgan district of Washington.

"Laura told me that she went over to Jenna's new apartment, and she and Maria [Galvan] spent the day with Jenna," Regan Gammon said. "She said they totally got the curtains hung. And she said, 'We got this great-looking rug. Jenna cleaned out the refrigerator. And I went in and I really cleaned out under the sink. You know how I really love that.' "

On February 16, 2005, the *New York Times* and the *Washington Post* ran front-page photos of Laura visiting *The Gates*, an installation by artists Christo and Jeanne-Claude in New York's Central Park in which 7,500 saffron-colored cloth panels fluttered over twenty-three miles of footpaths. Laura commented that the atmosphere in the park made people feel like children at play. It reminded her of childhood experiences recounted in Marilynne Robinson's *Gilead,* a novel Pamela Nelson had given her as an inauguration present.

The caption in the *Post* said that Laura had gone to New York to visit a friend, while the *Times* called it a personal visit. In fact, Laura was in New York to be fitted for dresses for a presidential trip to meet with European leaders and Russian president Vladimir Putin. In part, the first lady began buying from Oscar de la Renta because it was more convenient to go to New York than to the salons of Texas designers she had been using. In New York, she could shop with Jenna and with Barbara, who was especially interested in fashion.

Besides seeing the designer, Anne Johnson suggested a visit to the Museum of Modern Art. After decades of volunteer work in Texas, Anne had accepted a position as director of ART in Embassies, a State Department program that supplies 180 American diplomatic residences around the world with works by American artists. The full-time job involved certain drawbacks. A year after taking the position in May 2001, Anne took a half day off to have lunch and visit gardens in Middleburg, Virginia, with Laura and other friends.

"When the first lady's motorcade returned midafternoon, the president was throwing [a] ball for Barney on the driveway," Johnson recalled. "I tried to sort of hide behind the car because I knew what was coming. He saw me and yelled out, 'Anne Johnson, why aren't you at work?' "[8]

Laura invited Anne on the trip to New York with Barbara. After the Central Park excursion, they had lunch at Orso, a trattoria on West Forty-sixth Street, with Roland and Lois Betts. Laura ordered the sautéed calf's liver sliced thin with crispy onions and pine nuts. Barbara was talking about her forthcoming trip to South Africa to work on a project helping victims of AIDS. During the lunch, she kept in touch with Jenna on her cell phone.

In one of his last statements as Laura's press secretary, Gordon John-droe told the media that the Bushes would be doing more entertaining during the second term. What he didn't say was that the additional entertaining would include a monthly theme party. The first was on Valentine's Day, when sixty guests came to a black-tie dinner in the Blue Room. The second was on St. Patrick's Day, and the third celebrated Shakespeare.

The day before the St. Patrick's Day party, Pamela Nelson arrived for her monthly visit. That night, she had dinner with George and Laura; Barbara and Jenna; Jenna's boyfriend Henry Hager; J. Thomas "Tom" Schieffer and his wife, Susanne; Marvin and Margaret Bush; and Debbie and Craig Stapleton. Stapleton was about to be named ambassador to France. Schieffer, an investor in the Rangers and later a general partner, was about to assume his post as ambassador to Japan.

Doug Wead, a former aide to Bush and to his father, and the author of a book on presidential children, had just made public secretly recorded phone conversations he had had with Bush during the first campaign. Wead was described in the media as a friend, but he was never in the inner circle.

"Who?" Terry Johnson said when his name was mentioned.

The tapes revealed Bush in unguarded moments to be remarkably like the public Bush. Saying evangelicals wanted him to attack gays, Bush said on the tapes, "I'm not going to kick gays, because I'm a sinner. How can I differentiate sin?" The tapes made it clear that while he might have tried marijuana, Bush had never used cocaine, as Kitty Kelley claimed in her book.

Asked by Katie Couric on the *Today* show about Wead and his secret taping, Laura said she thought it was "very odd and awkward."

While the subject did not come up at dinner, Debbie Stapleton, along with other Bush friends and relatives, was outraged. Wead is a "fool," Debbie said. "He probably lost one of the greatest friends he could have had in life. You don't treat a friend like that. He will not be trusted again."

After dinner in the residence, Bush hugged his two daughters. The talk turned to Miss Beazley, who had just been taken to visit a second-grade cancer patient whose dying wish was to see the puppy. The boy could barely pet him. Soon after the visit, the little boy died.

Unlike Barney, Beazley did not yet have free rein in the White House. At night, she was confined to a holding pen in the residence kitchen. Still, she managed to pee on the Oval Office carpet. Johndroe said Beazley was toilet trained, but newspapers were being spread around where she slept just in case. "She knows what to do with the papers, which is a prerequisite for all Bush appointees," he said.

Jenna's boyfriend Hager, who had worked on the campaign and was the son of former Virginia lieutenant governor John H. Hager, wanted everyone to watch a parody of Bush by black comedian Dave Chappelle. So George, Laura, the daughters, and their guests hovered over Barbara's laptop and watched Chappelle pretending to act the way Bush would act if he were black.

"I didn't think it was very funny, but the kids did," Nelson said.

Two days later, Pamela and Laura went to a luncheon given for Anita McBride, Laura's new chief of staff, at the Georgetown mansion of Bonnie McElveen-Hunter, whom Bush had appointed chair of the American Red Cross.

"The woman sitting next to me at lunch was Sandra Day O'Connor," Pamela Nelson said. "She could sit next to a nobody because she wasn't really trying to work the room. She was as high as she wanted to go."[9]

The Supreme Court justice had just been at the St. Patrick's Day party at the White House. O'Connor told Laura's friend from Midland that growing up, she lived on a ranch in Arizona thirty-five miles from the nearest town. In order to go to school, she'd had to live with her grandmother in El Paso.

"My grandmother never stopped talking as long as her eyes were open," O'Connor said. "So I learned pretty young to just go, 'Uh-hum, uh-hum.' Sometimes on the bench, I'll start doing it, and I'll say, 'I better listen. This is important.'"

Laura and Pamela visited the Corcoran Gallery of Art around the corner from the White House, where Laura often dropped in unannounced.

"When she visits a museum, its status in the art world goes way up," according to Henry Moran, executive director of the President's Committee on the Arts and the Humanities.

23

DESPERATE HOUSEWIFE

For the Easter weekend, George and Laura invited Anne and Clay Johnson, the twins, and Barbara's boyfriend Jay Blount to the ranch. President 41 and Barbara and Regan and Billy Gammon stayed over Saturday night. As usual, Billy brought his chain saw in a case, leaving it just outside his room overnight.

On Saturday afternoon, Bush, his father, Clay, and Jay went fishing for three hours in cold rain. They returned wet and muddy. Clay went back to his guesthouse at the ranch.

"President 41 knocked on our door," Anne Johnson said. "He wanted to know if Clay had any wet clothes to throw in with his. I collected Clay's things, handed them to the president, and he put them in the dryer."

"What was that?" Clay asked.

"The president is drying your clothes," Anne said.

At dinner, "President 41 told the first part of a joke and Bar finished it," Anne Johnson said. "He said he could not remember the ending, but it was a little off-color, and I think he just wanted her to tell it."

The girls had been making Easter eggs. After dinner, they styled their grandfather's hair and made it stand on end. After the styling, "He looked like Lyle Lovett," Anne Johnson said.

"When they all talk around the table, the girls tell these stories about how President 41 is adorable but not hip, and they just go, 'Gampy, oh Gampy!' " Pamela Nelson said. "They have a kind of a code, and they just say his name, and everyone just sighs."

The next morning when she woke up, Anne Johnson looked across the lake.

"I saw three men on bikes, one being the president, biking along the sun-drenched shoreline, and three security cars following behind," Anne said. "The president took a bad spill at the end of the ride, but got up and dusted himself off. Said he had braked too hard."[1]

Because of an injured knee, Bush gave up running and instead takes treks of sixteen miles or more on a mountain bike. He continues to work out six days a week.

On Sunday morning, Laura put on Marvin Gaye full blast as they sipped coffee with whipped cream on the porch. They went to church at Fort Hood, where Anne noticed how the twins sat with shoulders touching each other. As Bar was leaving on Sunday, Anne hugged her and said, "You are so sweet."

"No, I'm not," Bar said. "I'm not sweet, but I AM funny."

"The 41s just adore Laura, you can tell," Anne said. "They all worked on a puzzle the whole time, and on Sunday morning, I saw Laura moving all the pieces to the side. She said they would be back in two weeks to finish it."

"You know," Laura said, chuckling, "I have to dust the table."

Laura left on April 21, 2005, for Midland and Mexico, where she would attend the wedding of Antonio Garza Jr. near Valle de Bravo west of Mexico City. A former county judge, Garza had been Bush's secretary of state in Austin and was now the American ambassador to Mexico.

In Midland, Laura saw her mother and slept overnight on an uncomfortable foldout bed at Jenna Welch's new retirement home. Kathy Robbins, Jenna's friend, called Laura a "faithful daughter" because she saw her mother so often and phoned more than once a week. That night, Laura called Johnny Hackney, the owner of Johnny's Barbecue, to say hello. The next morning, stewards went to Johnny's to pick up enough barbecue beef, sausage, and ham, along with beans, potato salad, and coleslaw, for Laura's entourage of twenty-nine people. They ate it on the plane to Mexico.

On the Gulfstream jet, Laura practiced her lines for the forthcoming White House Correspondents Association dinner, asking her assistant Lindsey Lineweaver if she thought they were funny. Stories in the press said the administration had deployed the first lady to step in and do the comedy routine because her husband's approval rating was more than thirty points below hers. In fact, the decision was a lot less Machiavellian. It went back to a conversation near the end of January between Gordon Johndroe and Dan Bartlett, the White House communications director, who had just been promoted to presidential counselor.

"Dan and I were shooting the breeze, and he said he had agreed to the president giving speeches at the Gridiron Club, Alfalfa Club, Radio-Television Correspondents Association, White House Correspondents Association, and White House News Photographers dinners," Johndroe said. "That's an awful lot of speeches, which all have to be funny. So the president came up with the idea of Laura doing one of them and had already asked her."[2]

When Johndroe talked with Laura about it, she was less than eager but said she guessed she could do the Radio and TV dinner. That dinner was to be on a Wednesday and was not as high-profile as the White House Correspondents dinner.

"She agreed to do the dinner on April 6," Johndroe said. "But then Pope John Paul II died on April 2. Dick Cheney went instead. So she and the president rolled over her talk to the White House Correspondents dinner on April 30."

Landon Parvin had already written a speech for Laura for the Radio and TV dinner, so she delivered it to the White House correspondents. Cheney was left with few funny lines and devoted most of his speech to a tribute to the pope.

Besides going over her routine on the plane to Mexico, Laura rehearsed in the White House theater in front of Johndroe, Bartlett, Parvin, Susan Whitson, and Ed Walsh, Laura's new speechwriter.

Meanwhile, as part of her Helping America's Youth campaign, she visited Homeboy Industries in Los Angeles, a program founded by Father Gregory Boyle to help ex–gang members acquire job skills.

"Y'all write to me," the first lady said to the former gangbangers and ex-cons.

Two days later, the media reported a sighting of an ivory-billed woodpecker in Arkansas. For sixty years, the bird had been thought to be extinct. The bird was nicknamed the "Lord God" because that is what people exclaimed when they saw it.

Through her friend Deedie Rose and her husband, Rusty, Laura kept up-to-date on bird events. Rusty had a bird-watching plank that extended outside their house in Dallas. Laura had just visited Death Valley with Deedie and Regan Gammon to see the spectacular wildflowers. She knew about the woodpecker sighting well before it was announced.

At 6:30 A.M. Dallas time, Laura called Pamela Nelson and mentioned the story about the bird in that morning's *New York Times*. Pamela had not yet looked at her paper.

"The White House Correspondents dinner was the next day, but that was all she could talk about," Pamela said. "I said, 'Laura, I just don't know about it.' She said, 'Well, I know Bill knows about it.' " Laura was referring to Pamela's husband, who used to ride a bike to work to save fossil fuel and likes to travel to places like the Galápagos Islands to see blue-footed booby birds, turtles, and sea lions that are threatened with extinction.

The day of the dinner, Laura did a final rehearsal of her lines with

Parvin, working on the timing. Laura has a natural wit. Asked by a reporter whether she or the president answers the phone at the White House residence in the middle of the night, Laura said, "We have phones on both sides of the bed. He actually can pick up the telephone. He actually is very, very competent in a lot of ways." Just before one of her four appearances on Jay Leno's *Tonight Show*, Laura had been in Las Vegas. So, Leno asked, did the first lady hit the slots or look in on a Chippendale show while she was there?

"Jay, what happens in Vegas stays in Vegas," Laura deadpanned.

After dessert on Saturday night at the Washington Hilton, President Bush was at the podium and heading into a joke about a city slicker's encounter with a cowboy. Coming up behind him, Laura interjected, "Not that old joke—not again." The president, who did not know what his wife was going to say, sat down.

"George always says he's delighted to go to these press dinners," Laura continued. "Baloney. He's usually in bed by now." As her husband beamed, Laura described the Bushes' typical evening. "Nine o'clock: Mr. Excitement, here, is sound asleep," she said. "I'm watching *Desperate Housewives*—with Lynne Cheney. Ladies and gentlemen, I AM a desperate housewife. I mean, if those women on that show think they're desperate, they oughta be with George."

Laura suggested that she and George must have been destined to be together since "I was the librarian who spent twelve hours a day in the library—yet somehow, I met George."

She and her husband are very different, she said: "I can pronounce *nuclear*."

Noting that Andover and Yale don't have strong ranching programs, Laura said, "But I'm proud of George. He's learned a lot about ranching since the first year [at the Crawford ranch] when he tried to milk the horse." Pause. "What's worse, it was a male horse."

Laura went on to poke fun at her mother-in-law.

"So many mothers today are just not involved in their children's lives," the first lady said. "Not a problem with Barbara Bush . . . People think she's a sweet, grandmotherly, Aunt Bea type," referring to Andy Griffith's TV aunt in Mayberry. "She is more like Don Corleone," Laura said.

While conservatives grumbled about the off-color jokes, Laura got a standing ovation from the normally anti-Bush crowd of 3,000 journalists and Hollywood celebrities.

John McLaughlin called it the best material he had heard in thirty years of attending the dinner, which has featured as the main entertainment presidents since Calvin Coolidge.

"It came as a complete surprise, and it knocked everybody's socks off," said Senator Charles E. Schumer, the New York Democrat. "It's not going to make everybody say, 'We're for Social Security privatization now,' but around the edges, it helps."

"I thought I could follow the president," Cedric the Entertainer said. "But the first lady—that's something different."

While Laura is not a prude and laughs when her friends make joking sexual references, she has never seen the racy ABC show *Desperate Housewives*. But the twins are fans, and they had filled her in on the characters and plot.

The next day, President 41 called Laura at the White House. When Laura answered the phone, he said, "Hold for Don Corleone," and put Barbara on.

"You are the star of the nation!" Nancy Weiss said to Laura the next time they talked.

"I was just surprised that they thought it was that funny," Laura said.

The day before Laura was to leave for her trip to the Middle East at the end of March, new violence erupted in Israel. Laura called Condi Rice to ask if any changes should be made to her itinerary. Laura had wanted to go to Afghanistan long before the security experts approved.

"The trip could change minute by minute," said Pamela Nelson, who had just arrived for her monthly visit at the White House. That day, she was appointed vice chair of her arts commission under Earl A. Porter III, director of the National Gallery of Art.

Pamela found that, with Maria Galvan's help, Laura was organizing and cleaning her bookcases. They contained hundreds of books the first couple had bought or were given during their first four years in the White House.

"She had all the books out of the bookcases so Maria could clean them with Windex," Pamela said. "They were all on the floor in the hall." The president said to Pamela, "Can't you help her put this in alphabetical order?" Laura arranged them by subject matter.

"When she is tense, she cleans," Pamela said. "She finds it soothing."[3]

Nelson was the one to break the news to Bush that Barney that morning had bitten a Park Service worker who was trimming trees. The man had not previously been on the White House grounds and was playing with Barney, pulling a ball from his mouth. The terrier, whom Bush has described as the son he never had, nipped the man's finger.

"The president looked stricken, as if his beloved child was a murderer," Pamela said.

"Laura, was there blood?" Bush said. "Are they going to sue us?"

Laura had had her hair done that morning, and had more blond highlights put in. For the new term, she had switched to Toka Salon, where cuts are eighty dollars and color is seventy. Monica Lewinsky had been one of its clients. For the inauguration, Laura had used Kurt Anderson of the Garry Cox Salon in Dallas. Anderson, who was Debbie Francis's hairdresser, had traveled with the first lady to every inaugural event.

Because of her workouts, Laura thought her neck had gotten thicker. To the necklace of turquoise beads she planned to wear on the Middle East trip, Pamela attached a longer wire.

Pamela showed the first lady the May 16 issue of *Newsweek*, which contained an article about William McDonough, an architect who specialized in buildings that generate more energy than they consume. Because of Laura, the ranch in Crawford is ecologically friendly, with geothermal heating and cooling. Rainwater and household waste are reused for irrigation. Wildflowers and native grasses are allowed to flourish. The Bushes agreed to preserve several hundred acres of hardwood forest that is home to the rare golden-cheeked warbler.

Newsweek had just run an item claiming that an American prison guard at Guantánamo Bay, Cuba, had flushed a Koran down a toilet. The item was based on an account from a single source. After the article appeared, the source said he wasn't sure if such an incident was, in fact, going to be contained in a Pentagon report, as claimed in the original story. In point of fact, a publication far smaller than the Koran—say, an issue of *Newsweek*—was too large to be flushed down a toilet. Finally, the magazine's editors retracted the story. But by then, in Afghanistan and elsewhere, it had touched off anti-American rioting in which sixteen people died.

"We need to change perceptions," Laura said to Pamela the day before the Middle East trip. "Americans have made terrible mistakes, not understanding how insulting some things are and how they can have ripple effects around the world." But she said, in reference to the reaction to the *Newsweek* item, that the people who engaged in the killings also bore responsibility. Later, in a press briefing on the way to the Middle East, Laura described the *Newsweek* item as "irresponsible."

"I don't want to see it," Laura said when Pamela handed her the issue containing the article on architect William McDonough. "I don't want *Newsweek* around the house."

The next day, Laura took off for the Middle East. She toured the pyramids of Egypt and visited Israel's Western Wall. She boldly challenged the region to allow women into the political process and the workplace and to allow democracy to flourish. As with her reading initiative, Laura's message fit with her husband's, encouraging democracy throughout the world as an antidote to terrorism.

At the World Economic Forum in Jordan, Laura said new freedoms granted to women in Afghanistan, Iraq, Kuwait, and Morocco prove that equal rights are compatible with Islam and Arab culture.

"Women who have not yet won these rights are watching," she said on the bank of the Dead Sea. "Freedom, especially freedom for women, is more than the absence of oppression. It's the right to speak and vote and worship freely. Human rights require the rights of women. And human rights are empty promises without liberty."

At the Western Wall in Jerusalem, the first lady, dressed in black from head to toe, placed a handwritten note into a crevice of the wall and quietly prayed.

"Each life is precious," her note said. "Each memory calls us to action to honor those lost. We commit ourselves to reject hatred and to teach tolerance and live in peace."

While the first lady prayed in silence, dozens of protesters shouted, "Free Pollard Now!" Jonathan J. Pollard, who is serving a life sentence, was a Naval Investigative Service analyst who gave a roomful of classified documents to the Israelis in return for $50,000 in cash.[4] As the protesters surged toward her, Secret Service agents and Israeli police hustled Laura back into her car.

At a mosque next to the golden Dome of the Rock in Jerusalem, where the prophet Mohammed is said to have ascended into heaven, a Palestinian worshiper shouted at Laura: "How dare you come in here! Why your husband kill Muslim?"

Laura's friends watched news accounts of the trip with concern. When she returned, Pamela Nelson phoned her. Laura told her the media had overplayed the danger and heckling.

"She said it was a memorable trip and not all that scary," Pamela said.

In July 2005, George and Laura prepared to celebrate both the nation's birthday and the president's birthday by spending the weekend at Camp David. With them were Anne and Clay Johnson; Nancy and Mike Weiss; Debbie and Jim Francis; Penny Royall; Regan and Billy Gammon; Dr. Charles Younger and his wife, Francis; and Susie and Don Evans. They played golf, swam in the pool, soaked in a hot tub, and worked an Elms puzzle. George bicycled furiously along tree-shaded roads for fourteen miles with Secret Service cars in hot pursuit.

As usual, the president held his birthday party on July 4. The weekend guests and more than a hundred other friends gathered in the White House's East Ballroom for a buffet dinner of fried chicken, minihamburgers, fried onion rings, and salads. They watched the fireworks from the Truman Balcony.

Two days later, the *Washington Post* noted that on Independence Day, Bush and Laura appeared briefly on the Truman Balcony to wave to staffers and their family members who had been invited to watch the fireworks from the South Lawn. The story said that illusionist Wayne Alan, who performed at the event, told the paper that George and Laura never even made it down to the lawn. "Those Bushes really know how to party," the *Post* snickered.

Meanwhile, inside the White House, the guests were singing "Happy Birthday" to the president over a three-foot-long chocolate cake. On top of the cake was a three-dimensional chocolate bicycle.

Just over two weeks later, Bush nominated Appeals Court Judge John G. Roberts Jr. to the U.S. Supreme Court. The next evening, the president and Laura had dinner in the residence with Pamela Nelson, her husband, Bill, and interior designer Ken Blasingame.

Like some other Bush friends, Pamela thought Bush might nominate White House Counsel Harriet Miers to the court. The first woman president of the Texas State Bar, Miers was named by the *National Law Journal* in 1997 as one of the Hundred Most Influential Lawyers in America. Moreover, after NBC's *Today* interviewed Laura from Africa on July 12, headlines across the country said LAURA BUSH WANTS A WOMAN TO FILL THE SUPREME COURT VACANCY. But the story was taken out of context. During the NBC interview, Ann Curry had asked Laura, "Do you want your husband to name another woman to the Supreme Court?" Laura responded, "Sure. I would really like for him to name another woman, but . . . I know that my husband will pick somebody who has—has a lot of integrity and strength, and whether it's a woman or a man, of course, I have no idea."

Later that summer, Laura announced her own appointment: Cristeta Comerford, the first woman executive chef in White House history. Second youngest of eleven children, Comerford was a forty-two-year-old naturalized citizen from Manila. Chef Walter Scheib hired her in 1995 as an assistant chef.

While she considered hundreds of applicants and held several tastings prepared by front-runners, Laura had been leaning toward Comerford for months. Cris had proven herself on everything from the president's cheeseburgers to a dinner honoring Indian prime minister Manmohan Singh and his wife, at which the 134 guests dined on pan-roasted halibut with ginger-carrot butter and basmati rice with pistachio nuts and currants. Laura considered Comerford inventive and liked the idea of appointing a woman to the top culinary post in the country. The fact that Comerford was a minority didn't hurt. Bonnie Moore, president of Women Chefs & Restaurateurs, said the appointment "sends a message around the world. Women make up more than fifty percent of food-service workers but hold fewer than four percent of the top jobs. And this is the top job."

Almost immediately, more than five hundred requests for interviews with Comerford poured in to Susan Whitson, Laura's press secretary.

Visiting Laura and George in Crawford in the middle of August, Pamela mentioned that she had seen a letter to the editor saying that Laura had not gotten her way on the choice of a Supreme Court justice but instead appointed a female chef. Laura told Pamela she really didn't say she wanted her husband to choose a female for the high court. "I just answered a question, 'Would you like to see a woman appointed?' " Laura said. "I wasn't going to say, 'Heavens, no!' "

After a dinner that ended with peach shortcake, Jenna Welch, who also was staying at the ranch, suggested they watch TV, as is her habit. Laura said that would not be very peaceful, so Jenna suggested that instead they go outside and look for the first star visible in the night sky. As they walked almost half a mile to the front gate, Laura mentioned that the moon would be full two days later. She was holding on to her mother's arm, helping her to keep her balance.

"I never thought I'd have to lean on you like this," Jenna said.

"It's only been a year that I've had to help you," Laura said.

As they looked up at the big sky, Pamela thought to herself that she now understood where Laura picked up her love of nature. But two weeks later, Mother Nature showed her dark side, dealing a knockout blow to New Orleans and the Gulf states with Hurricane Katrina. As flood walls collapsed and levees were breached, New Orleans was flooded, killing more than a thousand people and rendering most of the city's nearly half million residents homeless.

The president cut short his vacation in Crawford and returned to the White House on August 31. Laura had planned to attend the wedding of Regan Gammon's son Stayton that weekend. Instead, she returned to Washington on Friday, September 2. On the way back, she visited the Cajundome in Lafayette, Louisiana, where more than six thousand evacuees from New Orleans were being sheltered.

The night before, Debbie Francis and Katharine Armstrong were with Laura at the ranch as she packed. They tried to watch the tragedy unfold on Fox, but for reasons unknown, the cable channels were out of sync and they could only watch CNN. Laura was getting faxed updates from her office, and she talked with her husband as well.

Besides feeling the devastation that everyone felt, Laura knew that both she and the president would be shouldering the task of leading the nation toward recovery. At one point, Laura began going through bookshelves, dusting off books and weeding out duplicates. Briefly, her right hand trembled, a sign of her stress. But she displayed her usual resolve. When Katharine, whose mother, Anne Armstrong, grew up in New Orleans, said the city would never be rebuilt, Laura disagreed.

"San Francisco was demolished and rebuilt," Laura said, referring to the city's 1906 earthquake and fire that burned for four days. After the Great Fire of 1871, "Chicago was demolished and rebuilt," she said. "New Orleans will be rebuilt."

After Chief Justice William Rehnquist died, Bush nominated John Roberts as chief justice. He later nominated Harriet Miers to the Court to replace Sandra Day O'Connor. Bush withdrew Miers's nomination after she came under withering fire from conservatives. Then on October 28, a federal grand jury indicted I. Lewis "Scooter" Libby, Dick Cheney's chief of staff, for allegedly lying and obstructing justice in connection with the investigation into the disclosure of covert CIA officer Valerie Plame's name.

With Bush's approval rating at a low of 40 percent, the media depicted the White House as distraught and distracted. But they never got what Bush was all about. He did not seek office to win popularity or Chris Matthews's approval. He ran to achieve long-term fundamental change that would leave the country and the world a better, safer place. Like Warren Buffett, Bush kept his eyes on the horizon. Buffett invests in companies he believes have long-term growth potential. He holds on to those stocks regardless of short-term price fluctuations, negative media coverage, and downgrades by stock analysts. Today, Buffett is the second richest American, with $40 billion in assets.

Nor was Bush particularly interested in his place in history. Like any good CEO, he simply wanted results and viewed challenges as opportunities. But he was also aware of how transitory opinion polls can be. When Harry Truman left office, his approval rating stood at 25 percent. Yet today, because of his firm approach to national security, Truman—whom the press portrayed as a simpleton—is viewed as one of the great presidents.

"Instead of approaching each day saying, 'How do I get through the day?,' the president approaches problems by saying, 'How do we solve the problem?' " observed Ken Mehlman, who was director of White House political affairs and became chairman of the Republican National Committee. "Franklin Roosevelt did the same thing for the country. Ronald Reagan did that for the country."

Just before they were to have a tasting in the White House for an impending dinner in honor of Prince Charles and his wife, Camilla, Laura mentioned to Pamela Nelson that a friend had called her and said, "How *are* you?" in a voice of doom. Laura had a bemused expression on her face, suggesting the friend did not get it, either.

That night at dinner, the president was his usual ebullient self. While he was said by the media to be incurious, he pummeled a guest from Boston with questions about what had been going on lately in the city where Bush attended graduate school.

The following week, Adair Margo stayed two nights in the White House. Bush had just finished working out on the third floor at 5:30 P.M. when he heard Adair talking on the phone to her son Wake.

"Who's there?" Bush bellowed jokingly.

Laura was excited about the conference she had arranged at

Howard University as part of her Helping America's Youth initiative. The conference brought together five hundred researchers and other experts to share findings on successful methods to help kids at risk. At dinner in the residence the night before, Laura ruefully mentioned that Jason DeParle, the journalist whose *New York Times Magazine* piece had contributed to her decision to start the initiative, had just interviewed her. She said he seemed to be skeptical that someone like her—a first lady who is white—could relate to the problems of black youth.

The next day, Bush introduced his wife at the conference, and four of Bush's cabinet secretaries spoke. Laura introduced the Community Guide to Helping America's Youth, an Internet tool that allows people to find programs that help youth in their communities. Several speakers stressed the need to reintroduce a comprehensive reading instruction program—which includes phonics—to schools. Without being able to read, they said, kids develop diminished self-esteem, leading to behavior problems and setting them up for failure throughout their lives. But only the *Washington Times* covered the substance of the conference.

Kenyatta Q. Thigpen, the former drug dealer and pimp who was the subject of Jason DeParle's original article, sat ten feet away from Laura. DeParle's article the next day in the *New York Times* focused largely on Thigpen's anger that he was still only a pizza delivery man in Milwaukee and had given up two days of wages because he accepted the White House's offer of a plane ticket and lodging at a Hilton to attend the conference.

"The first lady has hope for young people struggling with problems," Adair said. "And they are making it. But then to have this reporter say in essence, 'You can't have hope.' It's so sad."

But being first lady has its compensations. Laura invited more than a half dozen of her friends to the 128-guest dinner for Prince Charles and Camilla. They dined on buffalo tenderloin, roasted corn, and wild rice pancakes. Afterward, cellist Yo-Yo Ma performed. The guests included an eclectic mix of celebrities and digni-taries ranging from Nancy Reagan and Chief Justice John Roberts to Kelsey Grammer and Tom Brokaw. But the presence of the Bush friends and the comfortable ambience made it seem like "going to someone's house for a very nice dinner," observed Katharine Arm-strong.

The royals were impressed. Thanking the Bushes in his toast, Prince Charles said he and his wife were especially grateful for their hospitality because the prince is "only too conscious of the enormous challenges and responsibilities which face the forty-third president of the United States. And I need hardly say that so many people throughout the world look to the United States of America for a lead on the most crucial issues that face our planet and, indeed, the lives of our grandchildren. Truly, the burdens of the world rest on your shoulders."

In private, the Prince of Wales and the Duchess of Cornwall were equally effusive in their praise, and Laura's dinner arrangements par-ticularly impressed them. To Donald Ensenat, the chief of protocol who accompanied the royals on trips outside of Washington, the prince's private secretary volunteered: "We could learn a thing or two from this."

Meanwhile, as Bush finally went on the offensive against Demo-crats who called for an immediate pullout from Iraq and voted against extending key provisions of the Patriot Act, the president's approval rating shot up to 50 percent, comparable to his winning margin of 51 percent in the 2004 election.

24

A VISIT BY THE FIRST LADY

I n October 2002, Condoleezza Rice was standing with President
Bush in the Oval Office discussing new terrorist threats against
the White House and other key targets. Vice President Dick
Cheney had already been taken to an undisclosed location.

Bush straightened and stood a little taller as he said to Rice: "You
know, they're going to have to come get me right here."[1]

A year earlier, on October 19, 2001, Laura had been at the ranch
with her friend Debbie Francis while George was in China. Laura's
Secret Service detail informed the women of a threat they had
picked up.

"They had me move from the guesthouse into the main house in
case we had to evacuate quickly," Debbie recalled. "I stayed in one
of the girls' rooms. For that one night, they didn't want us to have
any lights on in the house. So we closed all the curtains and just had
a little candle burning." Throughout the ordeal, Laura remained "totally calm," she said.[2]

It was against that backdrop of personal risk that both Laura and
her husband withstood daily vilification in the media. Bush was portrayed as a buffoon, a religious fanatic, or a monster with the temer-
ity to topple a man who had killed 300,000 people and to liberate 50

million people. Laura was described as a brainless Stepford wife who, according to detractors like Teresa Heinz, had never had "a real job."

Journalists and academics love stereotypes. Thus, Laura was said to be a "traditional wife" or a "traditional first lady." Even after she spoke out about the phony CBS documents concerning her husband's National Guard service, called *Newsweek*'s item about the Koran and Guantánamo Bay "irresponsible," and said the Democrats were leading a "witch hunt" against her husband over the National Guard issue, *Time* in its May 16, 2005, issue called Laura "the least outspoken first lady since Pat Nixon." Even though Laura turned the attention of the administration to global women's rights, liberals derided her as a prefeminist figure.

Writing in the *Detroit Free Press*, columnist Susan Ager described herself as a nontraditional woman who pitied Laura Bush's "placidity." Ager said, "She's demure. She's careful. And here's the nut of it: She knows her place."

"When I hear this, I realize how completely out of touch these people are with reality," said Ed Klein, a *Vanity Fair* contributing editor and author of a recent biography of Hillary Clinton. "Because we all know, and most of the country knows, that Laura Bush is a very smart, capable figure in this administration who has influence and has indeed accomplished a great deal. The fact that she doesn't fit the mold of the elite liberal class, in which women who claim to be feminists must also be aggressive in their behavior and their choice of language, just indicates how out of touch with the rest of the country these people are."

When talking with Pamela Nelson about these misperceptions, Laura said, "I'm the first first lady who made a radio address," referring to her November 17, 2001, address about brutality against Afghan women. "If Hillary Clinton had done that, they would have said she was trying to take over the presidency."[3]

While Laura's soft manner and Texas drawl have contributed to the misperceptions, prejudice has also played a role, just as it contributed to the caricatures of her husband.

"The East Coast prejudice is that if you're from Texas, you can't string two thoughts together," Pamela Nelson said.

For twenty years, Myra G. Gutin has taught a course on first ladies at Ryder College in New Jersey. In her 1989 book *The President's Partner*, she sorted first ladies into three categories: ceremonial wife (Bess Truman, Mamie Eisenhower), whose role was said to be mostly entertaining; emerging spokeswoman (Jacqueline Kennedy, Pat Nixon), who promoted issues important to them; and activist (Eleanor Roosevelt, Betty Ford).

While such theories give academics something to write about, they do not contribute much to an understanding of the subject. Like racial stereotyping, placing labels on people distorts the truth by focusing attention on apparent similarities while shifting attention from differences. Thinking outside the box requires looking at the world objectively rather than through a prefocused lens. For that reason, journalists and academics have had difficulty comprehending the unconventional approaches that Bush has taken to deal with the unique threat of terrorists who have no territory, don't care if they're killed, and are trying to acquire weapons of mass destruction.

Growing up in Midland, weathering sandstorms, Laura Bush had no idea she would become first lady of the United States. But the values she learned prepared her for the job and gave her the strength to support her husband as he faced relentless partisan attacks while shouldering the burden of keeping the country safe.

After 9/11, she became the comforter-in-chief, reassuring a frightened nation. Her intellect and good judgment have helped inform Bush's decisions and guide his actions and public comments. Doggedly, she has pursued initiatives to help kids learn to read and to help troubled youths earn a living. This Laura was the same one who went in on her own time on Saturdays to teach remedial reading to black kids in Houston. The Laura who told her high school boyfriend Harvey Kennedy "don't contradict me" was the same one who spoke out when the media demonized her husband. The same Laura who experienced the pain of causing the death of one of her best friends has never lost sight of the need to console the families of soldiers who died defending freedom.

From the woman who requested a podium to hide behind when she was to give a speech to Republican women in Dallas, Laura catapulted to star of the White House Correspondents Association dinner.

"She is getting better at having an impact," Craig Stapleton said. "When she talked about the Afghan women, she was just getting used to being first lady. Now that she has done it successfully, she really understands the power of the position. And she is going to use it." At the same time, since 9/11, George and Laura have "grown incredibly closer," Stapleton said. "She is just there with solid judgment about people and issues, and she knows George W. obviously backward and forward. I can't see how he could have done the job he has done without having her there."

"She has developed parts of herself that she may not have realized were even in there," Penny Royall said. "She has added to the person she was when I met her. But she has not lost those qualities that made her a wonderful friend thirty years ago."

"She doesn't have this ego," Pamela Nelson said. "She feels she has this short time in the White House to really make a difference— not [that] she has this time to promote herself."

Nancy Weiss expressed amazement that Laura has not become "spoiled," given the fact that "if she just voices an idea, it happens. But she is unaffected by it."[4]

Regan Gammon remembered only one time when Laura expressed a regret.

"When her dad had Alzheimer's and George was inaugurated as governor the first time, it had progressed to the point where her dad wasn't aware of what was going on," Regan said. "She said after he died, 'Maybe we should have taken him to Austin in a wheelchair. Maybe he would have been aware of more than we realized.' "[5]

"The word *wish* doesn't compute with Laura," Pamela Nelson said. "She doesn't wish for what isn't. She is very practical. She just deals with what is. She lives her life with a lot of gratitude."

Those who wonder how both Laura and George have remained so grounded can find a clue in their faith. "Part of what faith is is believing in God to make you humble," said Laura's friend the Reverend Kathi Card. "Understanding that it's not all about you. Those two understand that it's not all about them. They have good healthy egos, but they know it's so much larger than them."[6]

Through it all, Laura has kept her priorities straight: Her family and friends always come first. Her faith in America and optimism about the future are as unshakable as her husband's. And she has never lost the sense of wonder she feels about having the privilege of being first lady.

"She didn't aspire to be the first lady," Andy Card said. "I don't think that she aspires to be any more than Mrs. George W. Bush and a great mother to two beautiful daughters and to be a good citizen. We all know that politics is not her first, second, or third love. It may not even be in the top ten. She loves her husband, her daughters, her friends. She loves people."[7]

"I think the truth about Laura," said her friend Marge Petty, "is she fits wherever she is. I don't know that I know anybody that has more presence and more calm and more compassion. Her world is not about her. Her world is about what's around her."

"Some people go through life saying, 'It's not how I'm doing that's important as long as somebody else is doing worse,' " Don Evans said. "That's not Laura. She is always trying to find the good and the strength in other people. She is not trying to find the bad things or ways to criticize them."[8]

Laura "embraces whatever life brings her," Penny Royall said. "I don't think ever in her wildest dreams would she have imagined being in the White House, nor would she have sought it. But when life presented her with these opportunities, she said yes."[9]

At a dedication of Kentucky towns as historic communities in April 2004, Laura was asked to define her public role.

"Well, I don't really like the word *role*," she said, "because it sounds like an act that you're playing." What really happens, she said, is "we watch the people in the White House live their lives, and we learn lessons from them."

If that is so, Laura's lessons amount to a self-help book on life and its challenges. Rather than fitting neatly into one of Professor Gutin's conceptual boxes, both as role model and counselor to her husband, Laura as first lady is in a class by herself.

"In many respects, she epitomizes what President Bush refers to as the American spirit," said Harriet Miers, one of Laura's friends. "She did not choose to be a celebrity or to be in the limelight. She chose a service profession based on a keen intellect—teacher and librarian—and finds herself a perfect leading lady for the country, a perfect role model for young Americans. I daresay her strength, intelligence, composure, and genuineness endear her to all Americans except the most partisan."

In the end, a child had the best perspective. Preparing first graders for a visit by the first lady in Baltimore, Dr. Reid Lyon, Bush's reading adviser, was letting the kids know what to expect when she arrived.[10]

"I know her," said a six-year-old black girl. "She is the teacher of the whole world!"

ACKNOWLEDGMENTS

My wife, Pamela Kessler, is my partner in life and in writing books. A former *Washington Post* reporter and author of *Undercover Washington: Where Famous Spies Lived, Worked, and Loved,* she pre-edits my work and informs my decisions with her intellect and good judgment. If Pam had not supported my wish to leave newspapers and enter the risky business of writing books, this project might never have happened.

My grown children, Rachel and Greg Kessler, round out the picture with their love and support. My stepson, Mike Whitehead, is a loyal and endearing part of that team.

My agent, Robert Gottlieb, chairman of Trident Media Group, came up with the idea for this book. I am lucky to have him on my side.

Adam Bellow, executive editor at large of Doubleday, provided excellent editorial ideas at critical points along the way, turned the book into a better read with his deft editing, and enriched the tale with incisive questions that brought out new material.

Having written *A Matter of Character: Inside the White House of George W. Bush,* on which the White House cooperated, I should have had an easy time obtaining cooperation for a book on the first lady. Wrong. The public-relations people were focused on the campaign, and who wants to take a chance that a book about the president's wife might go awry? Into the breach stepped Laura's close friend Anne Sewell Johnson, who mentioned the project to Laura and began helping. Anne's husband, Clay Johnson III, Bush's friend from Andover, roommate at Yale, chief of staff when he was governor, and head of presidential personnel at the White House, had been my rabbi on the previous book. Anne provided phone numbers, leads, insights, and anecdotes. She has a sophisticated understanding of what's needed to make a good book. When friends or aides were hesitant to talk, she vouched for me. I called her my blond rabbi.

Laura had never cooperated on a book before, and her overwhelming modesty made her hesitate. But once she did, I became privy to a secret world that neither she nor her husband had allowed any outsiders to see. Either by checking with her directly or by going through Gordon Johndroe and later Susan Whitson, friends, family members, and aides got the word that the first lady thought it would be fine if they talked with me. Most had not talked to the media since before George Bush had entered the White House. Others, like Laura's former boyfriends and Judy Dykes Hester, who was in the accident with her at the age of seventeen, had never talked to the media. Laura's only desire, as related to me by Gordon, was that the book be accurate.

Pamela Nelson was the second close friend to help. Along with Pamela and Anne, Laura's close friend Nancy Weiss and Andrea G. "Andi" Ball, her chief of staff for ten years, went out of their way to make sure I got an accurate, inside portrait. In obtaining cooperation, I also received crucial help from Dan Bartlett, Gordon Johndroe, Margaret Spellings, and Collister "Terry" Johnson Jr.

Besides the remarkable level of cooperation, what made all the difference was the fact that the people around Laura Bush tended to be exceptionally smart, insightful individuals who were good at telling anecdotes. To the extent that the book succeeds, they and Laura Bush herself are responsible. I am grateful to them.

Those who were interviewed or helped in other ways included:

Charles Aiken, Don Aiken, Leilani Akwai, Oren Albright, Katharine Armstrong, Andrea G. "Andi" Ball, Jackie Stubblefield Ball, Dan Bartlett, Robert Battle, Dr. James H. Billington, Kenneth Blasingame, Joshua B. Bolten, Mary Bowhay, Marvin S. Brettingen, Nancy Brinker, Beth Ann Bryan, Laura Bush, Patty Bush, Andrew H. Card Jr., Reverend Kathleene Card, Alice Carrington, Kirk Casselman, Tony Chauveaux, Jane Purucker Clarke, Dalton H. Cobb, John V. Cogbill III, Betty Clarkson Conkling, Dewey W. "Skip" Corley, Dr. Rex Cowdry, Dr. Rebecca "Becky" Curtis, James K. Davis, Polly Chapell Davis.

Ambassador Robert J. "Rob" Dieter, Sharon Dodson, Sandra Moore-Dyrenforth, Dr. Harryette Ehrhardt, Ralph W. Ellis, Ambassador Donald B. Ensenat, Taylor Ensenat, Donald Etra, Jeffrey Eubank, Donald L. Evans, Susie Marinis Evans, Catherine S. "Cathy" Fenton, Mary Finch, Debbie Francis, James B. "Jim" Francis Jr., Regan Kimberlin Gammon, Christine Mast Gilbert, Dana Gioia, Bill Godwin, Rebecca "Becky" Turner Gonzales, Dennis Grubb, Tobia Hochman Gunesch, Vestophia Gunnells, Johnny W. Hackney, Judy Harbour, Bill Harlow, Erin E. Healy, Anne Heiligenstein, Mary Herman, Israel J. "Izzy" Hernandez, Judy Dykes Hester, Janet Kinard Heyne, Winton Holladay, David Holt, Martha Holton, Betsy Hurt, Marcia Jackson, Gordon Johndroe, Anne Sewell Johnson, Clay Johnson III.

Collister "Terry" Johnson Jr., Liz Johnson, Harvey Kennedy, Ed Klein, Felicia Knight, Dorothy "Doro" Bush Koch, Barnett Alexander "Sandy" Kress, James C. Langdon Jr., Sandy Langdon, Jay Lefkowitz, Isaac Lopez, Dr. G. Reid Lyon, Adrienne Abrahamson Madrid, Adair Margo, Marie Dodson Maxwell, Anita McBride, Delaney McCaghren, Jamie McCaghren, Robert D. McCallum Jr., Jimmy McCarroll, Robert McCleskey, Dr. John P. McElligott, Ken

Mehlman, Harriet Miers, Emily J. Miller, Henry Moran, Bill Nelson, Pamela Hudson Nelson, Noam Neusner, Jan Donnelly O'Neill, Raymond H. Patton, Marge McColl Petty, James Powell, Candice Poague Reed, William Addams Reitwiesner, Dr. Condoleezza Rice, Arland W. Richards, Krista Ritacco, Kathy Robbins, W. B. "Trey" Robbins III.

Noelia Rodriguez, Deedie Rose, Karl Rove, Penny Royall, Robert A. Shaheen, Tammy Smith, Margaret Spellings, Craig R. Stapleton, Debbie Stapleton, Anne Lund Stewart, Dr. William Stixrud, Ambassador Vygaudas Ušackas, Elsie Walker, Nicole Wallace, Peter Wehner, J. Michael "Mike" Weiss, Nancy Weiss, Peggy Porter Weiss, Ron Weiss, Mary Mark Welch, Susan D. Whitson, Ambassador Pam Willeford, Victoria "Vicki" Wilson, Linda Mills Wofford, Michael M. Wood, Bill Young, Dr. Charles M. Younger, Fred S. Zeidman.

NOTES

PROLOGUE

1. Andrea G. "Andi" Ball, February 8, 2004.

2. Pamela Hudson Nelson, October 21, 2004.

3. Gordon Johndroe, December 7, 2004.

4. Donald L. Evans, March 28, 2005.

5. Ed Klein, December 20, 2004.

6. Craig Stapleton, December 21, 2004.

7. Andrew H. "Andy" Card, March 10, 2005.

8. Condoleezza Rice, March 29, 2005.

CHAPTER I

1. Memo of May 14, 1945, from Major General Terry Allen to Lieutenant Colonel Sayward H. Farnum, commanding officer, 555th Anti-Aircraft Artillery Battalion, U.S. Army.

2. Jan Donnelly O'Neill, January 5, 2005.

3. Janet Kinard Heyne, December 13, 2004.

4. Mary Mark Welch, March 12, 2005.

5. Mary Mark Welch, March 12, 2005.

6. Kathy Robbins, January 9, 2005.

7. Jackie Stubblefield Ball, April 20, 2005.

8. Martha Holton, January 3, 2005.

9. *Midland Reporter-Telegram*, September 2, 2002.

10. Tammy Smith, January 3, 2005.

CHAPTER 2

1. Susie Marinis Evans, January 5, 2005.

2. Linda Mills Wofford, November 22, 2004.

3. Christine Mast Gilbert, December 12, 2004.

4. Susie Marinis Evans, January 5, 2005.

5. Dorothy "Doro" Bush Koch, April 26, 2005.

6. Barbara Bush, *Barbara Bush: A Memoir*, page 45.

7. Elsie Walker, February 4, 2005.

8. Antonia Felix, *Laura*, page 29.

9. Marge McColl Petty, December 28, 2004.

10. Pamela Hudson Nelson, October 21, 2004.

CHAPTER 3

1. Regan Kimberlin Gammon, February 6, 2005.

2. Ann Gerhart, *The Perfect Wife*, page 25.

3. As an editor of the Clark University student newspaper, the author called landlords and agents who had advertised rental apartments in Worcester, Massachusetts, and asked if their apartments were still for rent. Told that they were, the author said, "By the way, my roommate happens to be a Negro. I wonder if you would have any objection?" Of twenty-six landlords or agents, nearly 40 percent said they would object. *Clark Scarlet*, October 3, 1963, page 1.

4. Don Aiken, October 16, 2004.

5. Linda Mills Wofford, November 22, 2004.

6. Candy Poague Reed, December 4, 2004.

7. Peggy Porter Weiss, February 6, 2005.

8. Harvey Kennedy, November 28, 2004.

CHAPTER 4

1. Judy Dykes Hester, October 24, 2004.

2. Harvey Kennedy, November 28, 2004.

3. Dewey "Bud" Corley, February 24, 2005.

4. Regan Kimberlin Gammon, February 6, 2005.

5. Judy Dykes Hester, October 24, 2004, and February 5, 2005.

6. *Midland Reporter-Telegram*, November 8, 1963, page 3B.

7. Regan Kimberlin Gammon, February 6, 2005.

8. Jan Donnelly O'Neill, January 5, 2005.

9. Judy Dykes Hester, November 28, 2004.

CHAPTER 5

1. Sandra Moore-Dyrenforth, November 22, 2004.

2. Janet Kinard Heyne, December 13, 2004.

3. Pamela Hudson Nelson, October 2, 2004.

4. Harryette Ehrhardt, April 1, 2005.

5. Kitty Kelley, *The Family: The Real Story of the Bush Dynasty*, page 575.

6. Susan Byerly Nowlin, November 29, 2004.

7. *Wall Street Journal*, September 28, 2004. Nash declined to be interviewed for this book.

8. Jane Purucker Clarke, January 15, 2005.

9. Janet Kinard Heyne, December 16, 2004.

10. Mary Mark Welch, March 12, 2005.

CHAPTER 6

1. Janet Kinard Heyne, December 13, 2004.

2. Jimmy McCarroll, October 2, 2004.

3. Ralph W. Ellis, January 15, 2005.

CHAPTER 7

1. Judy Harbour, May 4, 2005.

2. Donald B. Ensenat, March 5, 2005.

3. Elsie Walker, February 4, 2005.

4. Jan Donnelly O'Neill, January 5, 2005.

5. Donald B. Ensenat, March 5, 2005.

6. Dorothy "Doro" Bush Koch, April 26, 2005.

7. Dorothy "Doro" Bush Koch, April 26, 2005.

8. Debbie Stapleton, February 26, 2005.

9. Janet Kinard Heyne, January 26, 2005.

10. Anne Lund Stewart, February 16, 2005.

CHAPTER 8

1. Dr. Charles M. Younger, January 5, 2005.

2. Mary Bowhay, April 20, 2005.

3. Nancy Weiss, April 18, 2005.

4. Regan Kimberlin Gammon, April 18, 2005.

5. Donald L. Evans, March 28, 2005.

CHAPTER 9

1. Nancy Weiss, January 4, 2005.

2. Dr. Charles M. Younger, January 5, 2005.

3. Jan Donnelly O'Neill, January 5, 2005.

4. *Washington Post,* July 25, 1999, page A1.

5. Winton Holladay, February 13, 2005.

6. Deedie Rose, March 15, 2005.

7. "Junior Is His Own Bush Now," *Time,* July 31, 1989, page 60.

8. Donald L. Evans, February 23, 2005.

9. Anne Sewell Johnson, September 24, 2004.

CHAPTER 10

1. Margaret Spellings, December 1, 2004.

2. Anne Heiligenstein, December 18, 2004.

3. Andrea G. "Andi" Ball, February 8, 2005.

4. Barnett Alexander "Sandy" Kress, December 27, 2004.

5. Adair Margo, October 4, 2004.

6. Pamela Hudson Nelson, April 2, 2005.

7. Penny Royall, January 21, 2005.

8. Anne Lund Stewart, February 16, 2005.

9. Anne Sewell Johnson, January 18, 2005.

10. Robert McCleskey, January 5, 2005.

CHAPTER 11

1. Donald L. Evans, February 23, 2005.

2. *Texas Magazine,* in the *Houston Chronicle,* July 20, 1997, page 8.

3. Nancy Weiss, January 4, 2004.

4. Noelia Rodriguez, February 11, 2005.

5. Andrea G. "Andi" Ball, February 8, 2005.

CHAPTER 12

1. Dr. G. Reid Lyon, September 30, 2005.

2. Beth Ann Bryan, December 20, 2004.

3. Nancy Brinker, March 2, 2005.

4. Dr. James H. Billington, March 29, 2005.

5. Pam Willeford, December 20, 2004.

CHAPTER 13

1. Joshua B. Bolten, April 15, 2005.

2. Dorothy "Doro" Bush Koch, April 26, 2005.

3. Marcia Jackson, March 15, 2005.

4. Rebecca Turner "Becky" Gonzales, March 2, 2005.

5. Adair Margo, October 4, 2004.

6. *New York Times,* October 11, 2002, A31.

7. Robert McCleskey, January 5, 2005.

8. Kenneth Blasingame, April 12, 2005.

CHAPTER 14

1. Collister "Terry" Johnson Jr., September 16, 2004.

2. *Austin-American Statesman,* June 8, 2001, page A1.

3. Regan Kimberlin Gammon, April 29, 2005.

4. Israel J. "Izzy" Hernandez, May 24, 2005.

5. Craig Stapleton, December 21, 2004.

6. Anne Sewell Johnson, January 21, 2005.

CHAPTER 15

1. Andrea G. "Andi" Ball, February 8, 2005.

2. Kathleene Card, March 21, 2005.

3. Katharine Armstrong, December 6, 2004.

4. Nancy Weiss, January 4, 2005.

5. Dr. Condoleezza Rice, March 29, 2005.

6. Catherine S. Fenton, March 30, 2005.

7. Joshua B. Bolten, April 15, 2005.

8. Fred S. Zeidman, April 20, 2005.

9. Craig Stapleton, December 21, 2004.

CHAPTER 16

1. Dana Gioia, February 10, 2005.

2. Clay Johnson III, February 22, 2005.

3. Henry Moran, February 14, 2005.

CHAPTER 17

1. Pamela Hudson Nelson, October 2, 2004.

2. JaneAnn Fontenot, January 18, 2005.

3. Regan Kimberlin Gammon, February 6, 2005.

4. Craig Stapleton, February 26, 2005.

5. Andrew H. "Andy" Card, March 10, 2005.

6. Victoria "Vicki" Wilson, November 20, 2004.

7. Peggy Porter Weiss, February 6, 2005.

8. Sandy Langdon, January 25, 2005.

CHAPTER 18

1. Andrew H. "Andy" Card Jr., March 10, 2005.

2. Israel J. "Izzy" Hernandez, May 24, 2005.

3. Pamela Hudson Nelson, May 2, 2005.

4. Donald L. Evans, February 23, 2005.

5. Adair Margo, April 20, 2005.

6. Dr. Condoleezza Rice, May 29, 2005.

CHAPTER 19

1. Dr. Rebecca "Becky" Curtis, March 6, 2005.

2. Leilani Akwai, May 7, 2005.

3. Donald Etra, August 9, 2003.

4. Debbie Stapleton, February 26, 2005.

5. Winton Holladay, February 13, 2005.

6. Pamela Hudson Nelson, November 2, 2004.

7. Alice Carrington, February 3, 2005.

8. Penny Royall, January 21, 2005.

9. Nancy Weiss, January 8, 2005.

10. Dr. Charles Younger, January 5, 2005.

11. Anne Sewell Johnson, October 15, 2004.

CHAPTER 20

1. James B. "Jim" Francis Jr., February 11, 2005.

2. Harvey Kennedy, November 28, 2004.

3. Collister "Terry" Johnson Jr., September 16, 2004.

4. Clay Johnson III, September 26, 2003.

5. Sandy Langdon, January 25, 2005.

CHAPTER 21

1. Dorothy "Doro" Bush Koch, April 26, 2005.

2. Anne Sewell Johnson, November 3, 2004.

3. Donald L. Evans, March 28, 2005.

4. Israel J. "Izzy" Hernandez, May 24, 2005.

5. Karl Rove, November 11, 2004.

6. Pamela Hudson Nelson, November 19, 2004.

7. Mary Mark Welch, March 12, 2005; Christopher Andersen, *George and Laura: Portrait of an American Marriage*, facing page 196.

8. Kathy Robbins, January 9, 2005.

9. Jamie McCaghren, January 4, 2005.

10. Vygaudas Ušackas, May 23, 2005.

11. Dr. Condoleezza Rice, March 29, 2005.

12. Deedie Rose, March 15, 2005.

13. Janet Kinard Heyne, February 16, 2005.

14. Sharon Dodson, February 19, 2005.

15. Pamela Hudson Nelson, January 7, 2005.

16. Regan Kimberlin Gammon, February 6, 2005.

CHAPTER 22

1. Gordon Johndroe, February 15, 2005.

2. Taylor Ensenat, March 5, 2005.

3. Anne Lund Stewart, February 5, 2005.

4. Regan Kimberlin Gammon, February 6, 2005.

5. Dr. Charles Younger, January 5, 2005.

6. Craig Stapleton, February 26, 2005.

7. Debbie Francis, February 7, 2005.

8. Anne Sewell Johnson, November 3, 2004.

9. Pamela Hudson Nelson, March 24, 2005.

CHAPTER 23

1. Anne Sewell Johnson, March 28, 2005.

2. Gordon Johndroe, May 19, 2005.

3. Pamela Hudson Nelson, May 21, 2005.

4. *The Bureau*, Ronald Kessler, page 207.

CHAPTER 24

1. Dr. Condoleezza Rice, March 29, 2005.

2. Debbie Francis, December 13, 2004.

3. Pamela Hudson Nelson, October 21, 2004.

4. Nancy Weiss, January 4, 2005.

5. Regan Kimberlin Gammon, February 6, 2005.

6. The Reverend Kathleene Card, March 21, 2005.

7. Andrew H. "Andy" Card Jr., March 10, 2005.

8. Donald L. Evans, March 28, 2005.

9. Penny Royall, January 21, 2005.

10. Dr. Reid Lyon, March 28, 2005.

BIBLIOGRAPHY

Anthony, Carl Sferrazza. *First Ladies: The Saga of the Presidents' Wives and Their Power.* New York: William Morrow, 1991.

Bruni, Frank. *Ambling into History: The Unlikely Odyssey of George W. Bush.* New York: HarperCollins, 2002.

Bush, Barbara. *A Memoir.* New York: Charles Scribner's Sons, 1994.

Bush, George W. *A Charge to Keep: My Journey to the White House.* New York: William Morrow, 1999.

Felix, Antonia. *Laura: America's First Lady, First Mother.* Avon, Mass.: Adams Media, 2003.

Frum, David. *The Right Man: The Surprise Presidency of George W. Bush.* New York: Random House, 2003.

Gerhart, Ann. *The Perfect Wife: The Life and Choices of Laura Bush.* New York: Simon & Schuster, 2004.

Hughes, Karen. *Ten Minutes from Normal.* New York: Portfolio, 2004.

Kessler, Ronald. *The Bureau: The Secret History of the FBI.* New York: St. Martin's Press, 2002.

———. *The CIA at War: Inside the Secret Campaign Against Terror.* New York: St. Martin's Press, 2003.

———. *Inside the White House: The Hidden Lives of the Modern Presidents* and the Secrets of the World's Most Powerful Institution. New York: Pocket Books, 1995.

―――. *A Matter of Character: Inside the White House of George W. Bush.* New York: Sentinel/Penguin Group, 2004.

Mansfield, Stephen. *The Faith of George W. Bush.* New York: Jeremy P. Tarcher, 2003.

Minutaglio, Bill. *First Son: George W. Bush and the Bush Family Dynasty.* New York: Random House, 1999.

Sammon, Bill. *Fighting Back: The War on Terrorism—from Inside the Bush White House.* Washington, D.C.: Regnery Publishing, 2002.

―――. *Misunderestimated: The President Battles Terrorism, John Kerry, and the Bush Haters.* New York: ReganBooks, 2004.

Schweizer, Peter, and Rochelle Schweizer. *The Bushes: Portrait of a Dynasty.* New York: Doubleday, 2004.

Stratton, Joanna L. *Pioneer Women: Voices from the Kansas Frontier.* New York: Touchstone, 1981.

Walsh, Kenneth T. *Air Force One: A History of the Presidents and Their Planes.* New York: Hyperion, 2003.

Woodward, Bob. *Bush at War.* New York: Simon & Schuster, 2002.

―――. *Plan of Attack.* New York: Simon & Schuster, 2004.

INDEX

abortion, Laura's views on, 88, 105
Adamkus, Valdas, 203
adoption, 17, 73
Afghanistan
    anti-American rioting in, 230
    U.S. invasion, 140–41
    women's rights, Laura's interest in,
      140–41, 170–71
Ager, Susan, 240
Aiken, Don, 33, 34, 35, 40
Akwai, Leilani (Peter), 176
Alan, Wayne, 232
Allen, Terry, 14
Ambrose, Stephen, 115
American Civil Liberties Union, 154
Andersen, Christopher, 201
Anderson, Kurt, 229
appointments, Laura's influence over, 6,
    7, 8, 156, 167
Armstrong, Katharine, 102, 139, 166,
    179, 234–35, 238
Austin
    Bush twins' drinking incidents,
      128–30
    Laura in, 61–62, 142

Ball, Andrea G. "Andi," 2, 94, 106,
    110, 169, 215
    and Bush twins' *Sex and the City*
      speech, 183
    on Laura and the press, 107

    on Laura's move to the White
      House, 106
    on Laura's reading and
      correspondence, 91, 92–93, 109,
      113
    on Laura's 2004 encounter with
      Harvey Kennedy, 188
    on poetry symposium cancellation,
      152
    on September 11 and aftermath,
      135, 136
Ball, Jackie Stubblefield, 18
Ball, Lonnie, 215
Bartlett, Dan, 225, 226
Battle, Robert, 13
Berman, Lea, 216
Betts, Lois, 218
Betts, Roland W., 176, 198, 214, 218
Billington, James H., 115
bin Laden, Osama, 141, 144, 167, 170
Blackaller, Cathie, 163
Blair, Tony, 160
Blasingame, Kenneth, 87, 124, 125, 232
Blount, Jay, 197, 200
Blount, Winton, 69
Bolten, Joshua B., 117–18, 142–43
Bolton, Michael, 128
books. *See* reading
Bowhay, Mary, 73
breast-cancer awareness, Laura's work,
    113–14